Youth cultures

Anthropology – the study of humankind – has dealt mostly with men, increasingly with woman, to some degree with children and old people but very little with youth. The analysis of the creation of youth culture is a long neglected topic across the social sciences yet is fundamental to our understanding of society. *Youth Cultures* broadens the scope for analysing young people's behaviour by moving away from notions of resistance and deviance and offers a range of ethnographically based studies of different kinds of youth in varied national contexts. From Nepal to Canada, Europe, the Solomon Islands and Algeria, it addresses current issues relating to globalization in Third World cities, ethnic diversity in European cities and consumption practices and places the lives of these young people in the contexts of the wider cultures.

Youth Cultures contributes to the general current concern in anthropology with 'rewriting' culture, even while it seeks to close particular gaps in studies on youth culture. By challenging the limitation of previous youth research and acknowledging children and young adults as agents to be respected rather than objectified, this book will be invaluable reading to students of anthropology, sociology, education, psychology, and cultural studies.

Vered Amit-Talai is Associate Professor in the Department of Sociology and Anthropology at Concordia University, Montreal. **Helena Wulff** is Lecturer in the Department of Social Anthropology at Stockholm University.

Youth cultures

A Cross-cultural Perspective

Edited by Vered Amit-Talai
and Helena Wulff

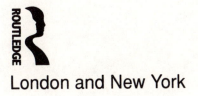

London and New York

First published 1995
by Routledge
11 New Fetter Lane, London EC4P 4EE

Simultaneously published in the USA and Canada
by Routledge
29 West 35th Street, New York, NY 10001

© 1995 Vered Amit-Talai and Helena Wulff

Typeset in Times by
Ponting–Green Publishing Services, Chesham, Bucks
Printed and bound in Great Britain by
T.J. Press (Padstow) Ltd, Padstow, Cornwall

Every attempt has been made to seek copyright permission
for the figures and tables used in this book.
Copyright holders should contact Patrick Proctor at
Routledge, London, with any queries.

British Library Cataloguing in Publication Data
A catalogue record for this book is available from the
British Library

Library of Congress Cataloguing in Publication Data
A catalogue record for this book has been requested

ISBN   0–415–10983–3 (hbk)
ISBN   0–415–10984–1 (pbk)

Contents

92847

Contributors

Vered Amit-Talai, Associate Professor, Department of Sociology and Anthropology, Concordia University, Montreal, Canada.

Virginia Caputo, Doctoral candidate, Department of Social Anthropology, York University, Toronto, Canada.

Allison James, Lecturer, Department of Sociology and Social Anthropology, University of Hull, United Kingdom.

Christine Jourdan, Associate Professor, Department of Sociology and Anthropology, Concordia University, Montreal, Canada.

Mark Liechty, PhD from University of Pennsylvania, USA, currently a post-doctoral fellow at the International Institute for Asian Studies, Leiden, The Netherlands.

Livio Sansone, Co-ordinator, 'The Colour of Bahia', Graduate Programme in Sociology and Anthropology, Universidade Federal de Bahia, Salvador, Brazil.

Marc Schade-Poulsen, PhD, Researcher, Centre for Development Research, Copenhagen, Denmark.

Helena Wulff, Lecturer, Department of Social Anthropology, Stockholm University, Sweden.

Chapter 1

Introducing youth culture in its own right

The state of the art and new possibilities

Helena Wulff

If anthropology is the study of humankind, why has it dealt mostly with men, to an increasing extent with women, to some degree with children and old people, but very little with youth as a subject matter? Perhaps, like many other adults, anthropologists view youth as not to be taken very seriously: occasionally amusing, yet potentially dangerous and disturbing, in a liminal phase. Recent writings on youth culture, mostly in other disciplines and by cultural journalists, have predictably focused on resistance and deviance. In this volume we intend to broaden the scope by way of offering a range of ethnographically based studies of different kinds of youth in varied national contexts: Canada, Britain, the Netherlands, Nepal, Algeria and the Solomon Islands. The studies deal with minority as well as mainstream young people, 'problem youth' as well as ordinary youth. The particular characteristics of youth as contrasted with both childhood and adulthood are analysed, and the lives of young people are placed in the contexts of the wider cultures. There is above all a consistent theoretical concern to show how young people are active agents – in different ways and with varying force – in the construction of the meanings and symbolic forms which make up their cultures.

Much writing on youth in terms of socialization, education or human development depicts youth as objects of adult activity. It is often more concerned with the institutional systems in which youth are implicated than with youth culture as such, or with the issue of the production and management of culture by adolescents in youth peer groups.

The analysis of youth cultural production raises questions which are at the very heart of contemporary debates in anthropology. It involves consideration of the relation between highly localized forms of cultural activity and more widely distributed practices and products; of the social context of meaning; of how anthropologists can deal with collectivities and cultural constructions which are ephemeral rather than enduring; of cultural reproduction, globalization and creolization, to mention but some issues that are dealt with in this volume. We hope to contribute to the general current concern in anthropology with 'rewriting' culture, even while we seek to close particular gaps in studies on youth culture.

IDENTIFYING YOUTH AS PROBLEMS, VICTIMS, RESISTERS

Since the aim of this volume is to show that anthropology can make major contributions to the study of youth culture, I will not offer a comprehensive review of this field as it has unfolded in all disciplines.[1] This section is therefore merely about the state of the art from the anthropologist's point of view. It is however restricted to publications in English, which is one limitation.[2] Trained in cross-cultural awareness, the anthropologist soon realizes that most major studies on youth culture have been about urban, Western male youth. A couple of rather recent exceptions are *Russia's Youth and its Culture* by Hilary Pilkington (1994)[3] and *Veils and Videos: Female Youth Culture on the Kenyan Coast* by Minou Fuglesang (1994). Other rare examples of studies on non-Western youth outside the West are *Kamikaze Biker* on Japanese motorcycle gangs by Ikuya Sato (1991) and *Adolescence in a Moroccan Town* by Susan Schaefer Davis and Douglas A. Davis (1988).

When studies on youth culture started to emerge in the 1950s they were mostly conducted by sociologists, not anthropologists, and this is still the case. To a degree they address other questions, work in different ways methodologically, and may hence arrive at somewhat different conclusions than do anthropologists. This is so mainly because of the fact that anthropological texts are constructed out of an interchange between ethnography and theory, not always to an equal extent; nor are the theoretical implications always supported by open-minded impartial ethnography; anthropologists are also products of their personal and political backgounds, let alone academic milieux. But the fact that anthropologists deal with living people in the midst of the flux of complexities of life (who by the way are continuously ahead of the current theoretical debate) is our distinguishing mark. It is furthermore quite common that anthropological research problems are being more or less altered in the field, since they proved not to be relevant out there in the field reality.

Some anthropological interest in studies on youth has been included in the traditional focus on family and kinship, such as in Margaret Mead's (1928) pioneering *Coming of Age in Samoa* (as well as in Wilson 1951), and on rites-de-passages (Turner 1967). Jules Henry (1965) was one of the first to formulate a youth anthropology. However, all of these early studies viewed youth as on their way to adulthood in the process of learning for later challenges, rather than producing something on their own which might not last in the long run but could still be significant for them at the time.

Talcott Parsons (1942/1964) seems to have introduced the term 'youth culture' to mean a distinctive world of youth structured by age and sex roles. He was in particular thinking of American middle-class youth who were preoccupied with having fun with the opposite sex, and who continued to enjoy the freedom from adult respons-ibility. James S. Coleman (1961) emphasized the separatness of youth culture from adult society and its closeness to the market through consumption of popular music. He wrote about it in terms of subculture, a concept that together with class were to be prominent in the burgeoning literature on youth culture. In the 1960s, Stanley Cohen (1972) and Jock Young (1974) were among those 'delinquency theorists' who applied American labelling theory to youth culture. Cohen's seminal study was particularly concerned with how the mass media created a societal 'moral panic' of youth as problem: 'folk devils'. Cohen particularly focused on how the mass media inflated an incidence of discord mainly between 'Mods' and 'Rockers' on the seaside of England by presenting it as a major disturbance.

More systematic studies of subculture and class were to come out in ample numbers from the Centre for Contemporary Cultural Studies (the CCCS) at the University of Birmingham, the renowned 'Birmingham School', in the 1970s and early 1980s, framing their studies in a Marxist perspective that was informed by a semiological interest. They depicted working-class youth culture – mainly that of white boys – as resisting class domination (on behalf of their parents) through spectacular forms of style. Working-class boys were por-trayed as temporary resisters fighting a symbolic class war that they will lose in the long run and hence end up as victims anyway.

Like all major theoretical sources of inspiration, the Birmingham School has had its critics (e.g. Jenkins 1983 and Lave *et al.* 1992). In fact, by now there is an entire industry of critique as well as some auto-critique where ex-CCCS scholars revise their own work (e.g. Johnson 1986; McRobbie 1991). (Like all influential schools of thought, it has also had a series of less competent followers, who perhaps have been more of a burden than an asset for the CCCS scholars, vulgarizing their work.) There has even been some internal critique with CCCS scholars scrutinizing each other, such as Angela McRobbie's (1980) early discussion of Paul Willis' (1977) lack of attention to gender.

Richard Jenkins (1983), from the outside, argued for a move away from the emphasis on deviancy and distinctiveness of subcultures to acknowledgements of cultural heterogeneity, similarities and connections between different cultural forms that may not necessarily be in opposition to a dominant culture. Tony Dunn (1986:73) points to the tendency of the Birmingham School for 'a determined politicization of culture'. McRobbie (1991) calls for more ethnography, as do Lave *et al.* (1992) more specifically of persons in social practice. Reviewing *Resistance through Rituals* (Hall and Jefferson 1975), the main collaborative work of the CCCS, Lave *et al.* note in passing that it largely represents CCCS work by its long, thorough theoretical analysis but short, insufficient empirical studies. Lave *et al.* argue that the Birmingham School never fully explored the connections between structure and subjectivity, nor paid enough attention to the significance of subjectivity.

The sheer volume of the critical work discussing the theoretical flaws of the Birmingham School must prove some evidence of its importance, even if reasonings of real intellectual originality in the CCCS work were rather far apart. It was very much a product of its time of Marxist paradigms and academic interdisciplinary collaborative setting. But it also grew out of a critique of sociological positivism, which has not been a major issue for anthropologists in a long time. This critique was however quite difficult to handle for the CCCS scholars, since ethnography and participant observation did not do for all of them. For instance, Dick Hebdige (1979) argued in *Subculture*, one of the most prominent books of the Birmingham School, that participant observation (in sociology) lacked an analytical framework and consequently failed to properly identify class and power. However, in his celebrated study *Learning to Labour*, a rare example of ethnography from the Birmingham School which succeeded in attracting anthropological attention (cf. Marcus 1986, Marcus and Fischer 1986), Paul Willis (1977) did exactly that.

Willis's book about counter school culture created by working-class boys was about the closest the Birmingham School ever got to the discipline of anthropology. For there was not one single anthropologist connected to it, which is a fact that has been something of a challenge for anthropologists working on youth culture, not least because of the longstanding anthropological interest in the concept of culture as well as culture theory (e.g. Hannerz 1992).

Setting out to do an ethnography of black teenage girls of West Indian origin in South London in the early 1980s, it gradually became clear to me that not only were these girls friends with other black girls of West African parentage, but also – more significantly – their friends included white girls (Wulff 1988). The issue of racism had to be reconsidered. But what about women's, or rather in this case, girls' assumed subordination? They were supposed to be invisible, hiding in their bedrooms, while the boys occupied the street corners (cf. the much quoted article by McRobbie and Garber 1976). Spending time with this group of girls and the boys they knew on an everyday basis over the course of a year and a half, made me realize that there was in fact no significant difference between girls and boys in this respect. Boys also stuck together in their bedrooms for hours on end, while the girls were 'muckin' around' on the street corner often waiting for the boys to appear, since the street corner was a meeting place for *both* girls and boys.

Another feature of youth culture studies is a closeness to applied and policy oriented scholarship. This is particularly common in education and studies on ethnicity and immigration in order to solve youth problems as perceived by adults. Scholars may then be ambivalent about having to produce results fast at the expense of the quality of their work. They may also feel that there is an expectation of certain results, while the ones they get are uncomfortable to deal with. A growing interest in youth from international organizations and development agencies may of course also be one way to finance research, at a time of budgetary cuts at universities and research councils. Many youth scholars have moreover worked as youth workers, teachers, journalists or musicians either before, during or after a period in academia. They may be regarded as latent fieldworkers, accidental ethnographers who possess empathy for young people. And if certain Marxist scholars in the 1960s and 1970s seemed more like 'armchair Marxists' viewing the world from the safe ivory tower of the university, hardly ever contributing to any political change, this charge could not really be levelled against this category of youth culture scholars. They have been or are still actively involved in trying to improve race and gender relations at youth clubs and schools in inner city areas, to activate young people, and to entertain them.

AGE, TIME AND GENERATION

The principles of age and generation have often been linked to youth, as if they only applied to or concerned young people. Age and generation seem to be acknowledged everywhere (Baxter and Almagor 1978) albeit in different, cultural ways. Kertzer and Keith (1984) point to the fact that most research on age has been about societies where physical ageing is structured by formal systems of age grades, groups and sets. This has more recently been followed by a life-course perspective, or ageing as a social process (e.g. Spencer 1990).

Biological generations are about the same in length, but cultural generations may vary considerably. The experience of being young is universal, but it takes many different forms, partly cultural and political, partly personal. In this volume we would like to open up the concept of youth culture from that of spectacular, deviant, oppositional, marginal groups to include *all* young people. Following Ulf Hannerz (1992) we advocate the view that people negotiate culture, or rather cultural processes, and are formed by them to a certain extent. When these cultural processes are formed by young people, we are dealing with youth culture. This is a much diversified and complex phenomenon, however, and one that not least contains different expressions defined by age sets; to be a young teenager is hardly equivalent to being an older teenager, for example. Young teenagers are often still at school, while older teenagers may have left school having completed compulsory schooling. Youth culture is often associated with teenagers, people between the ages of 13 and 19, yet the cultural boundaries separating youth from children on one hand and from adults on the other, may differ. Not only is 'youth' consequently a construction, as is the term 'children', but in fact so is 'adults'.

Furthermore, as Bennett M. Berger (1971) has pointed out, youthfulness may extend upwards in the ages. Not only teenagers are youthful, and not all teenagers would be defined as youthful according to Berger's American list of characteristic traits such as being spontaneous, energetic, exploratory, venturesome, vivacious, disrespectful, playful and erotic. Although many youth probably would be defined as such. Berger also discusses how certain professions and settings like those of intellectuals, athletes and artists may prolong youthfulness into middle age. There has been some attention to the fact that the state of youth tends to last over an increasing number of years, partly due to prolonged schooling, partly due to unemployment. This can be understood in terms of a cultural moratorium (e.g. Wulff 1993), a period when young people are extending their youth by way of experimenting with different roles and thereby delaying adult responsibilites. In his chapter on raï music and youth in Algeria, Marc Schade-Poulsen mentions that the youth period has become much longer in Algeria after the achievement of national independence. The young people appearing in this volume vary in age from children to young adults, but most of them are older teenagers.

Another problem, of a quite different nature but of vital importance for the study of youth culture and its reproduction, is the age of the youth culture scholars themselves – in particular the fact that they, like anyone else, get older. During the heyday of the Birmingham School, most of the CCCS scholars were young, since then they have grown older, which is something that some of them have reflected upon analytically. McRobbie (1993) confesses that she often has to struggle in order to combine her sociological interest in youth with being the mother of a teenage girl. At the same time as she feels too close to her daughter's experiences she also feels too old to study youth, and refers to Dick Hebdige (1987) who has described how nowadays he may find himself unable to sleep at night because of loud music played by his young neighbours. Getting up and out in order to take them to task makes him realize that there is a gap between himself and the people he used to write about.

While doing fieldwork on female youth culture when I was in my late twenties, it was quite useful that I was sometimes taken for a teenager by non-teenagers (such as youth workers and policemen) (Wulff 1988). A relatively youthful appearance is undoubtedly helpful when hanging around street corners with teenagers. To now and then 'go native' opens up vast understandings and rich data that should lead to more intriguing analyses. Now I do not believe that youth culture scholars necessarily have to be and look young; there are examples of grey-haired scholars who obviously have an ability to talk to teenagers, to get them to relax and open up, and to show them their world. Still, the ageing youth culture scholar remains a problem since few stay on in the field; most of them move on to other subject matters which is one explanation of the marginalization of studies on youth culture in academia. Distinguished scholars may have started out as youth culture scholars or they may comment in passing on the phenomenon, but the bulk of their work is usually about something else.

For youth culture scholars, time thus becomes an issue that they may apply to youth they study, since the state of youth – especially from an adult point of view – is something that will pass. Youth cultures are time-limited (Schwartz 1975); Vered Amit-Talai makes a special point of this in her chapter in this volume. She writes about a small group of mostly female English-speaking students at a Montreal high school in Canada who formed temporary but momentous friendships by constructing some personal space through accommodation, confrontation, or evasion of adults during their final year at school. Amit-Talai criticizes the assumption of friendship as private only, since these friendships were also public manifestations. Nor were they the outcome of much free time. These students were busy with full-time school and many had part-time jobs, on top of taking care of younger siblings and doing household chores as well. The management of the friendships consisted of a careful balance between developing intimacy through the sharing of confidences and limiting disclosures of information, opinions and feelings.

Among the following chapters there are two that discuss differences, similarities and continuities between children's culture and youth culture, by Virginia Caputo and Allison James respectively. Both deal with the concept of time. James writes explicitly about children's culture and youth culture as temporal forms of culture by exploring their distinct forms of language as an important medium of socialization, providing both form and content to the passage from childhood to youth.

YOUTH AS CULTURAL AGENTS

According to Anthony Giddens (1976:75), agency is 'the stream of actual or contemplated casual interventions of corporeal beings in the ongoing process of events-in-the world.' He links the concept of agency to that of practice. Tracing the origin of the concept of action or agency back to the Wittgensteinian tradition in Anglo-American philosophy he regrets that it leaves out Wittgenstein's own concern with social structure, institutional development and change. Giddens makes a point of distinguishing between agency and intention, contrary to these authors, bringing up the problems of if a person 'could have acted otherwise' (ibid.) and 'unintended consequences of intended acts' (ibid.:77). Later (1979), he developed his idea of dependency between agency and structure in terms of structuration implying a duality of structure, that social structure is both content and form of the practices of its system.

Charles Taylor (1985), the philosopher, argues that a responsible human agent is someone who has the capacity to evaluate desires, to rank them. And Margaret Archer (1988) says that structure and agency is much the same problem as that of culture and agency, that there is thus a need to combine the two aspects in social theory.

Zygmunt Bauman (1992) connects agency with habitat, which suggests that youth pick among what is available in their surroundings to form their identity. This is in itself one constraint of agency. Lave *et al.* (1992:269) compliment Hebdige (1979) and Willis (1977) for having acknowledged 'how young people appropriate and transform standard cultural artefacts'. Margaret Mead (1978) was one of the first to write about generational cultures. Her notion of cofigurative culture can in fact be seen as a kind of cultural agency. Because of some social change the parental postfigurative culture is not useful for the young generation to take over as it is. This is when members of the younger generation have to develop their own cofigurative culture together.

There is an interest in the following chapters in social structure and change, as well as habitat in relation to the agency of youth. It does, however, vary in strength as well as in expression and meaning. The weakest youth cultural agency of all that is reported on in this volume is discussed by Mark Liechty in his chapter on youth in Kathmandu, Nepal. Liechty portrays a situation where the terms 'teen' and 'teenagers' have just recently been introduced and signify a cultural space characterized by a tension between a glamorous consumption fantasy portrayed in the mass media (such as teenage magazines, films, videos, cassettes, etc.) and its negative emic or native designation referring to 'a category of anti-social, vulgar, and potentially violent young males'. Here the idea of youth as victims is again relatively close at hand; these young men have to form modern identities at the intersection of tradition and globalization, development and consumerism. They do have some room to negotiate a youth culture of their own, mostly expressed in public practice such as clothing, music, videos, or slang, but Liechty emphasizes that their choices are restricted.

When it comes to globalization or transnational connections youth cultures are in the forefront of theoretical interest; youth, their ideas and commodities move easily across national borders, shaping and being shaped by all kinds of structures and meanings. It may concern development and consumerism. But it also applies to the young men of Surinamese origin in Amsterdam who immigrated to the Netherlands as children who 'commute' back and forth between Paramaribo and Amsterdam which, in combination with an orientation towards Rastafarianism and the black heritage in the US, are phrased by Livio Sansone in terms of globalization. So are the youth styles of the young men. The youth styles of the black and white teenage girls in South London that I write about are also linked to globalization. The raï music in Algeria, discussed in Marc Schade-Poulsen's chapter, is certainly global, being played in other countries, as is the youth culture of the 'Masta Liu' in Honiara, the Solomon Islands. Christine Jourdan depicts how it is reformulating Western and Australian consumption and entertainment ideas.

Children's cultural agency has been underestimated in the literature, which is something that Virginia Caputo and Allison James both point out in this volume. If youth are not yet considered to be full adults, children are supposed to be even worse off, considered only 'partially cultural' as Caputo notes, knowing even less than youth what adult life is all about. The suggestion that children may have a different kind of knowledge, that they may be preoccupied with things that their adults are unaware of, may appear offensive to responsible parents and teachers. James furthermore describes how she had to 'learn to talk again', in mostly new vocabulary, in order to make conversation with the children she was studying. During the course of my fieldwork on young teenage girls in South London, I came to realize that I had forgotten how I used to think and perceive the world as a 14- year-old girl. By approaching the girls at a different angle from their adults who were enculturating them, intending to form them according to their cultural ideals and resources, I believe that I saw other qualities in those girls. I also had more time for the girls than did their parents. On one level, women may be able to bring back the memory of the excited discomfort of being in love at a distance – one of the central concerns of the girls – before one can be sure that it is actually possible to bridge it. Women may remember the experience of utter boredom and meaninglessnes, of a seemingly infinite number of days at school that they were once forced to endure without really believing that those days would ever come to an end. And they may now and then spend an idle thought on memories of successful pranks such as 'riding the trains' (i.e. going on the underground without paying), or shouting obscenities at male teachers in the school yard. But the difference is that women can ponder fleetingly over these situations from the safe distance of adulthood; to be absorbed by such situations while in the process of exploring them as a young teenage girl is a totally different matter. Spending long stretches of time meeting mostly teenage girls, relatively cut off from close adult relationships, one's adult perspective is momentarily displaced. I experienced flashes of insight when I understood that some of the girls' concerns were actually out of their parents' reach, and it was not only because the girls made an effort to hide them, especially from their parents' and youth workers' view, but because they were of an order that fell outside the adult enculturating relationship to the girls.

It ought to be an anthropological truism to have to state that young people may have things in common which the adults (parents, kin, teachers, etc.) in their lives do not necessarily understand or take an interest in, and which therefore are given little attention by adult observers and commentators. But because of the traditional social-ization perspective, youth (and children) still tend to be viewed as *incomplete adults*, not real, full persons who have understood what life is actually about; that is mainly the responsibilities and hardship that come with adulthood. According to this view, they know less than adults, as opposed to knowing something else that has to do with their particular situation and surroundings. Virginia Caputo emphasizes this predicament when it comes to those studies of children's culture that have left out the children's own perspective, failing to sufficiently disconnect adult relationships to children. As Caputo notes, however, William Corsaro (1985) has worked in this direction. Writing about children's peer culture he has, among other cases, a significant incident of two little girls who hide inside a large wooden spool and fire off long verbal curses into Corsaro's micro-phone, some of which he had barely heard himself and others that he had never used. The children were carrying out a naughty ritual as a part of their peer culture out of adult control. And they demonstrated cultural agency in the process.

Virginia Caputo gives children's musical production in metropolitan Toronto as examples of children's cultural agency. The children she studied, mainly girls, preserved a large repertoire of songs and passing them from one child to another, cultivating songs their teachers thought had been destroyed by the media. Despite progress in women's status in the adult world, these songs consisted of three- and four- note chants with themes on traditional female roles and matters such as females being treated as property. Allison James reports on cultural agency among children and youth in the north-east of England in the late 1970s and in a Midland town in the late 1980s. They challenge the limits of social action, established by adults, through restyling language – especially terminology, rhythm and cadence – thereby signifying their identities as 'child' and/or 'youth'. By way of ritualized phrases and formulae, verbal challenges and ripostes transform adult courtesy speech forms such as replying to 'Do you mind!' with 'No, I babysit'. James found that the children she studied used old Durham dialect words that are not a part of adult active vocabulary any longer and transferred them between generations of children, insulating them from adult influence. According to James, it is through developing their performative language skills that children progress into youth culture, which continues to be united with children's culture by the experience of marginality.

Caputo also discusses children's culture versus youth culture and finds that youth have more access to power especially over time (clothing, music to listen to, level of mobility) and money, but she maintains that children may have more control over their own worlds than adults understand.

Another ethnography from Britain, but in a quite different setting from the two areas that James writes about, is provided in the chapter on inter-racial friendship in South London. This is where I write about how a group of black and white teenage girls argued for a policy of ethnic equality by way of their youth styles that at the same time gave them an opportunity to experiment with teenage femininity. But it was not only ethnic conflict that they found repugnant. They also had to handle the more subtle, yet almost equally problematic *unfamiliarity* of most parents and teachers with ethnic mixture. A lack of knowledge of people from other ethnic groups and races may produce a basically friendly or non-committed distance. These phenomena are often misinterpreted as racism in the literature on youth and ethnicity, if they are recognized at all. Perhaps such seemingly delicate nuances can only be grasped through participant observation over a longer period of time. Since expressions of friendly distance are not as immediately forceful as racism, they are assumed to lack political significance and are therefore attracting less attention from scholarly as well as lay commentators. Because of its frequency, however, friendly and non-committed distanced ethnicity does have an impact on daily life in multi-ethnic settings.

Youth styles may again be transnational and occur in various forms in many places and managed according to local circumstances. They may also be national, regional, or put together out of even smaller settings. The twenty black and white girls in South London had their set of youth styles, some of foreign, others of national origin, that had to do with the particular constellation of girls in the group, such as best friends adhering to the same style. All the styles were promoting ethnic equality in an unconfrontational way.

Youth styles are also discussed in Livio Sansone's chapter on lower-class young black men of Surinamese origin in Amsterdam. For them, the aesthetic qualities of youth styles are important means to show off their blackness in public, aware of its attractiveness not least among many white youth. They are in the process of making a black youth culture out of influences from Paramaribo street corners, Western youth culture including white elements, and images of blacks in the mass media. This black youth culture is furthermore an example of older teenagers and young adults forming youth culture together – a cultural continuity – largely because they share the state of unemployment which is disguised as leisure. There is moreover a tendency for them to become involved with criminal activity such as petty pimping, pushing drugs and mugging.

Leisure is also the context in Marc Schade-Poulsen's chapter on young men in Algeria who listen to raï music: a mixture of Western instruments, local popular songs and rhythms, American disco, songs of Julio Iglesias, Egyptian instrumental interludes and Moroccan wedding tunes. Schade-Poulsen concentrates on the poetics of raï, arguing that raï lyrics reflect the contradiction between the desire of young men to establish love relationships with women and the fact that this implies a questioning of the authority of their mothers. There is 'dirty' raï about sexual lust that young men listen to outside the family, as opposed to 'clean' raï dealing with love, although hardly ever during happy circumstances. Schade-Poulsen does not believe that the raï lyrics mirror the social situations of the young men literally; current individual circumstances, just as intellectual, economic and social positions and interest in music, influence the listener's interpretation of these texts. He moreover points to the fact that raï music is commercial and mass-produced, that there is money being made by touching people's feelings and unsolved personal predicaments, but that raï lyrics above all should be seen in the wider perspective of the tension between a traditional orientation towards the mosque and a modern orientation to the West in Algerian society.

Schade-Poulsen makes a connection between the rural influx to the Western cities of Algeria and the rise of raï music there. It was a part of the urbanization process and a new kind of youth culture that grew out of it. How recent urbanization has brought forth a new combination of youth culture is also the theme in Christine Jourdan's chapter on the 'Masta Liu' phenomenon in Honiara, the Solomon Islands. Just like the young Nepalese men that Liechty writes about, these young people are the first generation to be exposed to Western consumption patterns, notably in the form of clothes (blue jeans and army garb), food (rice and take-away) and media (film posters and cassette players). Jourdan discusses this asymmetrical mixture of goods and customs from the West, Australia, Rastafarianism, and Malaita – the island from which most of the Masta Liu originate – in terms of socio-cultural creolization. There have been Masta Lius for quite some time, but a new form has emerged where both young men and women as well as girls are included. They have some schooling and come to Honiara to look for work and excitement. Their cultural creativity circles around the freedom to spend time with contemporaries window shopping, wandering around town in groups, and, especially for the girls, talking to boys, which is something of which their parents disapprove. Contrary to the life they left back home they have time for themselves, even if this easy existence is threatened by poverty and unemployment that may lead to delinquency.

COMPARATIVE YOUTH CULTURE: A UNIVERSAL EXPERIENCE DIVERSIFIED

In his comparison of youth cultures Michael Brake (1987) found that in America they tend to be defined by ethnicity, in Britain by class and style, while in Canada they do not occur to the same extent, and if they do they are often imported from abroad. This is so, according to Brake, because of the vast size of the country, the small population, and its diversity. To him identity and resistance are key concepts of youth culture, however, in line with the sociology of youth culture. This volume offers some new possibilities for study on youth culture. By way of anthropological theory and method we suggest a broadening of this field; youth culture does not only consist of resistance and delinquency on the part of white teenage boys in Western cities. Youth culture is what young people are concerned with, and there is more cultural agency in it than most earlier studies have acknowledged.

The contributors to this volume are presenting ethnographic cases of cultural agency such as young Canadian girls who had kept their song lyrics away from media influences, English children who create their own distinctive tongue of exclusive vocabulary, rhythm, and cadence, often in the form of ritualized challenges that were transformed adult courtesy speech. They had also kept and developed old dialect terms that were no longer a part of adult everyday talk. As their language performance skills increased these children were on their way to youth culture just as their compatriots were forming inter-racial friendship in South London. This group of black and white teenage girls was mostly defined by their idea of ethnic equality which they expressed through their particular set and versions of youth styles. Among black young men of Surinamese origin in Amsterdam, an aesthetization of youth styles was one prominent aspect, another was their criminality that may be viewed as a consequence of unemployment. In Algeria young adult men listen to 'dirty' raï music outside their homes; the lyrics of this music portray sexuality as dangerous and uncontrolled. Female English-speaking students at a Montreal high school in Canada establish temporary but significant friendships through accommodation and confrontation as well as evasion of adults. These friendships are characterized by both a private and a public side. And in Honiara, the Solomon Islands, new young urbanites lead an exciting but economically insecure life out of reach of their parents, a life that is much defined by more time to indulge in wandering around the streets with friends and for the girls to meet boys. In Kathmandu, Nepal, young men are beginning to form modern identities at the intersection of tradition and globalization, but their youth cultural agency is not very prominent.

Studies of youth culture have usually not made any substantial contribution to the development of the concept of culture; in fact it is rarely problematized and discussed in these studies. Instead there seems to be an implicit assumption of consensus on how to define the concept of culture, while as Vered Amit-Talai's conclusion illustrates, the conceptualization of culture would benefit greatly from findings on youth, especially of what she calls their multi-cultural strategies, or an awareness of cultural possiblities that may be of a contingent character.

It is time for anthropologists to make a more substantial contribution to the study of youth culture, to view young people as cultural agents and to illuminate their perspectives towards a wide range of general themes in social life: gender, class, ethnicity, race, globalization. At the same time, one must not lose sight of such particular youthful concerns as excitement, defiance, opportunities and exploration. When will the concept of youth culture have a place in our textbooks?

ACKNOWLEDGEMENT

I wish to thank Vered Amit-Talai for supportive comments on this chapter. It was written as a part of the research programme 'National and Transnational Cultural Processes' at the Department of Social Anthropology, Stockholm University, financed by the Swedish Research Council for the Humanities and Social Sciences.

NOTES

1 There is clearly a need for a comprehensive all-encompassing review article on studies of youth culture (not only youth).
2 There is a growing literature on youth culture in other languages than English, most notably in French (Louis and Prinaz 1990 is one example) and German (such as Ziehe 1982) of course, but also in Spanish (Feixa 1993) and Dutch (Sansone 1990). And more recently the Nordic countries, with Sweden (Fornäs et al. 1994) in the forefront, have produced an ample amount of work on youth culture, although most of it is not anthropological.
3 See also Soviet Youth Culture edited by James Riordan (1989).

REFERENCES

Archer, M. S. (1988) Culture and Agency, Cambridge: Cambridge University Press.
Bauman, Z. (1992) Intimations of Postmodernity, London: Routledge.
Baxter, P. T.W. and Almagor U. (1978) 'Observations about generations', in J.S. La Fontaine (ed.), Sex and Age as Principles of Social Differentiation, ASA Monograph 17, London: Academic Press.

Berger, B. M. (1971) *Looking for America*, Englewood Cliffs, NJ: Prentice-Hall.
Brake, M. (1987) *Comparative Youth Culture*, London: Routledge.
Cohen, S. (1972) *Folk Devils and Moral Panics*, London: MacGibbon & Kee.
Coleman, J. S. (1961) *The Adolescent Society*, New York: Free Press.
Corsaro, W. A. (1985) *Friendship and Peer Culture in the Early Years*, Norwood, NJ: Ablex.
Davis, S. S. and Davis, D. A. (1988) *Adolescence in a Moroccan Town*, New Brunswick: Rutgers University Press.
Dunn, T. (1986) 'The evolution of cultural studies', in D. Punter (ed.), *Introduction to Contemporary Cultural Studies*, London: Longman.
Feixa i Pàmpols, C. (1993) *La Joventut Com a Metafora*, Barcelona: Generalitat de Catalunya, Departament de la Presidècia, Secretaria General de Joventut.
Fornäs, J., Boethius U., Forsman, M., Ganetz, H. and Reimer, B. (eds) (1994) *Ungdomskultur i Sverige*, FUS Rapport Nr. 6, Stockholm: Symposion.
Fuglesang, M. (1994) *Veils and Videos*, Stockholm Studies in Social Anthropology, No. 32, Stockholm: Department of Social Anthropology, Stockholm University.
Giddens, A. (1976) *New Rules of Sociological Method*, London: Hutchinson.
—— (1979) *Central Problems in Social Theory*, London: Macmillan.
—— (1984) *The Constitution of Society*, Berkeley: University of California Press.
Hall, S. and Jefferson, T. (eds) (1975) *Resistance through Rituals*, London: Hutchinson.
Hannerz, U. (1992) *Cultural Complexity*, New York: Columbia University Press.
Hebdige, D. (1979) *Subculture*, London: Methuen.
—— (1987) 'The impossible object: toward a sociology of the sublime', *New Formations*, 1:47–76.
Henry, J. (1965) *Culture Against Man*, New York: Vintage Books.
Jenkins, R. (1983) *Lads, Citizens and Ordinary Kids*, London: Routledge & Kegan Paul.
Johnson, R. (1986) 'The story so far: and further transformations?', in D. Punter (ed.), *Introduction to Contemporary Cultural Studies*, London: Longman.
Kertzer, D. I. and Keith, J. (eds) (1984) *Age and Anthropological Theory*, Ithaka: Cornell University Press.
Lave, J. Duguid, P. and Fernandez, N. (1992) 'Coming of age in Birmingham: cultural studies and conceptions of subjectivity', *Annual Review of Anthropology*, 21:257–282.
Louis, P. and Prinaz, L. (1990) *Skinheads, Taggers, Zulus & Co*, Paris: La Table Ronde.
McRobbie, A. (1980) 'Settling accounts with subcultures: a feminist critique', *Screen*, 34:37–49.
—— (1991) *Feminism and Youth Culture*, Boston: Unwin Hyman.
—— (1993) 'Shut up and dance: youth culture and changing modes of femininity', *Cultural Studies*, 7:406–426.
McRobbie, A. and Garber, J. (1976) 'Girls and subcultures: an exploration',

in S. Hall and T. Jefferson (eds) *Resistance through Rituals*, London: Hutchinson.

Mannheim, K. (1952) 'The problem of generations', in *Essays on the Sociology of Knowledge*, London: Routledge & Kegan Paul.

Marcus, G. E. (1986) 'Contemporary problems of ethnography in the modern world system', in J. Clifford and G.E. Marcus (eds) *Writing Culture*, Berkeley: University of California Press.

Marcus, G. E. and Fischer, M.M.J. (eds) (1986) *Anthropology as Cultural Critique*, Chicago: University of Chicago Press.

Mead, M. (1928) *Coming of Age in Samoa*, New York: William Morrow & Company.

—— (1978) *Culture and Commitment*, Garden City, NY: Anchor.

Parsons, T. (1942/1964) *Essays in Sociological Theory*, Chicago: Free Press.

Pilkington, H. (1994) *Russia's Youth and its Culture*, London: Routledge.

Riordan, J. (ed.)(1989) *Soviet Youth Culture*, London: Macmillan.

Sansone, L. (1990) *Lasi boto*, Amersfoort: Acco.

Sato, I. (1991) *Kamikaze Biker*, Chicago: University of Chicago Press.

Schwartz, T. (1975) 'Relations among generations in time-limited cultures', *Ethos*, 3:309–322.

Spencer, P. (ed.) (1990) *Anthropology and the Riddle of the Sphinx*, ASA Monographs 28, London: Routledge.

Taylor, C. (1985) *Human Agency and Language*, Cambridge: Cambridge University Press.

Turner, V. (1967) *The Forest of Symbols*, Ithaka, NY: Cornell University Press.

Willis, P. (1977) *Learning to Labour*, Farnborough: Saxon House.

Wilson, M. (1951) *Good Company*, Oxford: Oxford University Press.

Wulff, H. (1988) *Twenty Girls*, Stockholm Studies in Social Anthropology, No. 21, Stockholm: Department of Social Anthropology, Stockholm University.

—— (1993) 'Moratorium on Manhattan', Paper presented at the 1st Annual Conference of the Swedish Anthropological Association, Kungälv, Sweden, 26–28 March.

Young, J. (1974) 'New directions in sub-cultural theory', in J. Rex (ed.), *Approaches to Sociology*, London: Routledge & Kegan Paul.

Ziehe, T. (1982) *Plädoyer fur ungewöhnliches Lernen*, Reinbek bei Hamburg: Rowohlt Taschenbuch Verlag GmbH.

Chapter 2

Anthropology's silent 'others'

A consideration of some conceptual and methodological issues for the study of youth and children's cultures

Virginia Caputo

INTRODUCTION

The concept of 'culture' has received considerable attention in anthropology recently. The representation of cultures in ethnographies as autonomous, integrated and bounded wholes has been called into question. In these depictions, differences between cultures are celebrated while at the same time differences within cultures are homogenized. Questions that challenge these kinds of representations of consistency are displaced by those that emphasize shared patterns and meanings. The spaces of culture wherein the inconsistencies occur, where meanings are contested or alternative ones articulated, are in turn marginalized. These spaces are the social sites of difference according to such factors as gender, race, class and age. Without these spaces, the practices of the creation of culture and the agents of its construction are absent. As Coombe (1991: 113) states, 'cultures become defined by their internal homogeneity and the characteristics that distinguish them from other cultural wholes.'

The social spaces of difference are important because these sites are constituted by the presence and activity of people whose voices continue to be silenced. These voices belong to those who occupy subordinate positions of power, including women and children. Culture, portrayed in terms of a unified system of meaning, privileges the voices of the powerful. In turn, cultural meanings that may be held by the groups that oppose dominant interpretations continue to be excluded in order to uphold this representation of culture.

This chapter considers anthropology's rethinking of the concept of culture and the issues of voice and agency in the context of children's lives. It suggests how current thinking about these issues has had repercussions for the study of children's cultures in the discipline. Using examples from my field research with children in various Canadian localities, I will argue two major points. First, the study of children's cultures requires a conceptualization of culture that is more dynamic and relational than traditional perspectives used in the past so that previously marginalized voices may be heard. In this way, culture is understood as a multiplicity of signifying practices rather than as a bounded thing. Agents of cultural production become centrally important from this vantage point. I argue that it is only with a more critical usage of the concept of culture that we can begin to understand the complexity of the subject of children as active agents engaged in the production and management of meaning in their own social lives.

The second point that extends from a rethinking of the concept of culture, pertains to the epistemological questions that guide much of this inquiry. More specifically, what are the linkages between anthropological knowledge and the subject of children? What are the structures of power that have deemed certain kinds of knowledge more important or valuable than others? What has this situation meant for the present state of studies of children and youth?

Three related themes serve to organize this chapter. First, the concept of culture is viewed in relation to the age/time based culture that encompasses the lives of children. Second, children actively engaged in the production of meaning in their lives is central. Third, categories such as 'childhood' and 'children' will be considered with a view to understanding how they have been constituted and maintained. Ethnographic examples, drawn from my own fieldwork with groups of children carried out in Toronto, Ontario in 1988 and 1993 and Halifax, Nova Scotia in 1991, will be used to illustrate some of these issues.

Finally, while the focus of this writing is directed to the subject of children's culture, one of the important linkages with the works that comprise this volume is the examination of some aspects of the relationship between the worlds of children and youth. The chapter concludes by stepping back from the primary focus on children to consider broader similarities, continuations and differences between children's culture and youth culture. In order to examine some of these points, definitional, conceptual and methodological issues pertinent to studies of children and youth are considered.

Organizationally, the chapter begins with a selected overview of the study of youth and children's cultures in the social sciences and in anthropology in particular. I go on to evaluate these approaches and suggest some of the problems that need to be addressed in order to understand the complexity of children's lives, providing details from my own ethnography. The next section of the chapter pays particular attention to methodological and conceptual issues that are important for the study of children's cultures. The chapter ends with an examination of some of the ways that the categories of children and youth are defined by arbitrary parameters. I suggest how research efforts help to construct and maintain these categories and offer some thoughts on how to empower children's voices in future research.

I A BRIEF OVERVIEW OF STUDIES OF YOUTH

Over the past several decades, interest in the study of youth has steadily increased in the social sciences. Various facets of the lives of young people have provided the impetus for ongoing research. Topics receiving scholarly attention include definitions of style, musical tastes, unemployment, delinquency, sexuality, resistance, and attempts to deal with 'difference', to name a few (Frith 1976; Hebdige 1979; McRobbie 1980; Campbell 1986; Mirza 1992). Much of this work has been carried out in the fields of sociology, psychology and cultural studies. In turn, particular types of frameworks to approach the study of youth have been implemented and developed through this research.

Anthropology has contributed to the literature on youth culture. Anthropological interest in age and age systems has been important to the development of research on youth.[1] Beginning with S. N. Eisenstadt's writings in the 1950s and continuing throughout the 1960s, interest in the stages between childhood and adulthood began to emerge. In the 1970s, the British Centre for Contemporary Cultural Studies became the site of a great deal of research on youth subcultures. These studies examined working-class youth subcultures as social groups through analyses of class structures (Cohen 1971; Hall and Jefferson 1976). While this work was highly influential in determining how youth were to be conceptualized, it remained at the level of the examination of facets of youth cultures as expressions of class conflict or the position of youth in future adult roles. These studies also helped to reinforce the view of youth as primarily passive. Youth, in a more active mode, were linked to the notion of resistance in response to conditions of oppression in their lives.

The view of the passive rather than active role of youth, reinforced through the discourse of resistance, is beginning to receive some scholarly attention and critique (see Amit-Talai, chapters 7 and 10 and Wulff, chapters 1 and 4, this volume). This is due, in part, to recent theoretical and methodological shifts that have occurred in the social sciences generally. Questions pertaining to the relationship between structure and agency and interest in cultural production are beginning to come to the fore in youth culture studies. The paucity of literature on the subject of youth as active agents of culture attests, however, to the continued marginalization of this subject.

The marginalization of research on youth and their depiction as passive receptors of adult culture in the social sciences has been clearly demonstrated. With regard to the issue of marginalization in particular, arguments for the position of youth on the periphery of social science concerns echo those heard in the past regarding the treatment accorded to other subordinate groups including women, for example. These concerns are extended further in order to point out the parallel marginalization experienced by children. While there has been an increased effort over the past decade to focus research on groups usually relegated to peripheral positions of importance, the study of children and children's culture remains marginal. Second, children, like youth, continue to be depicted as passive receptors of adult culture. There are very few recent studies that examine the worlds of children wherein they are depicted as active social agents in their own right (James and Prout 1990; James 1993).

In anthropology, the devalued status of the subject of children as active agents of culture arises out of a paradox. Children appear and disappear according to fluctuations in cycles of anthropological interest. In many of the societies where anthropologists carry out research, children are usually accorded a great deal of importance and concern. The problem remains, however, that anthropologists continue to exclude children by representing them as appendages to adult society. Therefore, while it would be unfair to argue that children have not been visible in anthropological writing, the problem of their inaudibility remains. The study of children as actively engaged in the production of meaning for their own social lives has been overlooked. In addition, anthropologists may have helped to uphold and perpetuate the trivialization barrier that surrounds the subject. This triviality arises not only from the absence of studies of children in ethnographies, but by other factors including the link between children and women, for example. This association has aided in the continued devaluation and in turn, absence of knowledge concerning children's lives from the anthropological record. While recent efforts by feminist researchers have targeted this issue for women, children, on the other hand, remain invisible. From their relative positions of powerlessness, they have been kept silent as well. The situation points to not only the double marginalization experienced by children, but forces one to question the kinds of power structures that are intertwined with the production of anthropological knowledge.

In the next section, an overview of some of the models that have been developed and implemented in the past for the study of children's cultures in the social sciences generally, and anthropology in particular, will be presented.

II THE STUDY OF CHILDREN'S CULTURE IN THE SOCIAL SCIENCES

In general, the treatment accorded to the subject of children across social science disciplines remains uneven. There has been an increased interest by some international agencies to make explicit the complexity of children's lives and the narrow view that is sometimes held regarding the concept of childhood. These efforts have resulted in a reconsideration of traditional concepts of childhood in some areas of the social sciences. In turn, many models previously utilized to view children's lives are being reshaped due to this wide range of critique.

Psychology has been the main arena for childhood research in the social sciences. Human development and socialization models have provided the frameworks for many of these studies. These models promote a view that children are part of a process in which social knowledge and competence is imparted to them from adults. In turn, children are transformed over time into mature adults.

Psychological Perspectives: Development framework

The development framework in psychology has had far-reaching implications for approaches to the study of childhood across many disciplines. This model links the biological facts of life to the social aspects of childhood. Rationality is an important feature of this model. Children are 'in process' of becoming full, rational adults and must move through biologically determined stages to achieve this goal. Children's activities, including their language acquisition and play patterns for example, serve to mark these developmental stages. Jean Piaget's work on child development has had an important impact on studies of cognition and children over the past several decades.[2]

Attempts have been made to extend Piagetian theory to consider the development of social cognition; that is, to identify levels of development of social concepts like friendship, for example.[3] However, this research continues to uphold the view that children are still culturally incomplete and require a progression through stages in order to attain the completeness attributed to adult members of society. More recent researchers involved in reassessing the work of Piaget are beginning to question this view by focusing their efforts on the importance of children's perspectives, social context and symbolic meanings (Light 1986).

Theories of socialization[4]

The psychological model of child development had a profound impact on theories of socialization that developed during the 1950s. Within a structural functionalist paradigm, the ways children learned to participate in society were viewed through their acquisition of social roles. Through the process of socialization, children were able to acquire knowledge of these roles. The socialization process has traditionally been viewed in two ways – from behaviourist and constructivist perspectives. The behaviourist view defines socialization as children's internalization of adult skills and knowledge. Through role models and reinforcement, the child is shaped and moulded by surrounding adult cultures and, in most cases, remains primarily passive.

The constructivist perspective stresses the active role of the child. Children are viewed as acquiring and constructing knowledge from what they interpret from the surrounding society. The constructivist view maintains that human learning transforms an individual through a process that generally occurs in a stage-like fashion rather than according to the accumulative view of the behaviourists. It promotes a primarily linear view of the developmental process. L. S. Vygotsky has made important contributions to the theory of human development.[5]

Vygotsky's arguments provided an alternative view of development in children's lives to a purely linear one. For Vygotsky, human development works in a dialectical relationship and involves the child's appropriation of culture through interaction with others. However his views continue to emphasize the goal of the developmental process to transform the child into a rational, full member of adult life. None the less, these constructivist approaches extended the views of the behaviouristic theories by articulating socialization as a more complex process.

One is able to see at this point that the issue of agency was becoming increasingly important in the models used to conduct research on children. In the work of Cicourel (1974) and Denzin (1977), one finds the emergence of another important factor in the study of children's worlds, namely context. Cicourel argued that children actively move through 'stages of child grammars, interpretive procedures and assumptions of the social world' (Corsaro 1985: 69). In this way, Cicourel's work focuses on social context by looking at children's interpretive abilities and how social actors link general rules to specific situations. While his views may be in line with the developmental perspective of Piaget and Vygotsky, Cicourel argues that models of adult knowledge and interactive competence should not be imposed upon the child. For Cicourel, like the developmental theorists, the child's everyday social interactions with adults and peers are the primary focus. In these frameworks, the study of peer interaction in children's worlds remains, however, of less central importance than adult–child interaction.

The importance of context and the acquisition of meaning by creative social actors were significant features of interpretive sociologies which began to emerge in the 1950s and 1960s. These approaches allowed children a more active role in the constitution of human society. The constitution of social life through an examination of the everyday life of actors fostered interest in the issue of children's agency and childhood as a particular kind of social reality. In turn, a critique of the conceptualization of childhood promoted by socialization theory was advanced.

For the study of children's cultures discussed in each of the models presented above, one sees that the issues of context and agency have become increasingly important. Despite this emerging focus, children continue to be viewed as reproducers of adult culture. Their lives are seen in relation to the lives of adults. William Corsaro's work on peer cultures throughout childhood and adolescence is an example of peer relationships that are viewed in relation to adult structures rather than in their own right. His research takes the view that children's peer culture is 'children's continual, communal attempts to grasp and control a social order first presented to them by adults but one which eventually becomes their own reproduction' (1985: 75). He presents what he calls an interpretive perspective wherein 'reproduction of the adult world [occurs] within peer culture. In the process, children come to more firmly grasp, refine, and extend features of the adult world in the creation of their own peer world' (1985: 62). This work reverts back to the notion of the child operating competently in the adult world.

In both the constructivist and interpretivist approaches, although one sees that the main focus is on children themselves, the models continue to render these voices inaudible. The focus is placed less on children than on other issues including developmental experiences, for example. The interpretivist views of development, unlike previous models, are primarily reproductive rather than linear. As Corsaro (1985: 74) points out, 'From this reproductive view of development, the child enters into a social nexus, and through interaction with others builds up a social understanding which becomes a core of social knowledge on which the child builds throughout the life-course.'

In sum, each of the models discussed above focuses predominantly on social learning; that is, the ways in which childhood knowledge and practices are transformed, whether dialectically or through stages of development, into the knowledge and skills necessary for participation in the adult world. As we have seen, most of this work has been carried out by looking at adult–child interactions with limited examination of children in peer cultures.

History

Apart from developments in psychology and sociology, it was in the area of history that one of the most dramatic changes in the study of childhood emerged. This movement, beginning in the 1970s, directed attention to critically examining received universalized categories and concepts including 'childhood'. Phillipe Aries' work is important to consider. He convincingly argued that childhood was not a universal notion but one that emerged in Europe between the fifteenth and eighteenth centuries. Through this work, he refuted traditional assumptions about the universality of childhood by tracing the gradual removal of children from adult society into a space of their own. Aries demonstrated that before the fifteenth century, Western society did not possess the idea of childhood. While Aries' ideas and work have undergone serious debate and critique, they none the less have had a lasting impact on the ways in which childhood has been conceptualized in the social sciences (Pollock 1983).

III ANTHROPOLOGICAL APPROACHES TO THE STUDY OF CHILDREN'S CULTURE

As noted earlier, in certain anthropological accounts of the past, children have retained a highly visible position. Except for a few studies, including John Blacking's *Venda Children's Songs* (1967), however, children's worlds have not been the primary focus of ethnographies. Most of the time, children have been discussed as part of a mother–child dyad in studies of child-rearing practices, as participants in initiation ceremonies, as members of kinship structures, as part of the schooling process in studies of language acquisition, or in connection with the importance of play in their lives (Sutton-Smith 1981; Herdt 1987; Shostak 1990). Consequently, children are most often relegated to a secondary position of importance in relation to adult cultures. It is ironic that this situation persists in anthropology in view of the preoccupation with children in many societies and the impact this has on broader social relations.

In anthropology, interest in aspects of childhood may be traced back to the work of early anthropologists from the culture and personality school including Ruth Benedict (1935) and Margaret Mead (1928). In both cases, the conventional view of socialization as a process wherein knowledge and cultural traits are transmitted by adults to children is upheld.[6]

Anthropological interest in age has been an important factor in encouraging studies of children as a specific age category. The notion that younger children inhabit a world with distinct social meanings was the premise for Charlotte Hardman's (1973) work, for example. Hardman developed the idea that there is in childhood a world that is not necessarily pre-rational or at a pre-adult stage (cf. 1973: 87). Her research pointed out the necessity to recognize the 'present' of childhood and to understand the importance of 'children as people to be studied in their own right, and not just as receptacles of adult teaching' (ibid.: 87). Unfortunately, Hardman's ideas have only recently begun to receive some attention by scholars of children's cultures.

New approaches to the study of children's lives

The subject of children and questions of agency and structure in children's lives is directly addressed in Alison James and Alan Prout's work (1990). The authors trace the development of a new and emerging paradigm for the study of childhood in response to the inadequacy of frameworks used in the past. The new paradigm that they propose involves the application of discourse theory to demonstrate the notion of childhood as a discursive formation within which different types of children and the notion of childhood are constituted (cf. James and Prout 1990: 22–31). Their work focuses on questions of social construction, subjectivity and authenticity in examining the role of children as active, meaning-producing beings.

James and Prout's emerging model is an important one because it moves away from development and socialization models to focus on the activity of children in their everyday lives. The authors outline several features of this emerging paradigm: first, is the importance of viewing childhood as a social construction: 'the institution of childhood provides an interpretive frame for understanding the early years of human life'; second, that childhood as a variable of social analysis can never be entirely separated from other variables including gender, ethnicity and class; and third, that childhood and children's social relationships and cultures are worthy of study in their own right: 'children must be seen as actively involved in the construction of their own social lives, the lives of those around them and of the societies in which they live' (ibid.: 3–4).

While the emphasis in Prout and James' work is on discursively made culture, they none the less acknowledge the importance of examining children's activities and cultural production. They are concerned however, to ensure that there is a theoretical space to understand the construction of childhood as a social institution that exists beyond the activity of any particular child (ibid.: 28).

IV RETHINKING MODELS FOR THE STUDY OF CHILDREN'S CULTURES

The development and socialization literature briefly reviewed above has contributed most substantially to our knowledge of children and their worlds. While many of the arguments made by theorists utilizing these models are useful and valid, each directs attention to particular questions and problems, thereby maintaining some biases and difficulties. The psychologically based literature, for example, emphasizes the individual child and his or her acquisition of a cognitive map to facilitate their eventual membership in adult society. This focus on the individual may obscure factors important to an analysis of a group. Similarly, the socialization literature focuses on the notion of the transformation, through various processes, of the child into a competent member of adult culture. Each of the models directs attention to the eventual incorporation of the child into the world of the adult. In effect, by focusing on what the child lacks, the models seem to imply that the child is in some ways incomplete. She or he is in the process of becoming a full adult member of society. This conceptualization depicts children as 'partially cultural'. Their contemporaneity with adult cultures is dismissed as well, along with the 'present' of their life experiences. It is a notion that is propelled by a similar logic that deems some cultures of the world, for example, as remnants of a previous time. Through this kind of exoticization, peoples are frozen in a conceptualization of time that negates the present. For children at least, this process reinforces the notion that children's lives are only significant in relation to some future state or in relation to adult cultures. In turn, these models promote the view, for the most part, of the passivity of the child while notions of agency are almost completely obscured.

This view of the passive, 'in process' child is therefore highly misleading. It is particularly incompatible with current conceptualizations of culture in anthropological theory that promote a more dynamic and relational view. In addition, the emphasis on passivity erases many aspects of children's lives including complex relationships of power. The passive model of the child promotes her as standing idly by awaiting to be filled with adult knowledge. For many adults that have been involved with children, this passivity is decidedly false. Children are actively engaged in the production of their own social worlds. This point was demonstrated very clearly to me during my field research with children in various Toronto grade schools in 1988 and subsequent research in Halifax schools in 1991.[7] I was interested in collecting songs from children that they created for themselves and then passed from child to child. After contacting local schools, several teachers attempted to discourage me from spending the time to collect songs that they claimed 'children no longer sing'. They were convinced that children did not retain the repertoire that they were sometimes familiar with from their own childhoods. They argued that technology and the media had all but destroyed the singing tradition. After working in many schools, it was thus to the great surprise of some of these teachers, that I was able to collect over two hundred songs after only six hours of contact. The experience left some of the classroom teachers astonished. On the other hand, the experience reinforced for me the idea that a rethinking of the question of agency used previously in models to understand children's cultures was long overdue.

Apart from the issue of children as active agents of culture, another problem extending from my earlier research has been the question of the temporal dimension of the way in which the category 'child' continues to be constructed. As demonstrated in the previous discussion, for the development and socialization frameworks that depict children in the process of becoming full adults, the 'present' of childhood is dismissed. The category 'child' is robbed of its immediate status and constructed as something of the past or as configured in a future adult world. There are numerous examples of the ways in which adults are complicitous in placing children 'out of time'. To name only one, in my recent 1993 field research in Toronto, I began to note the ways in which adults interacted with children at a downtown community centre. Many of the discussions I noted that occurred between adults and children who did not previously know one another centred around the adult asking the question, 'what do you want to be when you grow up?' The adults I spoke with thought that the question was an effective way to engage with children in order to establish rapport. In rethinking this argument, I could see that the question entirely dismissed the immediacy of children's lives in favour of some future time. While the children's responses were interesting, the question directed attention away from, instead of closer to, their everyday lives. Therefore, the temporal dimensions, along with the passive view of the child, help to perpetuate the continued marginalization of the subject of children's culture. Children, constructed without a 'present', are not studied in their own right. Accordingly, in order to understand children as active agents of culture, their presence and action in the immediate world must be acknowledged.

Children as cultural producers

One of the ways to facilitate an understanding of the 'present' of childhood is to look at the ways that children are actively involved in the creation of culture. As we have seen in the broad overview of literature on children's culture, the issue of cultural production has not been adequately dealt with in many of the development and socialization models in the past. As noted, most of the studies explore the ways in which facets of adult culture influence and permeate the lives of children. Children have been depicted as reproducers of culture. Children as consumers have been the focus of several studies as well, including children's role-playing, toy preferences, and television viewing (Sutton-Smith 1986; Fine 1987). Very few studies examine the ways in which children are active producers of their own culture. I have found through my own research with children that music can be an effective way to gain analytical access to this group.

Apart from my own work which examines the performative/ musical constructions of culture by children, however, limited attention has been directed to the subject by ethnomusicologists. The music remains a relatively unexplored resource. This situation persists despite the continued assertion by these scholars that they are interested in representing entire societies. Furthermore, music is said to be able to speak powerfully and directly to the realities of those people positioned in varying socio-historical locations. I would argue that for children in marginalized positions of power, it is a particularly important discourse. As John Shepherd writes:

> Music is ideally suited to coding homologously, and therefore to evoking powerfully yet symbolically, the structures, rhythms, and textures of the inner life of the individual; the structures, rhythms, and textures of the external social world; and the order of relations between them. . . . Because music can enter, grip, and position us symbolically, it can act powerfully to structure and mediate individual awareness as the ultimate seat of social and cultural reproduction.
>
> (Shepherd 1993: 52)

There are several reasons that may explain the lack of serious scholarly attention accorded to the subject of children's musical culture. Apart from practical considerations of research including lack of funding and time, there are broader issues to consider. In musicology, for example, there has been a continued marginalization for some time of music that is not part of the European art tradition. The boundaries surrounding musicology remain fairly rigid. Many analysts and theorists assume music's autonomy from society and culture and stress formalistic elements over other factors including the social location of the producers of music and experiences of the body, to name but two. Popular music, for example, is only just beginning to emerge as a legitimate research topic. Children's music falls within this marginalized space. However, if music is recognized as an important discourse, especially for those in subordinate positions of power, it should be considered vital to consider for an understanding of children's lives. Examining children's three- and four- note chants may be viewed as uninteresting by scholars studying the compositional styles of the 'master' composers, for example. However, when one considers that the children's songs, with themes that include female fear and physical abuse, are recited over and over again in a chant-like manner, few would dismiss the song tradition as trivial.

A similar hierarchical relationship to the one described in music circles is found in some areas of the social sciences. Children's culture is connected conceptually to women, is the subject of everyday life, is not explicitly tied to political economy and, as such, retains a devalued status. In order to rupture the devaluation process taking place, the work of scholars engaged in research 'from the margins' must be situated within the debates of the social sciences, drawing from them rather than working in isolation. The contradiction between the kinds of knowledge that are deemed important by those working to understand social worlds, and the marginalization of the voices of children and youth in their everyday lives, must be exposed. It is a contradiction that becomes obvious when there is a flurry of interest, for example, over issues of youth and violence. In my own research, I have concluded through my contact with children between the ages of 6 and 12 over a period of one year, that there is a significant increase in their tolerance of violence. This is an important finding, yet one which will remain inaudible unless new possibilities for the study of children's lives are explored.

V METHODOLOGICAL AND CONCEPTUAL ISSUES FOR THE STUDY OF CHILDREN'S CULTURES

Many methodological and conceptual issues important to the study of children's cultures need to be examined if the problems cited in the previous sections are to be effectively addressed. For instance, there are methodological problems particular to the study of children's cultures that begin when one asks the question: 'where is the child's perspective?' Only by answering this question can researchers begin to move away from the notion that the majority of elements of peer culture originate from children's perceptions of, and reactions to, the adult world (cf. Corsaro 1985: 172). This formulation serves once again to construct children's worlds as appendages to adult cultures. Children are not addressed on their own terms. Suransky notes this problem by stating that

> understanding the child from the perspective of his world is to hold the view that, despite biological and developmental determinants, the growing child is an intentional actor constructing a life project with consciousness, that becoming in the world involves a dynamic self-representation, that the child too, is a historical being, a maker of history, a meaning-maker involved in the praxis upon the world.

> (Suransky 1982: 36)

Methodologically and conceptually, children must be freed from the process of containment that produces them as 'Other' and in turn continues to silence them.

Moreover, it is important to understand the relationship between the researcher and her informants. Children experience much of their contact with adults in subordinate positions of power. I kept this point in mind when I designed the methodology for my own fieldwork. As a result, I made several choices including 1) choice of dress, i.e. flat shoes, casual and colourful clothes, and 2) physical proximity with the children, i.e. sitting on the floor with the children rather than on a chair above them. Apart from this practical focus, the relationship between the researcher and informants points to broader questions of how anthropological knowledge is constructed.

The fiction of the objective researcher has received much recent interest in anthropology. The notion that the fieldworker as participant-observer remains 'in a culture' in order to retain and record information about a particular group of people without including herself in the account, has been contested. She is, in fact, complicitous in whatever account of 'the culture' is produced in her interaction with the group of people under study. Clearly, the position of the field researcher is neither neutral nor insignificant to understand. It is a particularly salient point when one considers how categories such as 'childhood' and 'child' are constituted. I would argue that it is, in part, the relationship between the researcher and informants that produces these categories in particular situations. For example, early on in my recent research, I became aware that the concept of childhood I held was continually challenged by my interaction with my informants, as well as other adults. On the other hand, the children responded to my interest in understanding children's culture through their 'performance' of what they thought I wanted to see. For example, when I asked the children in the 1993 study to sing a 'children's song' for me, they usually offered a contemporary rap song. At other times, they would break out of rapping to provide a stereotypical children's song such as 'Pat-a-cake'. They would then wait for my reaction to their choice. In effect, they were responding to what they may have perceived as my interest in finding some kind of authentic childhood. In addition, by singing stereotypical children's songs for me, they were upholding, rather than subverting, the dominant formulations of the category 'child'. They were directly involved in the process of reinforcing the categories that otherwise exert control in their lives. The categories 'child' and 'childhood' were mutually shaped by our interaction.

An additional methodological problem for anthropologists of childhood is the fact that at one time or another they have experienced some form of childhood themselves. It is a feature somewhat unique to this kind of work. The difficulty lies in determining whether one can ever approach the ideal of fieldwork to put these preconceived notions of this time of life aside in order to become a full participant observer. Thus, working with an age/time based culture challenges the participant–observation framework in many ways.

On the other hand, there are positive aspects of the participant–observation method for the study of children's culture. As many researchers have noted in their continual call for an 'anthropology of childhood' (Hardman 1973; Suransky 1982), this methodology is particularly suited to working with children. It gives researchers the opportunity to experience at close hand aspects of children's worlds, including musical production, that occur spontaneously and in informal contexts.

Finally, there are, of course, several practical problems of method when working with children's groups. One important factor is to gain access to groups of children for extended periods of time. This proves to be difficult because of restrictions placed on children's time by adults, or restrictions on adults interacting with children because of concerns of abuse, for example. When one is able to work with children, there are issues of method, i.e. informal rather than formal techniques, contact time and attention span limitations that need to be considered for the particular research situation. In addition, new techniques can be devised when working with children who may not be accustomed to the formality of interviews. One of the ways that I have found to be productive for my research has been the use of a video camera. After instructing the children on how to use the camera, I allow them to take control of the images and sounds they wish to record. This kind of approach allows the children the freedom to express themselves outside the limitations of a question and answer format.

Problems of definition

In considering the methodological issues above, the question 'where is the child's voice?' was central. However, the usefulness of this kind of inquiry is diminished if the related question, 'what is a child?' is overlooked. The point to understand for the study of children's culture is that the terms used are ubiquitous and their referents are various. For example, various terms are scattered throughout the literature that sometimes fall under the umbrella term of 'children'. These include words such as adolescents, youth, teenagers and young adults. The boundaries between them seem to be placed arbitrarily. Discrepancies occur when, for example, people above the age of 13 are categorized as 'children' while at other times they are called 'youth'. It is the arbitrary nature of the constitution of the categories that becomes difficult. Age is one example of an important criterion that is used in our commonsense notion of how the categories of children and youth are defined. Yet it is a parameter that is arbitrarily placed. Moreover, this view that constructs the category of child by age is insufficient and reduces the complexity of the problem. Age should be a parameter considered not separately, but along with, others including ethnicity, class and gender.

Apart from age, there are other arbitrary features that are used to distinguish between the categories of children and youth. Some of these parameters include power, autonomy and consumerism. Depending upon which variables are chosen, the categories of children and youth may be conceptualized in different ways.

Power is an important component to consider in the lives of both children and youth, although it has been associated more so with the worlds of youth. The arbitrary ways that notions of power are used to distinguish between youth and children demonstrate, however, that more information concerning children's lives is required. For example, both children and youth have access to power. Their ability to retain this power or not depends on several issues: (1) to some degree, on the ability of others in positions of power who are able to oppress them. While the experience of this oppression differs, children and youth none the less may share in these experiences, and (2) whether researchers recognize the different forms of power in children's peer cultures. Most of these kinds of power relationships have not been examined. For example, the insistence of teachers that my search for children's songs would be futile exposes their unawareness of this oral tradition and the power relationships that facilitate its persistence. Furthermore, in many of the children's groups that I worked with, power was a key element of the group dynamic. This power was manifest when a visible leader emerged from a group to direct the activities of others. In sum, power is usually a defining characteristic to distinguish youth as a conceptual category. It is, however, very important to recognize power in children's lives. One of the problems has been that discussions of power sometimes focus on discursive power at the expense of non-discursive power. For both children and youth, the emphasis on discursive power is limiting, for it usually privileges those only in powerful positions to be heard.

Other variables used to define the categories of children and youth include access to resources such as money and time. Again, these variables are linked to the lives of youth more so than children. This may be due to the fact that younger children appear to have only limited access to these resources while youth may retain greater control. If they are able to secure employment, for example, they may have greater control over the choice of clothes they wear, the music they listen to, their level of mobility, and so on. In turn, they may be better able to define how to manage their own time, thereby exercising a greater amount of control over their lives than children. However, access to money is also an important consideration when examining the production of culture by children. The introduction of money undoubtedly allows people access to the market in different ways. From my research experience, for example, I have witnessed firsthand, for musical production at least, how musical tastes and production are driven by market forces as well as peer pressure. For example, the sample of songs that I collected from children in informal contexts in 1993 contains a minimal amount of what I defined as 'children's songs' in my previous studies. The children in

1993 usually sang and listened to rap and popular music in these informal contexts. As a result, their musical production diminished, while consumption rose significantly. These broad generalizations point to the complexity of the notion of precisely how to define cultural production itself. Therefore, access to resources, which is directly related to autonomy and consumerism, need to be questioned as the distinguishing variables of the category of youth alone. In sum, the point remains that the characteristics used to define categories are arbitrarily placed and need to be re-examined.

With regard to the issue of time, this element is significant for both youth and children. While one could argue that, for children at least, it appears that there is a connection between the loss of control over their time and a decrease in the production of culture, it cannot be substantiated. Adults are often unaware of the control children exert in their worlds within formalized spaces structured by adults. Until more work is carried out which examines the spaces of childhood from children's perspectives, wherein the complexity of power relationships that cross-cut axes of differences by age, ethnicity, class and gender are integral, an answer to the question of time and the production of culture cannot be effectively argued.

CONCLUSION: EMPOWERING CHILDREN'S VOICES

The rethinking of the concept of culture that has taken place in anthropology has made explicit issues to consider when formulating approaches to the study of children and youth cultures. Current conceptualizations of culture have helped to bring into view previously marginalized voices and have disrupted the maintenance of the subject/object dichotomy and the relations of power that have sustained anthropological research in the past. The search for the 'exotic' culture has been challenged in order for studies in a researcher's 'own backyard' to be deemed viable and legitimate forms of research. In addition, feminist efforts have aided in critiquing power structures that continue to devalue certain kinds of knowledge and have demonstrated the importance to consider subjective ways of knowing. This work has reoriented the focus on women's experience and agency in their everyday lives. Each of these efforts has had positive effects for the study of children's worlds.

For future studies that seek to empower the voices of both children and youth, it is important to consider the arbitrary ways parameters are used in the constitution of these categories as well as the cultural and historically specific nature of the categories of children and youth. To this end, Suransky notes, for childhood at least, that

> the meaning of childhood must be retrieved from adult structures of consciousness that are fixedly punctuated by a linear, 'rational' epistemology of human development. If childhood was acknowledged in the world of the ancients, formally denied in the medieval period, only to re-emerge in postfeudal Europe, does a dialectical approach not require us to understand these 'centuries of childhood' as a changing historical movement in consciousness directed toward the human future?
>
> (Suransky 1982: 17)

Following Suransky, important questions to gain an understanding of childhood include: How in the past, and how in the present does the child see herself – as a child? As a miniature adult? To what extent have adult constructions of reality misrepresented the historical child and to what extent do they continue to misrepresent the child's experience of 'being in the world?' (ibid.: 16).

Finally, the issue that has underlined this discussion has been agency. The brief overview of approaches to the study of children and children's culture demonstrated that the notion of children actively engaged in the production of culture has received little serious scholarly attention. One of the reasons for the persistence of this situation is that they have been contained in discourses that guarantee their passivity. In order to reposition the notion of agency for the studies of children and youth as active social actors, a dynamic concept of culture must be employed so that research can focus on their lives in the present and on their activity as producers of culture. They can no longer be seen as only 'partially cultural'.

For future studies of children and youth cultures, some may question whether or not to treat the subjects of children and youth separately or together. The answer is a complex one. As we have seen, the distinction between these categories is made according to a largely arbitrary notion of age, along with other variables including notions of power, autonomy and consumerism. On the one hand, we have been made aware by feminist researchers in the past of the problems inherent in trying to forge all-encompassing categories such as 'woman'. The end result may be the creation of homogenized categories, wherein all differences are levelled. In this regard, researchers should look to cues from feminist approaches to the category 'woman' that deal with difference. Some of these approaches may illuminate how to look at the whole without losing sight of the particular and relevant aspects of the lives of children and youth.

Moreover, the problem that may arise if children and youth are treated separately is that a ghettoization effect may occur. This means that anthropologists should be aware that their efforts to focus on one group or the other may again push the subject to the margins. Ultimately, one must keep in mind that the lines between youth and children are most often arbitrarily placed, and that research must not homogenize differences within the categories that are created. The creation of categories may be necessary to carry out certain kinds of research; marginalizing and silencing voices through the research process are not.

Accordingly, the question that becomes more important to consider is not whether children and youth should be treated together or separately, but rather how are researchers involved in the production and articulation of these categories as separate entities in light of how they are experienced by these people in their everyday lives? Concern should focus on the notion that through our representations of the worlds of children and youth, researchers are part of the process of creating, and to some degree, containing them.

NOTES

1 In her account of British youth research during the 1980s, Christine Griffin (1992) cites the emergence of two major perspectives for the study of youth – one mainstream and another radical. See Griffin 1992: 2.
2 Piaget's work focuses primarily on the conceptual abilities of the child as seen through her progression through a series of distinct levels of cognitive development. The goal of these stages is to achieve adult competence. His work follows a primarily evolutionary perspective that homogenizes the notion of 'the child' and produces a discourse of the universality of childhood.
3 In his work on children and development, Youniss (1980) extends Piaget's ideas, arguing that social development occurs as the result of children's interpersonal interactions in two distinct social worlds. He argues that it is children's entry into peer relations which gives development an innovative direction. This work relies almost exclusively, however, on clinical interviewing.
4 This overview is based upon a discussion in William A. Corsaro's book *Friendship and Peer Culture in the Early Years* (1985).

5 Vygotsky (1978) concentrated his work on the interrelationship of the practical activities of children in everyday social events.

6 Anthropological interest in the study of play has been another area that has received a significant amount of emphasis. In this work, play is defined as the process that gives shape as well as expression to individual and societal affective and cognitive systems (cf. Schwartzman 1978: 330). Schwartzman defined several categories of research on play including: the production of textual and contextual ethnographies of children's play including games of order and disorder; relationships between play and other social factors; cross-cultural studies of various developmental ideas, such as those of Piaget; and studies of children's verbal play and its relationship to adult/child speech acts (cf. Schwartzman 1978: 329–330). More recent researchers of play have explored the following: play and ritual; issues of context–text; play as context and adaptation; and interpretive perspectives of play, to name a few. For the most part, this research follows frameworks set up by development and socialization models.

7 Children's musical production was the focus of a previous study of mine (Caputo 1989). In this work, I was interested to find out what happens over time in a local branch of the tradition of Canadian English-language children's song. Initially, I set out to replicate the fieldwork undertaken by Edith Fowke between the years 1959 and 1964 in the Toronto area. With a second group of data generated in Toronto at a distance of twenty-four to twenty-nine years, I found that children maintain a large repertoire of songs, approximately one hundred, that are passed from child to child with little or no intervention from adults. For the core group of songs that persisted, approximately twenty-nine songs appeared mainly in the form of three-and four-note chants with highly gender-specific themes, and were played predominantly by girls' groups. This phenomenon occurred despite important cultural attempts to improve the status of women in society over the past several decades. These ideas seem not to have permeated the boundaries surrounding children's culture. Themes of songs dealing explicitly with issues such as female fear, females as property, physical abuse, control of the State, and traditional female and male roles, abound in the children's repertoire. Songs that carry these messages are repeated over and over again by children in predominantly 'chant' form. The chants indicate that they are not merely reflective of the surrounding adult world, but that children are actively engaged in the process of shaping their worlds.

REFERENCES

Benedict, R. (1935) *Patterns of Culture*, London: Routledge & Kegan Paul.
Blacking, J. (1967) *Venda Children's Songs Ethnomusicological Analysis*, Johannesburg: Witwatersrand University Press.
Campbell, A. (1986) *Girls in the Gang*, New York: Basil Blackwell Inc.
Caputo, V. (1989) 'Continuity and change in Canadian English-language children's song: a replication and extension in 1988 of Edith Fowke's

fieldwork 1959–64'. MA thesis, York University, Scott Archives No. 890056.

Cicourel, A. (1974) *Cognitive Sociology*, New York: Free Press.

Cohen, S. (1971) *Images of Deviance*, Harmondsworth: Penguin.

Coombe, R. J. (1991) 'Beyond modernity's meanings: engaging the postmodern in cultural anthropology', *Culture*, XI, 1–2: 111–124.

Corsaro, W. (1985) *Friendship and Peer Culture in the Early Years*, Norwood, NJ: Ablex Press.

Corsaro, W. and Eder, D. (1990) 'Children's peer cultures', *Annual Review of Sociology*, 16: 197–220.

Denzin, N.K. (1977) *Childhood Socialization*, San Francisco, CA: Jossey-Bass.

Donaldson, M. (1978) *Children's Minds*, London: Fontana.

Fine, G. L. (ed.) (1987) *Meaningful Play, Playful Meaning*, Champaign, Ill: Human Kinetics.

Frith, S. (1976) *The Sociology of Rock*, London: Constable.

Griffin, C. (1992) 'Forever young. Discourses of femininity and resistance in British youth research during the 1980's', unpublished paper.

Hall, S. and Jefferson, T. (eds) (1976) *Resistance Through Rituals*, London: Unwin Hyman.

Hardman, C. (1973) 'Can there be an anthropology of children?', *Journal of the Anthropological Society of Oxford*, 4, 1: 85–99.

Hebdige, D. (1979) *Subculture: The Meaning of Style*, New York and London: Methuen.

Herdt, G. (1987) *The Sambia. Ritual and Gender in New Guinea*, New York: Holt, Rinehart and Winston.

James, A. (1993) *Childhood Identities*, Edinburgh: Edinburgh University Press.

James, A. and Prout, A. (eds) (1990) *Constructing and Reconstructing Childhood: Contemporary Issues in the Sociological Study of Childhood*, London: The Falmer Press.

Light, P. (1986) 'Context, conservation and conversation', in M. Richards and P. Light (eds) *Children of Social Worlds*, Cambridge: Polity Press.

McRobbie, A. (1980) 'Settling accounts with subcultures: a feminist critique', *Screen Education*, 34: 37–49.

Mead, M. (1928) *Coming of Age in Samoa*, Harmondsworth: Penguin.

Mirza, H.S. (1992) *Young, Female and Black*, London: Routledge & Kegan Paul.

Piaget, J. (1950) *The Psychology of Intelligence*, London: Routledge.

Pollock, L.A. (1983) *Forgotten Children*, Cambridge: Cambridge University Press.

Schwartzman, H. B. (1978) *Transformations: The Anthropology of Children's Play*, New York: Plenum.

Shepherd, J. (1993) 'Difference and power in music', in R. A. Solie (ed.) *Musicology and Difference. Gender and Sexuality in Music Scholarship*, Berkeley, CA: University of California Press.

Shostak, M. (1990) *Nisa. The Life and Words of a Kung Woman*, London: Earthscan Publications Ltd.

Suransky, V. P. (1982) *The Erosion of Childhood*, Chicago, Ill: The University of Chicago Press.

Sutton-Smith, B. (1981) *A History of Children's Play: New Zealand, 1840–1950*, Philadelphia: University of Pennsylvania Press.

—— (1986) *Toys as Culture*, New York: Gardner Press.

Vygotsky, L.S. (1978) *The Mind in Society*, Cambridge, Mass: Harvard University Press.

Youniss, J. (1980) *Parents and Peers in Social Development: A Sullivan-Piaget Perspective*, Chicago, Ill: University of Chicago Press.

Chapter 3

Talking of children and youth

Language, socialization and culture

Allison James

INTRODUCTION

The ambiguity of the phrase 'talking of children and youth' is deliberate. First, it refers to the way in which these two phases in the life-course are commonly talked about, perceived and conceptualized; second, it draws attention to the forms of talking through which those social spaces of childhood and youth are shaped and experienced by young people themselves: the talk of children and young people. And, as a contribution to the burgeoning sociological and anthropological literature on childhood and youth cultures, these twin themes are brought together here through a consideration of the ways in which it is appropriate to talk theoretically about children and young people's experience of socialization in contemporary English society. Drawing on two periods of ethnographic fieldwork in different parts of England with children aged between 4 and 15 years olds I consider what the form, content and context of young people's language reveals about the nature and experience of growing up. From the perspective of these young people, some of whom were poised on the point of entry into childhood while others had relinquished their membership of the category 'child', I ask, how do young people of different ages talk of and about themselves and the Others they will become; how do they respond to being talked about and categorized by Others and what can all this talk tell us about the nature of the socialization process?

The explicit link drawn here between language and identity is no artifice for language acts as 'an emblem of groupness, as a symbol, a rallying-point' (Edwards 1985: 17). It is both a means of and for the communication of ideas about belonging and identity.

As work within the ethnography of speaking has established, language – whether realized through the medium of speech and/or writing – forms a cultural system and constitutes the shared symbolic resource of a particular speech community (Bauman and Scherzer 1974). Speaking a language – knowing its subtle connotations, sharing in its nuances and irregularities and abiding by (or deliberately rejecting) the conventions of conversational form – is, in fact, a prerequisite for belonging (Reisman 1974). Here I shall show how the children and young people with whom I talked both used the English language in particular and specific ways to mark out exclusive and excluding identities for themselves and how shifts in their use of language can be seen to facilitate movement in and between the different identities of 'child' and of 'youth' and thus to shape different kinds of belonging over time.

The first research project on which I draw was carried out in the north-east of England in 1979 where I worked in a youth club with young people aged between 11 and 16 years old who lived in a small mining village. Like many ex-pit communities, although coal-mining no longer provided an income, the working-class mining ethos remained. It was an industrialized rurality. The second project which I undertook in 1989 had a somewhat different location. While working again largely although not exclusively with working-class children, the research project took place in a large English town in the urban Midlands. Here my concern was with much younger children aged between 4 and 9 years old.[1] And yet despite such spatial and temporal differences, what struck me, as I carried out my second piece of fieldwork, were the remarkable parallels in language use. Given the strong links which have been established between social class and language use in Britain (Bernstein 1970) this was intriguing, suggesting to me the possibility that position in the life course, and not just in the class structure, may also have its part to play in shaping 'talk'. If the categories 'child' and 'youth' are constructed conceptually through the application of linguistic terms (see below) then it is not surprising that one critical source of children's and young people's identities may lie in the very words others (that is, adults) use to discuss and classify them. It is this observation about the generational nature of language use which is explored through the following ethnographic examples.

THEORETICAL PERSPECTIVES ON CHILD AND YOUTH CULTURES

Informing the way in which I talk about childhood and youth is a particular conceptual paradigm which has emerged from the studies of childhood variously carried out since the 1970s (Prout and James 1990). One important feature of this paradigm lies in its embrace of the idea that the concepts of childhood and youth are both social constructions of particular phases in the life-course which change their form and character across time and space. From this it follows that the biology of young people's maturing bodies is not the main invariant determinant of their categorical identity but instead is subject to different interpretive frames between and within cultures and historical epochs. Thus, the conceptual categories of 'child' and of 'youth' come into being through sets of prescriptive and proscriptive rules governing the social actions of category members. It is this which constitutes a pool of knowledge for the knowing Self (Hockey and James 1993; James 1993).

A second feature of this same paradigm stresses the participatory role which children and young people have in shaping the day-to-day experience and outcomes of their category status. Rejecting the passivity of functionalist roles/models, contemporary accounts of becoming social emphasize that young people 'are active in the construction and determination of their own social lives, the lives of those around them and of the societies in which they live' (Prout and James 1990: 8). With this theoretical orientation it has now become possible to speak of children possessing a 'culture of childhood', just as in the 1970s 'youth culture' acquired a sociological respectability. In both cases prominence is given to the symbolic practices and forms through which society is experienced by young people, reflecting their categorical positioning in particular phases of the life-course. One purpose of this chapter is to reveal – in young people's talk – how movement between these structural phases is accomplished.

In contrast to much research on 'youth' my focus, then, is not on subcultures *per se* (Brake 1985). Rather, it concentrates on exploring the cultural experience and structuring of the passage from childhood to youth. That is to say, I am interested in the process of becoming social, made manifest by children and young people in the contexts within which they are forced to socialize. This cultural experience may or may not take on ritualized and oppositional subcultural aspects (Hall and Jefferson 1976) as children and youth mark out their own passage to an adult world which forbids their entry just as it simultaneously engages their interest.

With this in mind, I take further the suggestion that children and young people's experience of the social world is one of social marginality, a consequence of the centrality of able-bodied adulthood within conceptualizations of the life-course in contemporary Western cultures (Hockey and James 1993). And, in emphasizing the marginality of children and young people within the social world, some of the insights to be found in Eisenstadt's (1956) early work on generations prove illuminating. Eisenstadt highlighted the structural regulation of youth on society's margins and pointed to the structured routes of transition from the stage of youth to that of adulthood. For Eisenstadt, youth 'culture' essentially represented an antidote to this problematic experience of marginality and had 'the general function of smoothing the transition from child to adult, (Frith 1984: 21). Although his theory of generations was formulated within a functionalist framework and is now seen as problematic, the idea of social marginality and generational culture remains a useful insight. For me it offers a theoretical lens through which to understand the process of socialization when placed alongside other later anthropological work on rites of passage and liminality (Turner 1974; and see James 1993). It allows me, for instance, to focus upon the cultures of childhood and youth, not as subcultures seemingly fixed in their opposition to the adult world or in jeering mockery of it, but instead as Geertzian contexts within which the generational experience of being denied access to and participation in central social institutions can be thickly described. Further, it allows the processual quality of children and young people's social lives to be explored as participatory experiences of transition, rather than zones of exclusion, in the life-course.

What I am suggesting, then, is that the differences which exist between children's and young people's social experiences and those of adults be understood first as characteristics of temporal, rather than sub-, cultures (Schwartz 1976). Seen in these terms, the differences and/or similarities between child and youth cultures become comprehensible in terms of the gradual easing of social restrictions or the imposition of further controls which accompany the transition to adulthood. Thus, the parallels to be found in the cultural forms and styles of expression used by young children and older youth can be seen as illustrative of overlaps in social transition,

of the movement into youth from childhood in successive generations. Ultimately, in a Western culture such as Britain, it is time
itself, visibly displayed in the developing body and numerically
quantified in passing years, which is said to provide the passage into
adulthood.[2] What unites children and youth, then, is their shared
cultural experience of the denial of the full social personhood which
adulthood will bring (Carrithers *et al.* 1985; Hockey and James
1993). It is this experience of generation, therefore, which overlays
and meshes with those other experiences derived from class position,
gender or ethnicity. Traditional studies of youth subcultures have
made these latter aspects of young people's lives their primary focus
at the expense of ideas of generation. In this chapter I endeavour to
redress the balance by bringing the two streams together.

My concern, then, is to depict the experience of the transition
between childhood and youth, envisaged as a gradual movement
towards the social centre, through describing how particular kinds
of 'talk' facilitate and image that transition. I will suggest that
through 'talk' social knowledge is both reproduced and created so
that, in the movement into and out of the loquacious 'culture' of
childhood/youth, is imaged the process of becoming social – being
socialized – which is the mark of full personhood. I shall show
how the verbal motifs and motives which structure childhood talk
gradually become extenuated in youth, that formality yields to
informality and dogma to innovation, as the sociality of the social
world falls at last within the orbit of individual competencies.[3]

LEARNING TO 'TALK' – AGAIN

While sitting with a group of boys one evening in the 1970s,
sheltering in the youth club from the cold north-eastern night,
one lad remarked conversationally, 'It's nice coming here – to
talk'. 'Talking' was seen by them not just as a means of and for
communication but as an activity in itself. But this 'talk' was
distinctive both in its resources and its performance; as an adult I
had to learn to talk again to be able to join in their conversations.
And later, in a Midlands school, in the 1980s I heard younger
children of 6 and 7 years old similarly beginning to re-learn their
native tongue. They were learning to restructure their 'talk' – they
practised a particular narrative style, tried out jokes, softly swore and
drew enthusiastically upon a repertoire of smutty rhymes.

It was Iona and Peter Opie who first drew attention to the fact that

British children have their own lore and language which is peculiar to them and passed between generations of children without the aid of adult intermediaries. In their two seminal texts on children's language and games (1959; 1969), they detail the resources of this special language which, for the Opies, makes children's language first and foremost a location for childhood identity. Their opening words make this abundantly clear: 'the scraps of lore which children learn from each other are at once more real, more immediately serviceable, and more vastly entertaining to them than anything which they learn from grown-ups' ([1959] 1977: 21).

This language has a distinctive form and structure, having a long and continuous tradition and a tenacious uniformity across class and community. At the same time, however, new words and phrases are speedily assimilated and quickly transmitted between children. This lends to childhood language a dynamic and creative flexibility, rather than fixing it as a static and unchanging form. Like other largely oral traditions children's language also has distinctive streams or genres. In this case, a 'slangy superficial lore of comic songs, jokes, catch phrases, fashionable adjectives, slick nicknames, and crazes' sits alongside a dialectal lore which is 'the language of children's darker doings: playing truant, giving warning, sneaking, sniveling, tormenting, and fighting' (Opie and Opie [1959] 1977: 34–35). In both my research contexts, though distant from each other in terms of years and miles, I encountered this exclusive tongue. Familiar words spoken in a peculiar form or strange adjectives and obscure but resonant phrases peppered the conversations I heard. In the playground and on the street I listened to children talking with a cadence and rhythm which was both singular and excluding. And I heard repeated in a primary school in a Midlands town of the 1980s many of the songs and rhymes I had previously encountered in the 1970s, tripping smartly off the tongues of near-Geordie lads of 12 and 13 years old as, in the streets of a small rural community, they teased and argued with their Geordie lasses.[4] The tradition and continuity of childhood lore was obvious; what was perhaps less certain was the purpose it served. How do children come to grasp the subtleties of this particularized lore and language, why are some children more adept than others and why, in time, as youth encroaches, do they lose or abandon a previous and cherished facility with it?

In detailing the linguistic resourcefulness of children through these comparative ethnographic contexts, the role of language as a social and a socializing medium for young people will become clear for, as Giddens notes:

> becoming social cannot be understood in 'monological' terms: as a series of competencies simply 'stored' in the learner. Rather becoming social involves, on the level of cognition, mastery of the 'dialogical' contexts of communication. Such mastery is by no means wholly discursive, but involves the accumulation of practical knowledge of the conventions drawn upon in the production and reproduction of social interaction.
>
> (Giddens 1979: 129–130)

For children and young people 'talk' is a primary medium of social exchange through which, as Rapport notes, the 'contours of the social world [are] continuously firmed up' and declared as common, in the same moment when, as individuals, children and young people announce loudly their individuality and uniqueness. This seeming contradiction in talk and conversation arises from the fact that 'Individuals depend upon [the] common attributes of their culture for the capacity to make meaning, and yet, the vitality of the forms depends on individuals with meanings they endemically want to express through them' (Rapport 1993: 170).

In the conversational style, which shapes the 'talk' of childhood, are writ large the themes which characterize the temporal culture of child/youth: as I have shown elsewhere, emphases on hierarchy and equality vie with those on individuality and conformity and, in each individual's competence and ability to negotiate these conflicting cultural demands, lies the source of their identity as child among other children (see James 1986; 1993). I shall go on to illustrate how these same cultural motifs shape children's growing verbal facility and fluency, a form of 'talk' which, in youth, becomes translated as a stylistic emblem of their practical mastery, to be demonstrably revealed through competitive performances (Bourdieu 1977).

RESOURCES AND RESPONSES

'Talking' involves first knowing how and when to use language and young children soon recognize that 'rules of appropriateness beyond grammar govern speech' (Hymes 1971: 56). Over time, through successful acts of speaking, these rules are made manifest through repetitive occurrences and, like the games they learn to play (James 1993), it is through taking careful cognizance of the speech styles of

those who are older, more competent performers that little children
begin to learn which are appropriate and inappropriate speech forms
and contexts of speaking. This process takes both time and practice
which is why, when first working with 4- and 5-year-old children who
had only just begun to join the child's social world, the lore and
language of childhood seemed glaringly absent. Only later did I
realize that, as mere novices, they simply had not yet had the time
to accumulate the necessary specialist resources.

One of the prime resources which children draw upon, for
instance, are sets of specialized words, what Brake (1985) terms the
'argot' of youth subcultural style. Through the articulation of these
words children and young people separate themselves off from the
adult world and, at the same time, identify for themselves those who
are, or who are not, stylish speakers; that is, those who do or do not
yet belong. Classificatory children they might be, but competent
child persons they are not. The 4- and 5-year-old children with whom
I worked had yet to get to know these words but, by 7 and 8 years
old, the children were beginning to know that bum should always be
used instead of 'bottom' when talking to friends, that dibby means
thick, i.e. stupid, that the use of bagsy can stake out one's claim.
Such words, often localized and particular, provide an important
passage into the language of 'talk', as children who move between
schools or localities soon realize (Opies and Opies [1959] 1977: 35).
Newcomers may not be understood and, being unable to 'talk'
appropriately, may find themselves on the fringes of the child's
social world. Other words – for example, the adjectives mega and
wick meaning exceedingly good – may be appropriations of the adult
tongue, a form of fashionable slang which, as the Opies noted, may
be less enduring. But knowing, and correctly using, these words is
also a prerequisite for belonging.

This facility with language develops slowly over time. Thus, the
young people I knew in the 1970s – then aged between 11 and 14
years old – had by this age an extensive and excluding vocabulary
which I, as an adult, had to learn. Places in the village were identified
by special terms and parts of the body were always referred to by an
alternative terminology: *gob, rattle, trap, hole* or *hooter* were always
used as replacements for the mouth; *sneck* or *beak* described the
nose, while ears were *lugs* and *lid* stood for head. Gradually
becoming conscious fashion followers, for them, shoes were never
just shoes. Representing a particularly significant item of clothing,
a specialized vocabulary allowed particular types of shoes to be

identified and their wearers to be categorized. Boys, identified as 'the lads', never wore shoes. Instead it was *docs* (Dr Marten boots) which always graced their feet. Those other boys, observed to wear *sannies* or *slip-ons*, clearly did not aspire to the status of 'lad'.

Some of these words are old dialect words which have died out in the adult tongue (Opies and Opies [1959] 1977). As the property of children and young people, therefore, these words register not only the continuity of verbal traditions between generations of children; they simultaneously celebrate their insularity as a social category. Words, now marginal in the adult lexical world, are thus taken as symbolic emblems by those who are marginalized. For example, the word kets in Durham dialect, originally meant something rotten or decaying and applied particularly to meat and carcasses. In the north-east in the 1970s only elderly people still used the term and then usually only as an adjective, *ketty*. But the noun *kets* was still used by children as a noun, to refer to the kinds of sweets which they prized most highly; it was children's food over which children had control (James 1979a). The younger children whom I worked with in the 1980s were only just beginning to familiarize themselves with such esoteric linguistic usages and would tentatively practice half-heard phrases or try out on their peers the jokes which older children or siblings had recently told them.

However, despite the frequent localized nature of particular terminologies children and young people's simultaneous membership of the generational culture of the young is evidenced by the fact that these specialized words reproduce many of the structural features and resources of children's language – suffixes, formulaic phrases and rhymes – which have been noted as characteristic by the Opies [1959] 1977). The musicality of the language of childhood, for instance, immediately struck me as a feature of young people's 'talk' in the 1970s, an observation which was to be repeated in the 1980s when I worked with younger children. Conversations would be peppered with short, snappy words ending with 'g','y','a' and 'z': *hag, bag, bog, lug, mug clemmy, spuggy, chowy, gadgy, gobby, sissy, manky, hacky; spacca, snacker, knacker, mega; soz, bas, lez, proz*.[5] Some of these were abbreviations, made to fit the childish tongue by adding suffixes and, among the older children, the nicknames by which they knew each other also echoed this patterning of sound: Baz, Daz, Caz, Cribby, Banny, Pewsy, Stoker, Mogga (James 1979b). Thus, through the active shaping and reshaping of the English language the young people created a distinctive 'youthful' language whose terminology, rhythm and cadence styled their 'talk'. In doing so it therefore signified not only their membership of a local group of children or young people, marked by neighbourhood and class, but also their participation in the wider generational culture of the young. As the older boys teased each other and made jibes at the girls, and those same girls nicknamed those they despised, so the younger children listened, ready to learn the art of youthful conversation. A second feature of the 'talk', which took place among the children and young people I worked with, was their use of ritualized phrases and formulae, verbal challenges and ripostes. Again, this characteristic is noted by the Opies ([1959] 1977). In the 1970s I listened to 11- 12- and 13-year-old children delight in tripping each other by invoking traditional verbal ploys. If a child, irritated by another, asked rhetorically, 'Do you mind!', the provoker might insight further annoyance with the reply, 'No, I babysit'. There were many comparable pairings:

    A: Well!
    B: That's what you get water from.

    A: Aye!
    B: Comes before J.

These couplets, invariably brought into verbal play whenever an opportunity arose in the flow of ordinary conversations, were used deliberately to misconstrue an intended meaning and to out-perform another child.

Listening to these frequent contests of wit and verbal dexterity revealed to me early on the value placed by young people on careful and creative wordsmanship. Those who were fluent in this language style were the more popular boys, central characters within the social group. That it was a skill which needs to be developed was later confirmed for me when I heard 8- and 9- year-old children practising in the school playground in the 1980s. They were articulating the same play upon a common homonym which, some ten years earlier, had been a continuous refrain among the 12- and 13- year-old children I was working with.

To the concerned question, ' Are you alright?', the correct answer was 'No, I'm half left.' By this means, the questioner's trickery is exposed and the challenge correctly deflected. The skilled practitioner could, however, always engineer another's downfall. He or she might casually ask, 'How are you?', thereby inviting the common and unthinking response, 'Alright.' To this would be countered the joyous rejoinder: 'No you're not, you're half left' or 'No, you're centre down the middle.' A myriad of similar opportunities could present themselves in the flow of many ordinary conversations:

A: Are your shoes wet?
B: No.
A: Well they should be, There's a big drip in them.

A: When did you have the operation?
B: What operation?
C: Do you mean to say you've always looked like that?

What is significant about many of these sets of challenges and ripostes is that they are built upon expressions which, within the adult world, are courtesy speech forms, part of that armoury of verbal platitudes with which, as adults, we oil the art of conversation and smooth the course of social interactions. As adults we inquire routinely how others are; we exclaim, sympathize and work with rhetoric. It is this ritualized, empty social conventionality which young people creatively dismember in their conversational style. It is a form of symbolic usage which 'intentionally deconventionalizes the conventional (and unintentionally conventionalizes the unconventional; a new meaning has been formed (and an old meaning has been extended)' (Wagner 1975: 28).

Thus the 'talk' of childhood and youth marks out its own boundaries and conventions of communication, setting out parameters of identity in relation to degrees of linguistic facility as, through threat and counter-threat, challenges to belonging are issued between peers.

A third feature of this generational language is the frequent use of rhymes in conversation, which enhances the rhythmic, musical quality which ordinary 'talk' possesses. This is partly facilitated by the use of the particular suffixes noted above, but also because, as the Opies note, 'rhyme seems to appeal to a child as something funny and remarkable in itself, there need be neither wit nor reason to support it' ([1959] 1977: 37). In both periods of fieldwork this was clearly the case. As with jokes, rhymes were rarely separated out as a distinctive speech act; no introductions were given to the incorporation of verse within 'talk' as would occur in an adult conversation. Instead, rhymes would appear as part of the normal flow of conversation. Listening to young children talking in the

1980s they might burst spontaneously into rhyme in mid-sentence, the rhyme appearing to serve no extrinsic purpose, such as provoking laughter or delivering insults. It was simply a conversational filler, part of the flow of 'talk'. Among the older children I knew in the 1970s, however, it was clear that the ways in which rhymes were spoken – and which rhymes they were – was more important and that great value was placed upon the demonstration of verbal skill and performative style in displays of recitation. Again, this requires time and practice. Verbal skill was something which the younger children had yet to learn.

The following rhyme, for example, might commonly serve as a conversational filler for little children. It would just be dropped into a conversation or chanted exuberantly when there appeared to be nothing else to say:

> Mrs White had a fright
> In the middle of the night
> She saw a ghost eating toast
> Halfway up a lamp post.

Spoken by a young child in the company of others, such rhymes would be told and retold, time and again, each child rehearsing his or her delivery style and verbal competence. Other rhymes, however, served the more important purpose of allowing children to deal in scatological thoughts and taboo topics through the inclusion of sexual terminology, swear-words and profanities. Like the process of linguistic creation manifested in the specialized vocabularies and nicknames described above, these kinds of rhymes would often be deliberate parodies of songs from the adult world, their reworking by children and young people serving as similar signs of a shared generational identity. The old music hall song received this rendering in the 1970s:

> Daisy Daisy the cops are after you
> And if They catch you They'll give you a month or two
> They'll tie you up with wire
> And set your knickers on fire
> So ring the bell and pedal like hell
> On a bicycle made for two.

Similar treatment was given to a traditional Christmas carol:

> We three kings of Orient are
> selling ladies underwear
> Knicker elastic
> How fantastic
> Two shilling a pair.

That such rhymes help constitute the linguistic resources of a generational culture is established by the fact that a similar reworking was told to me in the 1980s and that, as a child in Birmingham in the 1960s, when Beatlemania gripped the pop music world, I too learned to re-cite this carol:

> We four Beatles of Liverpool are,
> John in a taxi, Paul in a car,
> George on his scooter,
> Tooting his hooter,
> Following Ringo Starr.

This was itself a transformation of an original transformation, cited by the Opies as being current in Birmingham in 1959, prior to the Beatles era:

> We three kings of Orient are,
> One in a taxi, one in a car,
> One on a scooter,
> Tooting his hooter,
> Following yonder star.

Such is the nature of a generational culture.

TALKING IN PERFORMANCE

The 'talk' of children and young people draws, therefore, on a variety of linguistic resources which style the form and content of the language they use among themselves. In its deliberate misuse of the language of the adult world the 'talk' of children and young people affirms their distinctive identities as 'children' and 'youth', in the same moment as it declares their status as non-adults. Working with children it was I who, as an adult, was found wanting, just as children, in adult defined environments at home or in the classroom may find their language deemed similarly inappropriate. As Labov argued many years ago, although children originally learn to speak through contact with their immediate family circle, their language becomes increasingly 'reconstructed to fit the rules used by their peer groups' (1969: 208). These 'rules' derive first from the set of resources already outlined: ways of speaking demand the use of a particular and particularized vocabulary, a distinct syntax and rhythm. But to be able to speak in this language – to be able to 'talk' and participate in this generational culture – requires more than the art of translation. It necessitates knowing how to use language; it means giving a good performance. And it is their performative skills which children hone as they progress through childhood into the cultures of youth.

For example, the mildly scatological rhymes cited above, commonly recited to me by 8- and 9-year-old boy bravados in the 1980s, were replaced by more explicit ones among older children; a discreet reference to knickers giving way, for example, to a more direct sexual reference. The following poem was popular amongst 11- and 12-year-old boys in the 1970s:

> Mary had a little lamb
> She also had a duck
> She put them on the mantelpiece
> To see if they would. . . .

In its recitation, the last word would not be spoken and the listener was left to silently fill in the gap with a knowing and acknowledging smirk. Such performances contained a hidden challenge because the listening boys had to demonstrate their own affiliation to the generational culture by visibly 'getting the point' of the rhyme or joke, joining in the crude conspiracy with a ribald and obvious guffaw.

Using the familiar nursery rhyme format provided some clues as to the length and sound of the missing word, and therefore those who failed to find a fitting rhyme risked being marginalized within the social group for any admission of ignorance. Strategic action was often necessary and, in the 1970s, it was the tentative and nervous laugh or weak, uncertain snigger which belied the knowing air with which 11- and 12-year-old boys would watch and judge other boys' performances. At times this could become an anxious game of bluff and counter bluff when the 'point' of a rhyme eluded them all, including the teller, because of its more obscure sexual or scatological allusions.

The telling of jokes proves to have a similar classificatory function beyond entertainment. It sorts out those who are competent in the generational style from those more marginal members of the group.

As with rhyming, to 'get the point' of the joke means that the listener must literally demonstrate, through direct and appreciative laughter, that the joke has meaning. Joke-telling, like rhyming, is thus built around an active communicative exchange between speaker and listener. Only then can a good performance be counted as such. In the youth club one evening in the late 1970s an 11-year-old boy asked me the following riddle:

'What's the dirtiest thing in the world?'

Before I had time to reply he added triumphantly,

'Second-hand toilet paper.'

I didn't laugh. Perturbed and anxious, lest his performance be thought lacking, he asked, 'Get it? Get it? Covered in shit.'

Such explicit kinds of 'talk' were rare among the older girls in public. In contrast to the loud and voluble 'talk' of the boys, the girls would feign a bashful, quiet ignorance of such vulgarities. In the desegregated world of the youth club the admission of such knowledge was deemed inappropriate, unfeminine or indicative of shaky morals. However, this was a fictive ignorance for, privately between themselves, the girls too would trade their knowledge of sexual matters and laugh at 'dirty' jokes together at a later time. This disparity in language use, as evidenced in the strutting, public utterances of the boys and the more private whisperings of girls, I witnessed in its infancy among 8- and 9-year-old children in the 1980s. Literally sidelined in their own playground games – those built around the traditional songs of childhood lore – the girls would watch and listen to the boys' more public competitions of wit and counter wit, of insult and verbal injury and, though making no public contribution to it, would none the less still adjudicate these male performances privately among themselves (James 1993).

Knowledge of linguistic resources and the acquisition of performance skills thus registers children and young people's relative positions within the generational cultures of childhood and youth. The accomplished actors of early childhood may become central players in later youth cultures through their active and keen demonstration of these verbal arts. Those others, silent watchers or mumbling jokers, may find the transition through this generational culture less easy. In the late 1970s, for example, it was with great derision and scorn that one boy marked out another's identity through the observation that he couldn't even 'swear properly'.

However, it is an ability to 'talk', rather than simply knowledge of the resources of language, which acts as the primary identifier, an ability which, as the following two tape transcripts reveal, develops through the generational experience of marginality, which ties childhood to youth culture. The first conversation took place between two 12-year-old boys in the 1970s in the north-east of England, the second between three 7-year old boys in the Midlands in the 1980s. What is significant about these conversations is their remarkable similarity: words and phrases are woven into a jerky cadence of conversing voices as turn-taking gives way to interruptions, accents are mimicked, rhymes recited and insults rhythmically exchanged.

Extract 1.

D: It's not taping.

K: It is taping you idiot

D: Is it?

K: Aye.

D: Well, say something then.

K: Ducka is a nutter

D: Shut yer trap now, son.
(*pause*)
(*laughter*)

K: Ducka is a nutta

D: Shut yer trap Kev now or I'll beat yer brains out (*laughs*)

K: Go back to Sandby where you belong, Ducka.

D: What's that? Is it taping?

K: Why aye. . . . Ducka is a nutta, Ducka is a nutter,

D: Shut yer mouth Kev now, you stupid idiot...
oh, shut up man.
(*threatens to thump him*)

Extract 2

A: Knock, knock

C: who's there

A: Hen,

C: Hen who?

A: Knock knock.

C: Who's there?

A: Water . . . water . . .

L: I know that one . . . water in majorta
tastes more like it oughta.

C: Ba, ba black sheep, smack your bum (*all giggle*)

L: Ba ba black sheep . . .
A: Who knows Humpty Dumpty.
A: Humpty Dumpty sat on the wall
     Eating up bananas,
     Where do you think he put the skins,
     Down the king's pajamas,
L: I know this one . . . Humpty Dumpty sat on a wally....

The second extract, although containing more traditional verbal formulae and ritualized expressions which bear witness to less accomplished players, none the less prefigures the first in its experimentation with word endings, rhymes, jokes, insults and retorts. Thus in these conversations is found confirmation that childhood prefigures youth, not just as an earlier phase of biological development nor simply as a less socialized condition, but as a cultural context through which young people's identities are actively created and marked out as the patterns of belonging are laid down.

THE LANGUAGE OF TALK

In the ethnographic accounts which I have presented it has been shown that the language which is used commonly to talk about children and young people and the language which children and young people themselves use, meet and/or clash in moments of definition, in the act of establishing conceptual boundaries and in the staking out of identity and personhood. Children and young people explore the limits on social action set for them by adults through the application of identifying labels by restyling language as a distinctive feature of their categorical identities as 'child' and/or 'youth'. In doing so they illustrate Hymes' (1971) point that within any community, shared rules for the conduct and interpretation of speech provide lines of discrimination for distinguishing between competencies and belonging. Further, they underline Bauman and Scherzer's (1974) observation that speech is a cultural system. The talk of children and youth bears two distinctive marks. The first is the resources of young people's language: an implicit knowledge of particular linguistic practices upon which they draw when speaking. As I have shown, the language of childhood and youth contains codes which specify categories of thought, genres that style the forms which speech can take, norms and values which govern rules of turn-taking, which shape public and private cursing and provide gender specific language forms. These resources, constituting a tacit knowledge, are rarely made explicit, and yet they pattern any talk, locating any individual speaker within the specific speech community of the young.

A second linked aspect of speaking as a cultural system, borne out by the ethnographic examples given above, is that of performance. In the young people's performances can be seen the interplay between an individual speaker and the resources of his or her speech community noted by Bauman and Scherzer. For them, specific speaking occasions – that is, particular individual performances – have an 'emergent quality, structured by the situated and creative exercise of competence' which accounts for the differences between discrete speech acts (1974: 7). This heterogeneity of speaking has been demonstrated among the young people with whom I worked: some individuals were able to draw creatively and poetically on their language's resources while others remained ensnared by a nervous formalism. None the less, there is ever a dynamic quality to each act of speaking: every young person can offer a unique performance (even though this might take place within a highly routinized or ritualized narrative genre) through the active resourcing, at a particular moment in time, of the language which identifies his or her speech community. It is this which contextualizes the changing identities of young people.

In brief, this chapter has argued that talk is one important medium through which children and young people carve out for themselves particular cultural locations for the Self and for identity. And it is in the social spaces of the playground and the school, spaces peculiar to children, that these identities take shape through the process of being and becoming social.

NOTES

1 Acknowledgment is given for financial support from the SSRC (1977–80) and from the British Academy (1988–91) and to the many children and young people who, in the course of these projects, I got to know. It is an irony of anthropology and the academy that now as entirely different people – as adults no doubt with children of their own or as emergent teenagers – they will not realize the valuable contribution their conversations with me are still making to the sociological understanding of childhood, youth and socialization. As ever, thanks to Nigel Rapport for his insightful comments on an earlier draft of this chapter.
2 Jenkins (1990) argues that mentally handicapped people never achieve

full adulthood and remain infantilized as children, despite their chrono-
logical age.
3 The idea of motif and motive was inspired by Nigel Rapport's associate
section at the ASA Decennial Conference, Oxford 1993. The word 'play'
underlines the strategic and multivariant nature of symbolism and is
appropriate in this context to allude to the complex ways in which
children use, rather than simply speak, their language.
4 Geordie refers to someone identified as a north-easterner, more strictly
thought of as belonging to Newcastle-upon-Tyne. Hence, Geordie lad
(young male), Geordie lass (young female, but can also refer to older
married women: 'my lass' is 'my wife').
5 In the north-east dialect the endings 'er' are pronounced as a short 'a',
as in cat; 's' is pronounced as a 'z', as in measure.

REFERENCES

Bauman, R. and Scherzer, J. (1974) *Explorations in the Ethnography of Speaking*, Cambridge: Cambridge University Press.
Bernstein, B. (1970)'Education cannot compensate for society', *New Society*, 26 February, 344–347.
Bourdieu, P. (1977) *Outline of a Theory of Practice*, Cambridge: Cambridge University Press.
Brake, M. (1985) *Comparative Youth Culture*, London: Routledge.
Carrithers, M., Collins, S. and Lukes, S. (eds) (1985) *The Category of the Person*, Cambridge: Cambridge University Press.
Edwards, J. (1985) *Language, Society and Identity*, London: Basil Blackwell/ Andre Deutsch.
Eisenstadt, S. N. (1956) *From Generation to Generation*, New York: Free Press of Glencoe.
Frith, S. (1984) *The Sociology of Youth*, Omskirk: Causeway Books.
Giddens, A. (1979) *Central Problems in Social Theory*, London: Macmillan.
Hall, S. and Jefferson, T.(eds) (1976) *Resistance Through Rituals*, London: Hutchinson and Co.
Hockey, J. and James, A. (1993) *Growing Up and Growing Old*, London: Sage.
Hymes, D. (1971) 'Sociolinguistics and the ethnography of speaking', in E. Ardener (ed.) *Social Anthropology and Language*, London: Tavistock.
James, A. (1979a) 'Confections, concoctions and conceptions', *Journal of the Anthropological Society of Oxford*, 10, 2: 83–95.
—— (1979b) 'The game of the name: nicknames in the child's world', *New Society*, 14 June, 632–634.
—— (1986) 'Learning to belong: the boundaries of adolescence', in A. P. Cohen (ed.) *Symbolising Boundaries*, Manchester: Manchester University Press.
—— (1993) *Childhood Identities. Self and Social Relationships in the Experience of the Child*. Edinburgh: Edinburgh University Press.
James, A. and Prout, A. (eds) (1990) *Constructing and Reconstructing Childhood*, Basingstoke: Falmer.

Jenkins, R. (1990) 'Dimensions of adulthood in Britain: long-term unemployment and mental handicap', in P. Spencer (ed.), *Anthropology and the Riddle of the Sphinx*, London: Routledge.

Labov, W. (1969) 'The logic of non-standard English', in P. P. Giglioli (ed.) *Language and the Social Context*, London: Penguin.

Opie, I. and Opie, P. ([1959] 1977) *The Lore and Language of School Children*, St. Albans: Paladin.

—— (1969) *Children's Games in Street and Playground*, Oxford: Oxford University Press.

Pollock, L.A. (1983) *Forgotten Children: Parent – Child Relationships from 1500–1900*, Cambridge: Cambridge University Press.

Prout, A. and James, A. (1990) 'A new paradigm for the sociology of childhood? Provenance, promises and problems', in A. James and A. Prout (eds) *Constructing and Reconstructing Childhood*, Basingstoke: Falmer.

Rapport, N. (1993) *Diverse World Views in an English Village*, Edinburgh: Edinburgh University Press.

Reisman, K. (1974) 'Contrapuntal conversations in an Antiguan village', in R. Bauman and J. Scherzer (eds) *Explorations in the Ethnography of Speaking*, Cambridge: Cambridge University Press.

Schwartz, T. (1976) 'Relations among generations in time-limited cultures', in T. Schwartz (ed.) *Socialization as Cultural Communication*, London: University of California Press.

Spencer, P. (ed.) (1990) *Anthropology and the Riddle of the Sphinx*, London: Routledge.

Turner, V. (1974) *Dramas, Fields and Metaphors*, London: Cornell University Press.

Wagner, R. (1975) *The Invention of Culture*, Englewood Cliffs, N.J.: Prentice-Hall.

Chapter 4

Inter-racial friendship

Consuming youth styles, ethnicity and teenage femininity in South London

Helena Wulff

Cultural mixture is very much on the increase in terms of types and amounts; growing numbers of people and places are mixing culturally, and becoming mixed culturally. Not only do new antagonisms occur as a result of this, but new and equally important alliances are also being formed. The latter circumstance has attracted theoretical interest, producing concepts such as bricolage, syncretism and hybridity.[1] Cultural and ethnic mixtures are particularly obvious among young people in urban areas (see Wulff 1992), and these concepts have contributed to illuminating their conduct. Explanations however, have mostly been framed in macro perspectives focusing on issues of class and ethnicity. As a complement I am going to suggest the usefulness of a micro perspective. My purpose is to show that larger forces influence the small-scale phenomena but also that face-to-face social relationships may contain agency, providing individuals with a certain ability to form cultural meanings out of their specific experiences that in their turn may have an impact on the larger forces.

My ethnographic miniature is an ethnically mixed group of young teenage girls who met at a local girls' club in South London in the early 1980s and subsequently became friends.[2] They managed the contradiction between racism and ethnic hostility in the wider British society, and their practice of socializing with girls of the other colour, primarily by way of composing their own kinds and combinations of youth styles. These expressed a policy of ethnic equality, at the same time as they reflected the dynamics of personal relations of friendship among the girls in the group. The girls put together their youth styles through consumption of clothes, shoes, cosmetics and music – all significant ingredients in their teenage femininity. Consumption has mainly been treated in macro perspectives, often assuming victimization. This has recently shifted somewhat to an interest in how consumption is utilized in processes of identity formation. A micro perspective such as this shows how these girls consumed youth styles in much the way they liked and that again fitted with their ideas of ethnic equality. It also suggests another tantamount but neglected theoretical implication which however is supported by Roger Hewitt's (1986) work on black and white adolescents; it is possible that many girls are more prone to mix culturally than boys, more open for identity experimentation, and perhaps in fact often in the forefront of cultural mixture.

There were four clusters of friendship in the group of altogether twenty girls, each with one girl in the centre. Doreen, who was black and of Jamaican descent, was at the centre of one of the mixed clusters. She was tall as well as the most developed physically and socially, the first one to have a boyfriend. And she was regarded as beautiful by the other girls. Agatha was also black, born in Nigeria; she was to eventually move back there. In the group she represented someone who dared to break school rules. Yet her most important characteristic was her warm friendliness towards everyone in the group which made her very popular and not only the centre of a black friendship cluster, but the centre of the entire group, the *kernel friend*. Then there was Rosemary, at the centre of a mixed cluster. She was white, well developed physically and socially, and also known for her friendliness. Sarah, the centre of a white cluster, was white, and profiled herself by breaking school, club and home rules.

It should be pointed out, however, that the most significant friendship choice was not whether the girls had chosen black or white or a mixed friendship cluster as their closest friends, but the fact that they went to a mixed girls' club. Not everyone did in their inner city area, nor did they in South London (Wulff 1988).

It is still common that studies on youth culture deal with different and conspicuous youth which are marginal or subordinate to an unclearly defined mainstream culture. These studies often rely on early work from the Birmingham School focusing on what they then saw as subcultural resistance among working-class youth against the dominant culture in England. According to this view youth cultures are strongly connected to class; they emerge in the working class because of class conflicts. One of the central arguments of the Birmingham School (Hall and Jefferson 1975; Hebdige 1979) was that working class youth were fighting a symbolic class war in the place of their parents by way of spectacular youth styles. Writing about 'the politics of feminist research', Angela McRobbie (1991: 64–65) modifies in retrospect the importance of class in the lives of young teenage girls that she studied in Birmingham in the 1970s: 'I brought in class wherever I could in this study, often when it simply was not relevant . . . but being a *girl* over-determined their every moment' as she urges for new questions and wild strategies to do feminist research. Richard Johnson (1986: 302–303) has also conceded in an auto-critique that 'there is a pressure to present lived cultures with which one sympathizes deeply as peculiarly homogeneous and distinct. Indeed, sometimes the "cultures" replace the people and the social relationships.'

MICROCULTURE: PERSONALITIES, LOCALITIES, EVENTS

Now a small-scale youth cultural analysis can most fruitfully be developed by way of the concept of *microculture* (cf. Wulff 1988). In this case it is very much about cultural mixture, but it does not necessarily have to be so. The theoretical point of departure here is the view that culture consists of flows of meanings that people create and interpret when they communicate with each other both directly face-to-face and also indirectly by way of media. Ideas and their externalizations are unequally distributed over a social structure (Hannerz 1992). Microcultures are thus flows of meaning which are managed by people in small groups that meet on an everyday basis. Much of our social life is in fact enacted in such small groups between three or four people up to about a hundred individuals. I am thinking not only of groups of teenagers and school classes, but also families, people at places of work and groups of friends. They choose cultural concerns that relate to their specific situation and reformulate them in their own terms as far as it is possible. Microcultures are thus distinguishable among other forms of culture. The particular combination of personalities, the localities where they meet, and certain momentous events that they experience together, are three elements in every microculture. The beautiful Doreen, the kernel friend Agatha, the friendly Rosemary and the daring Sarah are examples of important personalities in the microculture of the group of twenty girls. The four arenas – usually the girls' club and a street corner nearby, but also at school and in their homes – were the localities where they met and experienced exciting events, such as being chased by the police after swimming in a closed public swimming-pool or dancing on tables at the girls' club one evening that all of a sudden turned into a hilarious party (Wulff 1988). In analyses of microcultural process such small-scale variation is not abstracted away. And, what is even more important here; agency is extra visible. Agency, or the fact that people do form or influence their culture, albeit in varying degrees.

The microculture of these black and white girls circled around concerns about ethnic equality and teenage femininity.[3] These themes were unequally distributed in the group of girls; for example, some of the girls were dealing more with one of them than the others. And they were also unequally distributed over the four arenas. With time however, the microculture changed, and actually faded away after about a year, much because Agatha went back to Nigeria (Wulff 1988). Some girls left the club; they became too old for it or moved out of the area, and others who had not been there from the beginning joined in.

'BLACK PEOPLE WHO ARE ENGLISH INSIDE'

The black parents had moved to England during the wave of labour migration from the colonies and ex-colonies between the late 1950s and before it was stopped by way of the Commonwealth Immigration Act in 1962 (Wulff 1988). In the early 1980s they worked in unskilled manual to semi-professional jobs. Most of the fathers had manual jobs while the mothers tended to be employed in service or care unless they were housewives, which for some was a way to hide the fact that they were unemployed, a strategy the few fathers who did not have jobs were unable to sustain.[4] The teachers of the girls were mostly white English, however, and middle class, as were the youth workers who were running the club that the girls attended. Taken together, the media content of television, radio, song texts, music videos, newspapers and magazines that they took in was predominantly about white matters which contradicted the reality of the girls living in this ethnically mixed area with more non-white residents (Asian, West African and Caribbean) than white.

The girls were continuously synchronizing messages about ethnicity from their parents, other kin, teachers, youth workers and the media with their everyday life in the ethnically mixed group, not least their contacts with girls of the other colour. The most significant and problematic of these messages maintained that there was racism and ethnic inequality in the national social structure. They were aware of the fact that blacks were a minority in England and that more white people had influential positions in the country. There was a generational difference when it came to ethnic attitude and behaviour between the parents of the girls who had grown up in monoethnic situations and the girls having lived in an ethnic mixture as long as they could remember. It was thus mostly a question of habit that led the girls to mix more ethnically than their parents, who in general had nothing against the fact that their daughters went to a mixed club and a mixed school (Wulff 1988). At one point, Vicky, who was white and precociously intellectual, phrased this as something black and white girls had in common in relation to their respective parental generation:

> There's no difference really between black and white girls. There's a difference because of parents, and their music – reggae. I don't know about their different religions, about the black religions, or what Jamaican religions are called. People used to live in poor countries. Their food's different. Sometimes their clothing's different. . . . There are black people who are English inside.
>
> (Wulff 1988: 153)

The remarkable mixture of national, ethnic, and racial origins in the group of girls dissolved into a black and a white dichotomy when they met, especially on their own without adults on the street corner. Parents, teachers, and youth workers tended to refer to the countries of origin of the girls' parents, whereas in the group it was much more important whether the girls were black or white and the fact that they were black and white together. It was a way of identifying each other (rather than oneself), especially in conversations about appearance and boyfriends (Wulff 1988).

BEST FRIENDS: GIRLS AS CONFIDANTES AND EXPLORERS[5]

The girls provided each other with joy and comfort through their friendships in the group. The principal activity was talking, mostly about boys, singers and actors, preferably male. Connected to that topic of conversation was the one on appearance; they thus talked about the latest hairstyles, clothes, youth styles, cosmetics and jewellery which sometimes made them consider the teenage boys' gaze. But they also listened to records together, went to the pictures, parties, and discotheques. They needed each other for such excitement that was clearly also connected to their femininity, growing up into young women, as well as to a certain extent to ethnicity.

If the friends in the group were important for the girls, some a bit more than others such as those in one's cluster (there were also a few hostilities), the most interesting and gratifying link of them all was the best friendship. It had certain similarities to close sibling relationships, but differed in the important way that it was acquired and had to be confirmed over and over again. And it entailed an exploration of each other as well as the sharing of particularly exciting events, let alone secrets. Best friends thus went 'bunking' (i.e. left school too early in the day), or indulged in pranks like trying to embarrass young male teachers by shouting obscenities to them in the school yard. But the girls kept coming back to the significance of trusting and comforting in best friendships; a best friend is 'someone you can share things with, like problems, and also someone you can trust'. It is thus 'somebody you can talk to, tell secrets and all that and you know that they won't bother to tell anybody else'. There was a consistent focus on their conversations which can be viewed in terms of what Berger and Kellner (1964) have written about another dyad, the marital union. They argue that married couples create a shared perspective on the world by way of conversations and keep their relationship going in the process. It was obviously what these best friends were also doing.

Not every girl in the group had a best friend, however, at least not all the time. But I observed and was told about eighteen best friendships in the group of which six were reciprocal. Some girls had best friends outside the group. Two of the girls claimed two best friends, none of which were reciprocal. The idea of having two best friends at the same time was moreover a contradiction in terms, since best friendships could only consist of two people according to the other girls, just as a best friend by definition had to be a girl. There was also consensus about certain norms of best friendship behaviour; a best friend was thus expected to spend more time together with her best friend than with any other girl, keep secrets within the best friend union, and refrain from exciting events with another girl.

Best friendships lasted from between two weeks up to five or six years, the average being somewhere around two years. There was some competition over certain girls as best friends, especially Agatha, which in a couple of cases led to virtual dramas when someone was abandoned for someone else. The mother of Sarah's best friend saw to it that their best friendship ended; she did not approve of Sarah's obstinate behaviour.

The girls were restricted in their choice of best friends by their age, gender, class, and to a certain extent by their ethnicity. Again, the girls preferred this ethnically mixed group of friends, but when it came to best friends most of the girls chose and accepted girls of their own colour. (This might of course have been more or less incidental since my sample is rather small.) Best friendships in the area tended not to be ethnically mixed, however, and neither was the majority of marriages.

In discussions of intimate friendships the private and personal aspects are usually emphasized (Jerrome 1984; Paine 1969). Friendships, especially close friendships, are moreover often assumed to be voluntary, acquired relationships (Du Bois 1974; Paine 1969, McCall 1970; Jerrome 1984); yet Allan (1989) outlines a number of constraints on the forming of friendship of which class and gender are the most applicable for my purpose here. Still, close friendship is an informal social relationship and it may be expected, even an ideal, for young teenage girls in the West to establish best friendships. Girls who fail to make best friends, are never offered best friendships or lose their best friends, or (for reasons of individuality) stay indifferent towards best friendships, are in any case not running the risk of stigmatization.

KEEPING SECRETS AND HAVING A LAUGH

Most of the best friendships were between girls the same age, or one year apart. Their femininity was often expressed in an interest in what older teenage girls and young women were doing. It was mostly explored in the comfortable seclusion of the bedroom of one of the friends – the private sphere in other words – by way of experimenting with cosmetics, hairstyles and clothing. Trying on the high-heeled shoes of an older sister while smoking cigarettes and in their still puerile manner copying the posture, gestures and way of talking of the older teenage girls who were more used to sexuality, was a kind of exploration of what it might be like to be an older teenage girl. Best friends could spend entire days during weekends and holidays, as well as long evenings pretending to be older teenage girls, talking and giggling. They would often play records either as background music or would sing and 'skank' to them which they called black dancing (performed by both black and white girls) to reggae while they checked what they looked like in a mirror. And if no one else was at home, they might turn up the volume and throw themselves into the blasting reggae beat, reaching a magical state of hilarious excitement. McRobbie (1984) has analysed fantasy and daydreaming that dancing produces for women and girls as a component in their resistance. This was certainly the case for these girls; they were engaged in an oppositional endeavour against their parents, testing how far they could go without the commotion and throbbing music being discovered, hoping, a little ambivalently, that they would be discovered and fearing the adult reaction at the same time. But they were just as much involved in an exploration; the girls were looking for new sensations through dancing like this, sensations that had to do with the fact that they were in the process of growing up. Their conversations revealed that the dancing often meant that they nourished fantasies of how they would appear to a certain boy and how it would feel to be dancing with him.

With an emphasis on the impact of the teenage leisure market of girls getting together like this, such endeavours have been called 'the culture of the bedroom' (McRobbie and Garber 1982). These girls were not, however, confined to the bedroom; on the contrary, they were prominent and visible actors out on the street corner, in the school yard, and of course at the girls' club, busily exploring life.

YOUTH STYLES AND CONSUMPTION

The girls' youth styles were obviously a type of consumption that contributed to their teenage femininity and process of growing up into young black and white women, in other words, to acquire a sexually mature gendered identity and to manage ethnic equality and experience excitement.

Consumption has been linked to youth culture all the way back to the 1950s when the concept of the teenager was introduced by the flourishing Western market creating special teenage goods and items for consumption by this growing cohort in a phase in the life cycle when they had some money and time to spend. It soon became a feminist concern to picture women consumers as compensating patriarchal and class oppression through shopping. Teenage girls were assumed to be of the same category. Later women and teenage girls were seen as resisting oppression by way of consumption. Writing about the contradictions of consumerism, Mica Nava (1992:

167) has nuanced her earlier point of view by stating that consumerism cannot be fully explained through economic structures, since this activity also has to do with 'dreams and consolation, communication and confrontation, image and identity'. The girls were growing up in an ethnic paradox, acquiring an identity, a gendered ethnic identity in Alan Tomlinson's (1990: 18) words through 'the emergence of new "identifications"', a situation which is not all about domination. For as Paul Willis (1990) says, consumption is a kind of symbolic work. Placed rather low in the English class hierarchy, the girls noted with discomfort that in the wider scheme of things the black girls were ranked below the white girls. This did not make sense to them and it became one of the ideas that preoccupied them in their microculture; not least by way of their youth styles that more or less actively, but never in a confrontational manner, favoured ethnic equality (Wulff 1988). In general, many youth styles are high in 'blackness', providing an interesting revenge against the low-class position of most blacks.

John Clarke (1983) has suggested that youth styles are significant boundary markers between groups. This implies a hostility that still lingers in much work on youth styles, presenting them as conspicuous and violent with only one style per group which may be more common among boys who have received most attention in studies on youth styles. However, in the group of twenty girls under discussion, there were in fact several styles that were dealt with and interpreted both individually as well as collectively. Another important characteristic of youth styles is that some youth styles are transnational and appear in different versions in many places around the world according to local circumstances, while others are national or regional, or the products of even smaller areas. The styles of the twenty black and white girls were their versions of foreign and national styles. There were youth styles that the girls picked up via the music; singers they admired promoted them, and other styles were provided by the fashion industry (Wulff 1988). These youth styles came about during a special moment of effervescence in the early 1980s, when a number of the classic post-war styles such as Skinheads, Rastas, Rudies and Soulheads co-existed with, for example, the ephemeral New Romantics. They were later to be replaced by fewer styles such as Raggamuffin, a black style that some whites also assume.

The youth styles, or 'fashions' or 'groups' as the girls said, were defined by appearance (clothing and hairstyle), music taste and ethnicity. One of these elements was accentuated in every youth style which may reveal its origins and distribution among the girls in the group. Best friends always had the same youth style, but might change to new ones when they split up (Wulff 1988).

Like most of the girls, beautiful Doreen and friendly Rosemary, as well as their respective best friends, called themselves Rebels (as did many other young teenage girls in South London). This was the style the girls had for the longest periods of time. There was not a male version of this style, despite the fact that most youth styles tended at first to be conceived in male forms. The Rebel style attracted both black and white girls; this style was a political statement for ethnic equality. A number of the white girls emphasized this by pointing out that they were black Rebels, at the same time as they to a certain extent projected themselves as interesting people because of their black friends. Contrary to their name, Rebels looked quite properly dressed in box-pleated skirts and tie-up blouses in inexpensive materials copying brand namestyles. They listened to reggae music. Some of the white girls, such as Sarah, the opposi- tional girl, and her best friend, were Rude girls or Rudies. They also liked reggae music, but as one of them described herself, 'a Skin(head) that isn't racist. You like black people' (Wulff 1988: 101). And they dressed in stay-press shirts, denim jackets, had cropped hair with a fringe and wore loafers. A couple of the black girls, among them Agatha who was the most popular girl in the group, and her best friends were Soulheads, which meant that they dressed casually in jeans and listened to reggae, soul and lovers' rock. There were other styles which girls in the group claimed to adhere to, such as the black Sticks-girl known for being elegantly and expensively dressed, the white New Romantic mostly connected with a certain kind of music, and even the white anti-black Skinhead that also in this context primarily had to do with a particular music form, not the racist message. When one of the white girls went out with a Skinhead for a while, she regarded herself as a Skinhead. Her boyfriend at the time (who had a black grandparent) was mainly using the Skinhead label as a way to decide for himself and others that he had chosen a white identity. Styles were thus either ethnically unmarked or ethnically marked yet unconfrontational (Wulff 1988). The concern with and the search for expressions of ethnic equality run through them all.

Most of the girls' consumption was directly connected to their *bodies*, and they cultivated their own esthetic of ethnic equality through their youth styles. The view that the body is culturally constructed is clearly in line with this; the girls constructed their public physical appearance through clothing, jewellery, hairstyle and cosmetics. If it was detached from any youth style, their clothing was 'colourless' in this context, i.e. they did not connect blackness or whiteness with any kind of clothing unless it had the red, green and yellow Rastafarian colours. This also held for jewellery. A hairstyle might be black – usually numerous thin plaits (which are often mixed up with the tangled dreadlocks of Rastafarian men which none of the girls had) or white such as the cropped hairstyles of the Rude girls. There were cosmetics for sale in the local stores: strong colours for black complexions and milder hues for white complexions. The girls used mascara, eye-shadow, lipstick, nail varnish and eau-de-toilette that they kept on top of small chests of drawers in their bedrooms, but which they also carried with them in handbags or tucked into jeans pockets so that they could improve and change their looks, often with the help of a best friend, wherever they went.

The girls' presentation of themselves thus meant bodily pleasure both external, to look good, which made them feel good, but also other internal pleasures such as to eat, drink, and inhale (!) commodities that caused sensuous enjoyment occasionally up to the point of intoxication. Apart from the food their mothers, the youth workers and the school provided that is of less interest here, they ate sweets (preferably Mars or Cadbury chocolate bars and long, soft, raspberry flavoured laces). They often bought small bags of 'chips' (*pommes frites*) drenched in tomato ketchup at classical English (and hence white) fish and chip shops instead of having school lunch. It was usually the boys they knew who tried drinking alcohol on the street corner, mostly beer in cans, or gin. The boys would also sometimes inhale the contents of Tipp-Ex bottles, or glue, which was more widespread among white teenagers in South London, and occasionally connected with Skinheads. And the girls also experimented with this, taking turns at inhaling the glue from a plastic bag which resulted in excited giggling rather than real intoxication. This tended furthermore to be the case with 'spliffs' made of 'ganja' (marijuana cigarettes) that the older black girls and boys brought to the street corner and sometimes to the club, despite the fact that the youth workers had banned them there on legal grounds. 'Fags' (cigarettes made of tobacco) were allowed, however, and some of the girls, black as well as white, smoked them at the club, on the street corner, and sometimes in their homes.

Not every commodity had a 'colour', but some were definitely identified as either black or white. Still, it happened that the black girls talked about 'white' commodities as 'English' and 'black' ones as 'West Indian' or 'Jamaican', for example. That is to say, if they did not take it so much for granted that the colour of a particular commodity that they were consuming just did not matter to them. They may at some point have become aware of the blackness of some commodity through the white context, for example, a comment by a parent or teacher. These black and white girls were on the whole consuming the same kinds of commodities, sometimes mixing black and white ones on purpose, sometimes without thinking about it. This consumption was internalized; it became a very obvious bodily sensation of positive value for the girls. In line with Bourdieu's (1977: 93–94) notion of body hexis, their consumption was thus remembered as are bodily experiences. This is especially the case for young teenage girls who are in a momentous phase in their physical and psychological development.

All this external and internal consumption raises the question of how these young teenage girls got hold of the commodities. Most of their clothing was paid for by their parents, usually their mothers, who also often took them shopping at Woolworth's, Marks & Spencer or at some other local shop. It happened that they went by train to a shopping mall nearby or even occasionally to sales in the centre of London. The mothers also taught their daughters to buy cheap clothing, sometimes second-hand, at the Portobello market. And of course the mothers saw to it that the girls wore handed down clothes from older sisters and cousins.[6]

But the girls went on shopping sprees on their own. They regarded those sprees as even more important, since they were able to indulge in window shopping which fed daydreams of growing up to be an older teenage girl. Trying on clothes and shoes that were far too expensive for them to buy was indeed a part of the window shopping experience. They did not have much money to spend; most of them got about £3 per week in pocket money (some of them in exchange for household work), some held Saturday jobs or worked a couple of hours after school in the afternoons at hairdressers, restaurants, dry cleaners, etc. making about £1.20 per hour. They bought sweets, girls' magazines, single records, cosmetics, cheap jewellery (especially earrings) and cigarettes with the money. If they saved up for a while they could afford to go to the pictures, a concert or a discotheque (Wulff 1988).

So they did not have a lot of money, in fact they often complained that they were short or had run out of money. As a way of experiencing excitement some of the girls occasionally 'snatched' commodities from the small department stores or shops in the area, usually small items such as chocolate bars or cosmetics that were on display, or cassettes containing song tracks that they liked. If some commodities were *stolen* in this way, others were *borrowed* on a long or short-term loan, usually clothes and shoes from older sisters or female cousins or friends, but also records and magazines. The girls moreover received some of their petty commodities as *birthday* or *Christmas presents* from best friends, friends, family or kin. Consumption consequently not only requires regular shopping but may also be derived from commodities that are stolen, borrowed or given as presents.

The youth styles of the girls were connected to the media through music in particular. Here we have the most obvious example of how culture, microculture, is constructed via indirect communication. The media were also linked to the girls through their bodies, if somewhat more remotely than was the case with the youth styles. But the girls used their bodies, i.e. they listened to music on cassettes and the radio, watched music videos, films and television, and read girls' magazines. Their media consumption hence had a considerable impact on them at the time, and they would remember it later.

It was clear that the girls interpreted the media according to their own situation, emphasizing the growing up or new sensation that the presence of boys might cause, the importance of ethnic equality, and of course excitement that tied in with the first concern. Yet the girls were not completely autonomous agents in their endeavour to manage media flows: the microcultural meaning they created from them was socially and ethnically structured to a certain extent; they were aware of the ethnic inequality in the wider English world, especially among adults, but also among teenagers both elsewhere in South London and in their own area. This awareness made them accentuate their notion of ethnic equality, at the same time as they were unable to move away completely from the class and ethnic belonging that the wider English society had assigned to them. All the girls knew that the white girls were better off than the black girls when it came to education and job prospects, if not all that much (Wulff 1988).

Susan Willis (1991) points out that in American advertising blacks are most often portrayed as the 'other' (contrary to Asian-Americans and Hispanics). This applied on the whole to the media that the girls consumed. Music and fashion in the media were rather black, if mostly mixed with white components. Some of the black girls listened to radio programmes playing black music. Many of the girls, black as well as white, enjoyed breakfast shows and the pop charts. They bought the hits as single records and played them incessantly at home and at the club. Albums or cassettes were not as common. They defined their favourite music as reggae, ska, disco, soul, new wave, lovers' rock, futurist, Skinhead music and jazzfunk. And they identified reggae, soul, ska and lovers' rock as black music, whereas disco, new wave, futurist and Skinhead music were white, and jazzfunk was a mixture of black and white music. All of them listened to black, white and mixed music, yet the black girls and a substantial number of the white girls ranked black music as the most interesting. The ethnic theme of the black songs reminded both the black girls and the white girls of the history of the black girls,[7] which made the black music more important to them than it possibly could be in all-white contexts.

Reggae, but also soul, was 'music with meaning', according to the girls. Most reggae songs were about the Rastafarian idea of black people living in exile in the white, oppressing Babylon, yet promising freedom for all blacks some day in Africa ruled by blacks. The song *Rivers of Babylon* illustrated this idea, for instance. Reggae lyrics may also feature romance and love such as in *Could you be loved?*; it was however more typical of white songs. A much played hit was *Ebony and Ivory* presented by Paul McCartney and Michael Jackson, urging harmony between black and white people (Wulff 1988).

Despite the dominance of whiteness in the media it also provided the girls with a ready-made ethnic mixture, as well as ample opportunities for them to pick and mix, making their own ethnic syntheses out of the media messages that were available to them. And this they did, happy to find a way to express and deal above all with their notion of ethnic equality, just like the youth styles that they primarily had on the street corner and at the club, but also occasionally in their homes, their bedrooms being the backstage for preparations and experimentations with these styles. At school, however, the girls had to wear school uniform; anything else was banned. But of course the school uniform could easily be changed into the Rebel style, the two types of clothing inveriably being indistinguishable for outsiders. Also the media were present at all the girls' arenas, but they were kept at bay at school. With the aid of portable radios and Walkmen provided usually by the boys, the media flourished even on the street corner. And it happened on a mild summer afternoon that someone put loudspeakers in an open window nearby which blasted out the throbbing reggae over the street corner for hours, until it was stopped by some homecoming parent or angry neighbour. Both youth styles and music were thus prominent in the lives of the girls, permeating their entire existence.

Taken together, the girls emphasized the black elements in their youth styles which in this white context resulted in a cultural mixture. Many of the black elements such as reggae, rastafarian colours in clothing and a mass of thin black plaits had black origins of which the girls were aware.

Looking back at the microculture of this ethnically mixed group of girls primarily formed through friendships and youth styles, I would argue that it is likely that the idea of ethnic equality will stay with them as they grow up to be young women. Not in the particular version they were managing in the early 1980s, but it will change according to new circumstances. My point is that since they have internalized ethnic equality with their femininity through bodily consumption of youth styles and music, it was – like bodily sensations are – a formative experience that will be useful for them in the long run as they go on dealing with multi-cultural England through other microcultures consisting of new friends and boy-friends, their own families of procreation further in time, and people at workplaces (which in fact they already have). To these girls, ethnic mixture was both attractive and self-evident, something they managed as cultural agents in their everyday lives. And up on a macro perspective it is obvious that they are far from the only ones who have grown up acquiring the habit of multiracial friendship, which is bound to have an increasing political impact in the long run.

ACKNOWLEDGMENTS

I am very grateful for comments by Vered Amit-Talai, Ulf Hannerz, Roger Hewitt and Daniel Miller.

NOTES

1 This was hinted at by Dick Hebdige already in the late 1970s (1979), in terms of the Lévi-Straussian concept of bricolage of youth styles. More recently, Roger Hewitt (1992) has suggested the term 'polyculture'

for an assemblage of cultural entities that are not distinct wholes of uniform nature, but interact together and are connected to change. And Paul Gilroy (1987) writes about black cultural syncretism indicating mixtures of different black cultures in Britain, different combinations of the Afro-Caribbean and the African diaspora. Also Ålund (1991), in a study on immigrant youth in Sweden, has found evidence of cultural syncretism of ethnic mixture with indigenous youth. Recently, Paul Gilroy (1993) has discussed youth cultures in terms of social and political hybridity. There is furthermore the concept of creolization (Drummond 1980; Hannerz 1987; 1992) as a way to understand cultural mixture that has grown out of unequal relationships between world centres and peripheries.

2 By coincidence there were ten black and ten white girls in the group. Although none was of mixed parentage, one or both of their parents came from Jamaica, Guyana, Nigeria, Ghana, Zaire, the US, Finland, Malta, France, Scotland, Ireland or England. In the early 1980s they were between 13 and 16 years old. Except for one girl, they were all born in England.

3 See Wulff (1988) for an extended discussion of these focal concerns, or themes. They had to do with the fact that the girls were in the process of growing up into young women, the implication being of ethnicity and the occurrence of excitement (and to a certain extent danger) in their lives.

4 The occupations of parents, or rather fathers according to the Western principle, is of course in many ways an unsatisfactory measurement of people's sense of class membership since it is often formed by experience of some social mobility upwards or downwards in the parental or grandparental generation. Immigrants who move from one country to another are also likely to experience some kind of social mobility.

5 The following section is a development of Wulff (1988). I have added data from my participant observation of the girls and interviews with them.

6 See Angela McRobbie (1989) on how girls and women buy second-hand clothes at ragmarkets in order to cultivate 'retrostyles', and even create new styles. This was not really fashionable in the early 1980s. Besides, the black and white girls in South London were still busy 'dressing away from' their school uniform as soon as they had an opportunity, which often meant 'dressing up' socially in copies of brand name clothes, or stating ethnic equality by way of youth style clothing.

7 This was how they talked about it, expressing an awareness of poverty in the countries of origin of the families of the black girls and (the black girls) about the slavery.

REFERENCES

Allan, G. (1989) *Friendship*, Boulder: Westview.
Ålund, A. (1991) 'Wrestling with ghosts', in A. Ålund and C.-U. Schierup (eds) *Paradoxes of Multiculturalism*, Aldershot: Avebury.

Berger, P. and Kellner, H. (1964) 'Marriage and the construction of reality: an exercise in the microsociology of knowledge', *Diogenes*, 46: 1–24.

Bourdieu, P. (1977) *Outline of a Theory of Practice*, Cambridge: Cambridge University Press.

Clarke, J. (1983) 'Style', in S. Hall and T. Jefferson (eds) *Resistance through Rituals*, London: Hutchinson.

Drummond, L. (1980) 'The Cultural continuum: a theory of intersystems', *Man*, 15: 352–374.

Du Bois, C. (1974) 'The gratitutious act', in E. Leyton (ed.) *The Compact*, New Foundland Social and Economic Papers No. 3. Institute of Social and Economic Research, Memorial University of New Foundland: Toronto University Press.

Gilroy, P. (1987) *There Ain't No Black in the Union Jack*, London: Hutchinson.

—— (1993) 'Between Afro-centrism and Euro-centrism: youth culture and the problem of hybridity', *Young*, 2: 2–12.

Hall, S. and Jefferson, T. (eds) (1975) *Resistance through Rituals*, London: Hutchinson.

Hannerz, U. (1987) 'The world in Creolisation', *Africa*, 57: 546–559.

—— (1992) *Cultural Complexity*, New York: Columbia University Press.

Hebdige, D. (1979) *Subculture*, London: Methuen.

Hewitt, R. (1986) *White Talk Black Talk*, Cambridge: Cambridge University Press.

—— (1992) 'Language, youth and the destabilisation of ethnicity', in C. Palmgren, K. Lövgren, and G. Bolin (eds.) *Ethnicity in Youth Culture*, Stockholm: Youth Culture at Stockholm University.

Jerrome, D. (1984) 'Good company: the sociological implications of friendship', *Sociological Review*, 32: 696–718.

Johnson, R. (1986) 'The story so far: and further transformations', in D. Punter (ed.) *Introduction to Contemporary Cultural Studies*, London: Longman.

McCall, G. J. (ed.) (1970) *Social Relationships*, Chicago: Aldine.

McRobbie, A. (1984) 'Dance and social fantasy', in A. McRobbie and M. Nava (eds) *Gender and Generation*, London: Macmillan.

McRobbie, A. and Garber, J. (1982) 'Girls and subcultures: an exploration', in S. Hall and T. Jefferson (eds) *Resistance through Rituals*, London: Hutchinson.

—— (1989) 'Second-gand dresses and the role of the ragmarket', in A. McRobbie (ed.) *Zoot Suits and Second-Hand Dresses*, London: Macmillan.

—— (1991) *Feminism and Youth Culture*, Boston: Unwin Hyman.

Nava, M. (1992) *Changing Cultures*, London: Sage.

Paine, R. (1969) 'In search of friendship: an explanatory analysis in "middle-class" culture', *Man*, 4: 505–524.

Tomlinson, A. (1990) 'Introduction', in A. Tomlinson (ed.) *Consumption, Identity and Style*, London: Routledge.

Willis, P. (1990) *Common Culture*, Boulder: Westview Press.

Willis, S. (1991) *A Primer for Daily Life*, London: Routledge.

Wulff, H. (1988) *Twenty Girls*, Stockholm Studies in Social Anthropology, no. 21. Stockholm: Department of Social Anthropology, Stockholm University.

—— (1992) 'New mix, new meanings', in C. Palmgren, K. Lövgren and G. Bolin (eds) *Ethnicity in Youth Culture*, Stockholm: Youth Culture at Stockholm University.

Chapter 5

The power of love

Raï music and youth in Algeria

Marc Schade-Poulsen

INTRODUCTION[1]

This chapter is inspired by a growing range of suggestions within anthropology questioning the classical approach to societies as being self-sustained communities in terms of cultural production (Marcus and Fischer 1986; Fabian 1978; Hannerz 1987; 1992; Barth 1989; Appadurai 1990). The increased worldwide interconnectedness in terms of systems of cultural communication demands the integration of new fields of understanding and research into the anthropological discipline.

One field of increasing importance today is the growth of Third World cities and the numerically and politically important groups of youths living there, who consume mass-produced cultural goods in their leisure time. In the area of the Middle East and the Maghreb, studies focusing on the significance of this interrelation or taking it as a point of departure seem only to be in the beginning.[2]

In Algeria however, in the early 1980s a new musical style came into being. It was called raï music and was sung by young singers entitled *chebs* (youngsters), using Western instruments and mixing local popular songs and rhythms with such music forms as American disco, songs of Julio Iglesias, Egyptian instrumental interludes and Moroccan wedding tunes. It was from Oran, the second largest city of Algeria, that hundreds of commercial songs were to be spread over a much vaster territory the following decade, to make raï the most popular musical style of Algeria.

This coincided with profound changes that had taken place in Algeria since independence, such as the doubling of the number of inhabitants, a profound renewal of the population of the cities and the large proportional growth of youth, many of them today without any higher education or employment, working in the black market or in poorly remunerated jobs.[3]

Here I will focus on this group and deal with the social significance of raï in relation to the conditions of *male* youth in Algeria of the 1980s.[4] It thus represents an attempt at using an analytical approach to mass-produced commercial music and texts, in order to contribute to an understanding of non-musical and non-poetic social dynamics.[5] This attempt demands a concern for the form and style that surrounds this art, its production, performance and consumption. Starting out with these matters I will arrive at the poetics of raï.

The main topic will be, not surprisingly when dealing with pop music, men's relationship to women, one of the most important aspects for male youngsters being to establish a relationship to a person of the opposite sex in order to leave the age of youth (for the Muslim world it can be termed as the age from fasting to wedding (cf. Davis and Davis 1989)). In dealing with these matters an underlying background will be that the concept of youth in Arabo-Muslim societies might differ from the one developed for the Western, industrialized world (B'Chir & Zghal 1984; Zghal 1984; Mortensen 1989). Furthermore, the conflicts in gender and family relations which we have found involved in our topic are not new in an Algerian or Maghrebian context, but have been part of a public debate that has taken place at least since the 1930s (Merad 1967; Camilleri 1973; Bouzar-Kasbadji 1988; Déjeux 1989).

Nevertheless, the social changes which have taken place in Algeria since independence might have sharpened these conflicts. The creation of a huge amount of wage labour jobs in the 1970s and the population influx to the cities seem to have led to changes in the family structure, bringing the couple as a unit to the centre and weakening the foundations of patriarchal power (Boutefnouchet 1982; Messaoudi 1990). At the same time, the economic conditions in Algeria have worsened severely throughout the 1980s, leading among other things to a severe crisis in housing (Messaoudi 1990; Sari 1990).

Finally, the period of youth has lengthened considerably since independence,[6] and at the same time Algeria has witnessed for the first time in its modern history an important arrival of *women* into the public spheres.[7] The above mentioned aspects are, I believe, strongly related to two important movements to be found among male youth in Algeria today, i.e. one towards the mosque and

Islamism, the other towards the West. An analysis of raï can contribute to some nuances into the understanding of these currents.

THE HISTORY OF RAï[8]

The emergence of raï is generally associated with the rural influx to the Western cities of Algeria (Belkhadem and Miliani 1981; Miliani 1983; Virolle-Souibès 1988a),[9] the first great movement following the depression of the 1930s, a second influx coming after the Second World War and the latest following the exodus of the European population at the time of Algerian independence.

The period of interest here however, is the late 1970s in Oran. At that time a number of groups versed in European music[10] were playing pop and rock at concerts and amateur contests in cinemas or rented halls, as well as in the numerous cabarets along the coastline. The entertainment in the cabarets consisted of at least two orchestras, one playing Western music and the other Oriental, Moroccan or Wahrani styles.[11] But in that period these latter genres seem increasingly to have been replaced by the acoustic raï genre. Musicians talk about how the two orchestras in that period would get together, creating such a success in terms of people taking to the dance floor that it subsequently became the standard fusion in the cabarets.

This coincided with the appearance of a new generation of singers,[12] all of them born around the time of independence, and thus representing the first generation of Algerians not having experienced the colonial period. It furthermore coincided with the final 'death' of the gramophone in Algeria, and its replacement by the cassette tape. The latter, being a cheaper and easier medium to handle in terms of production and distribution, opened the possibilities for a wide-scale production of music and – being more mobile than the record – for extending consumption in space and time. All in all a more democratic medium which, at the time led a new generation of producers into the business, many of them without previous musical experience and originating from occupations such as workers, small traders, etc.

During the following three to four years the new raï style spread with a speed and success which indicate that it expressed elements of acute concern in Algeria. And the fact that this spread took place outside the official channels is a further indication of a genre reflecting an autonomous socio-cultural change among youth. It was not until 1984 when the radio started releasing some raï songs on the French language Channel Three,[13] and in August of 1985; when the national party, FLN, sponsored an official raï festival in Oran. This was followed by two concerts in the first half of 1986 in Paris.

Together these events meant a decisive breakthrough for raï music, in Algeria as well as among a certain Western audience. The following years seem to have been the golden years of raï. In Algeria a series of party-financed public concerts was held and there was a constant source of new cassettes and singers. Western journalists and film teams travelled to Oran, and leading singers such as Cheb Mami, Cheb Khaled and Sahraoui and Fadhela were giving concerts in Europe, North America and Japan.

Today however, the raï boom has peaked. Most singers have not had the expected international breakthrough, with the exception of Khaled who has recently been relaunched on the international scene.[14] In Algeria the October revolt of 1988 and the Islamist take-over of the municipalities at the 1990 local elections (apart from the Kabyle region) have had serious repercussions on public raï performances. At the time of my fieldwork raï seemed to be nothing but the established and main pop genre of the country.

THE MUSIC

As the short history of raï suggests, its emergence has not taken place in a vacuum. In fact, there is a whole debate surrounding the growth of the genre, in which the musical aspect however has been little addressed.[15]

The basic form of raï is simple and strongly repetitive: a vocal or musical introduction will set the atmosphere of what is to come, i.e. a popular rhythm (often binary) upheld during the whole song, setting the time for simple song phrases, which will be duplicated by the instruments or by a responsive choir.

The process of actualizing raï has also been simple, taking place by way of analogy. Thus the drum sets, drum machines and bass guitars have replaced the acoustic percussion, and the synthesizers have replaced reed flutes, trumpets, accordions or violins.

But new instruments open up new musical possibilities. The bass can play harmonic figures, the electric guitar can enter on the upbeat (as in reggae), the drum machine can create a complex mixture of rhythms and sounds (bongos, congas, reverb, etc.), and the synthes-

izer can create backgrounds of violin orchestras, riffs of brass
sections, solo lines on piano, organ, qanun, pan-flute, etc.

This is in fact what has happened in a basically oral and
improvised process. Today the instrumental recording sessions last
no more than a week for a cassette of thirty eight minutes. The
outcome depends on the musicians, abilities, their familiarity with
the genre and their flair for integrating formulas (cf. Lord 1960) that
they have captured from outside the genre. The rules of the game are
simple. They are established by the basic dance rhythm and by the
melodic formulas proposed. But to this are added rhythmic 'conventions', musical sentences, sound ideas, formulas or motives from the
global world of music, which in all creates the unique and complex
blend appreciated by a wide audience in Algeria.

THE TEXT

In Algeria the debate has dealt mainly with the textual aspect of raï.
First, because a number of raï songs contain words and lines that are
not supposed to be heard within a family context. Second, because
raï rarely conforms to any poetic standard as found in other Algerian
genres.

Commentators have hinted at the fact that raï can be seen as an
expression of an ambivalent or fundamental duality in the identity
of Algerian youth (Miliani 1986; Virolle-Souibès 1988a; Mazouzi
1990). Others have seen it as a form of resistance to official,
legitimate culture or as a social outcry of the Algerian youth faced
with social, political and sexual misery (Chebel 1989; Mezouane
1992).[16] On the other hand, opponents to raï have stressed that it is
to be seen as a product of colonial acculturation and destruction or
as the failure of post colonial society in terms of its cultural policy
(c.f. Virolle-Souibès 1989; Schade-Poulsen 1993b).

Both points of view thus reflect a well-known debate of high
culture versus popular culture, but they have at the same time
neglected the most important aspect of any artistic production: its
poetic form, the context of the performance and the consumption. If
we want to deduce anything of social significance from raï music,
we have to deal with this matter.

The textual form of raï is most intriguing to the uninformed
listener. At first it seems to be contradictory, diffuse and disrespectful of any poetic standard. Thus in one and the same song, a
refrain deplores the miserable state of a woman having lived the life

of a whore, whereafter you will find sentences invoking people to
leave her alone; sentences talking about women's acts of sorcery
towards men, letters received by the singer from people the audience
does not have a chance to know, love 'at first sight', a person leaving
Algeria for France, spoken dedications to people unknown to the
listeners, and so on.[17]

But this apparent confusion will mainly tend to embroil a listener
devoted to poetry in a written tradition, with a high investment in
metaphorical richness and in time spent in finding and developing a
poetic line and idea. Mainly it will confuse the consumer of Western
popular music, the latter being 'sectionally structured, goal-oriented
[having] discrete units with a clear sense of dramatic climax and
closure' (Manuel 1988: 23).

The basic form of raï has its roots in an oral, improvised
performance, one of the main stages being at wedding parties. It is
an art mainly performed by female singers, either *sheikhâts*, singing
for men, or *meddahâts*, singing for women (both in an acoustic
tradition). On the basis of an ongoing dance rhythm, they will choose
a catchy key phrase to which they repeatedly return. During the
singing they will have a whole range of standard phrases at hand to
keep the movement ongoing. But in between they will improvise by
entering into a dialogue with the audience. They might make
comments on the people present, flattering them or offering them
dedications, the whole idea being the one at the centre of all
professional musical entertaining, i.e. to touch people (cf. Guignard
1975; Frith 1983), which can subsequently lead people to give a bank
note to the orchestra.

The *chebs* (young male singers) have built their profession on this
tradition. They will tend to improvise less than their female colleagues and in a performance they will often associate with a *berrâH*.
He is a man supposed to be gifted in the 'psychology of partying',
with a great knowledge of poetry, proverbs and so on. At the
weddings he is the one who collects money from the male audience,
asks for their favourite songs, and is in charge of announcing
publicly the names of those who have paid for the songs and to whom
the donors have dedicated the songs. He does this by means of poetic
sentences or proverbs intended to create a propitious atmosphere for
an audience in search of good entertainment and musicians looking
for a good pay.

The entertainment will often take the form of a competition, with people paying for a song in order to insult people present at the party. This will create a counter-order, and raise the money invested in the orchestra. Sometimes people will compete in having their particular song sung, thus overbidding one another. All this is mainly to create fun, but sometimes, when the *berrâH* does not possess the verbal finesse or psychological insight, it can result in serious fights.

It is this whole basic idea from live performances that you find repeated in the recorded songs on cassettes, i.e. a form that can be described as a repetitive movement in time, embedded in a person-to-person social game, with sentences sung to an audience in order to touch people, and with a continual return to a key phrase.

The singers are aware of the fact that the most important thing needed in order to create a hit lies in finding a key phrase that will touch people. For this they will draw on their life experience in their densely populated, popular districts of Oran (or from neighbouring cities). Most singers have no high degree school certificate and are sons of small employees, handicraftsmen, traders or divorced women.

They will often go consciously for popular subjects, have poet friends helping them, or they will use sentences or ideas from a berrâH's stock of proverbs and poetry. Others will take up old songs and rearrange the sentences according to the raï format. Finally, a number of stars receive fan letters which include raï poetry, from which they will select sentences according to their professional intuition.

With this they will enter the recording studio. The six songs required for a cassette will be recorded in one day, and the singer will pursue the habit of keeping a person-to-person contact with an audience. Thus nearly every song is introduced by dedications to people present in the studio at the time of recording or to acquaintances outside. These dedications will often continue during the song, sometimes even taking the form of a whole song line, and in the most improvised situations the singer will contact people directly, either by joking:

Mâlîk w Ben `Alî anâ galûli Hbâb
Malik and Ben Ali told me they were friends (Cheb Khaled; *dellâli,dellâli*; my guide, my guide)

ya lamen hbâla, `abdallah, Hseb l-birra sherrbet
He is crazy, Abdallah, he thinks beer is like sugar water (Cheb Khaled; *rrây shîn*; evil raï)

Or sometimes by sending out personal messages:

> *yekber `abdallaH w nrrabih `ala yedi*
> Abdallah will grow up, and I'll educate him by my own means
> (Cheb Hasni; *âna ndabbar râsi*; I will manage on my own)

> *yana bghit meHHenti ya shkûn ysalni?*
> I wanted my passion, who has the right to question that (Cheb
> Sahraoui; *deblet galbi*; torment of my heart)

Thus the consumers are offered the possibility, when dancing to a
raï cassette, of being taken into an atmosphere of a live performance.
When listening to the text the cassettes offer the setting of a peer
group of male friends where jokes can be told, women talked about
and problems expressed.

LISTENING TO RAï

There seems to be a wide consensus among young men in considering raï music as being light (*khafîf*) and good for dancing. They
tend to appreciate the use of electric instruments and label the music
as 'pop-raï', 'disco-raï' or 'raï-reggae' in opposition to the acoustic
city-based raï which is termed 'old raï' or the rural-based form which
is termed 'raï of *gaSba*' or 'raï of the *shîkh*s'.[18] Finally it is said
that the success of raï is due to the fact that it has modernized an
older repertoire and put it on the level of universal pop music while
keeping its Algerian character.

People who enjoy raï cassettes are aware of the poetic form from
their participation in weddings and so on. They are not surprised (but
sometimes irritated if it is not done skilfully enough) to hear the
praise of a blonde, a redhead and a brunette in one and the same song,
a song dealing with a woman living in Oran as well as in Arzew,
Marseilles and Paris. They know that one sentence might touch them,
but not other people, who might be touched by other sentences. With
this knowledge in mind, they will say that raï deals with the problems
of Algerian society and youth, and often express it in phrases such
as: 'When I hear the singer, it is as if I hear my own story', or 'When
I hear this and that song, it makes me remember a time when. . .'.

The listeners tend to identify with the persona of the singer.
Through the cassettes and the 'street telephone' (gossip) they get an
image of the life conditions of the singer. They will 'know' that one

singer has serious housing problems, the mother of another has to work in the public sphere as a cleaner, the wife of a third has left him, a fourth has been bewitched by a woman, a fifth has married a raï singer, and of course that several singers have had success in the West.

Thus the consumers ascribe a personality to the singer according to which they will tend to select their cassettes. One is known as a *meriûl*, a man enjoying the good life (women, food, drink); another is known for his sentimentality and is good to listen to when you are in love; a third is known as a serious man who always sings proper words, and so on.

In my encounters with the singers and young raï consumers I have found no significant difference, in terms of ideology and life-style, except for the fact that the singers live a professional life in a leisurely style to which most youngsters cannot afford access.

STYLE

The same holds true for the use of clothing. Most singers are dressed and pictured on cassette covers in a 'simple style', which means a short haircut (or haircuts modelled on Afro-American disco style), a T-shirt (or shirt) and trousers (often jeans) of good quality – which in Algeria means non-Algerian clothes from Spain, France, Italy or Morocco purchased on the black market.

In Algeria you will have difficulty in finding styles of dressing signalling the existence of any subculture or counterculture as is found in the literature on Western youth (Fornäs *et al.* 1984; Frith 1983; Hebdige 1979). Differences do exist however, the most significant being that Islamists wear *qamîS* (a long day shirt) and grow a beard (in honour of the Prophet). The style of dressing is however not specific to the youth, but is characteristic of all age groups within the movement. And many raï fans do not tend to consider themselves as being in opposition to the Islamists. They talk about them as being 'real Muslims', and they know that their style signals, among other things, that the wearer has forsaken women, music and alcohol for the benefits of a pure, sacred life.

Raï fans do, however, term themselves in opposition to other categories of youth. On the one hand, people originating from Tlemcen or Kabylia are known not for a different style of dress but for having a dialect or language which differs from the Oran dialect, plus a musical tradition of their own. According to the stereotypes, the Kabyles and Tlemcenians possess an advantageous social position in Oran, and they do not marry their women to non-Kabyles or non-Tlemcenians.

On the other hand there are the *tchi-tchis*. The expression is synonymous with rich, spoiled youngsters who are snobbish, drive their fathers' cars, go abroad on holidays and imitate Western life. According to the stereotype, they avoid doing their military service, are physically weak and only obtain women because of the money and cars they possess. And once they have such women, they let them do as they please. All in all, they are effeminate men through their imitation of the West and their possession of Western material goods.

In this sense, they resemble a final category: young men – many of whom have visited Europe – who wear ear-rings, long hair or ponytails. Raï fans tend to dislike this fashion: they say that every man is free to do as he likes, but that they do not know the context in which Western men dress like that, and that it is not good for a man to imitate a woman. Thus this latter category is stereotyped in the same way as the Kabyles, Tlemcenians and the *tchi-tchis*, i.e. according to notions of gender and according to their access to material power. These topics will be central to the discussion of the poetics of raï below.

EXPRESSION

Raï is not as incoherent as it might seem – although it involves a low investment of money and time. A fundamental duality in the identity of Algerian youth cannot be deduced from the narrative form of raï songs.[19] These songs consist of a series of independent sentences, each containing a story or a message meant to touch people. In what follows I will analyse the raï poetics by extracting sentences from the songs and rearranging them in thematic order.[20] I will consider them as what they are, a bricolage theory (Lévi-Strauss 1962) of what the producers of raï believe will move people in Algerian society. The following section will go into detail with some main themes of raï, in order to give a background for a theory of emotional concern in Algerian society. I will start with the period of the early 1980s and trace how the themes of raï mainly evoked spheres of pleasure in Algerian society. I will then continue with a discussion of raï songs dealing with matters outside those spheres, i.e. songs of love which became the dominant trend after the official breakthrough in the mid 1980s. But before doing this a reservation must be made in the light of the previous discussion.

Raï words are not factual, spoken words, but expressive words put into music and song. Taken as a total expression, a song can have another direction than when listened to for its literal textual value. In one of the most famous songs, for example (*hadha rrâykum*: this is your opinion), the singer is telling how the husband of today is asleep while his wife goes out; how people do as they like, etc. – all in all, a song which can be said to deplore the disintegration of Algerian family values. But at the same time the song moves in a good dance rhythm with a call and response character. When heard live, one of the pleasures it gives to the audience is to sing along to the reply. Later on in the recorded song the singer goes on offering dedications to women present in the studio, indicating that he himself does not inhabit a world which conforms to the family ideal. Thus if the song can be said to deal with a rather serious matter on a discourse level, it becomes a song of pleasure on the level of musical expression, of singing along and making fun of a world turned upside-down.

PLEASURE

The spaces into which the raï of the early 1980s takes its audience are actually the ones from which it originated: the male spheres of pleasure, alcohol and women, i.e. 'women without men' (Jansen 1987). Jansen has described how, in Algeria, women who lack a man's financial support and moral control will tend to be found in occupations generally considered to be impure or to transgress public morality. Included in these professions are singers, but also courtesans.

Jansen uses the term *qaHba* for these women, but in Oran men will make a distinction between *qaHba* and *meriûla*. The former is associated with women working in public or private brothels; the latter with women working more freely from a home base, in bars, cabarets and big hotels, as the mistress or entertainer of one or several men – thus all in all being closer to a lover than the *qaHba*.

Raï of the early 1980s brings its audience into a relationship with the 'free women':

> *metdheblet l-shfâr w tji `andi l d-dâr, nsherrebha w r-rikar,*
> *khuya `aeynâni*
> The woman with the drooping eyelashes will come to my

house, I will make her drink Richard believe me brother, openly (Cheb Mami; *ghîr l-beyDa w âna*; only the blonde and I)

In fact, the 1980s borrowed a great deal of its verbal stock from the repertoire of the older acoustic performative context, in which *sheikhâtes* (female singers) entertained men at weddings, in brothels or at pleasure parties.

A great number of lines thus take us into a close description of such pleasure parties, known as *basTas*, first, by mentioning the pleasurable things brought along in order to create a propitious atmosphere:

> *baytîn fi zebûj w Hshân w l-rûje*
> We spend the night under the wild olives, with a meal and red wine (Cheb Khaled; *mâ netzûj ma rabi kebda*; I won't marry, I won't tie my sentiments up)

> *âna njîb el-wiski w el kuka 'alîk*
> I will bring the whisky and you the Coca-Cola (Zargui; *Dyâf rabbi*; the invited of God)

> *l-mizân w l-`aqliya w nSabihu l-hal*
> The hand drum, and hashish, and we'll find a good time (Cheb Khaled; *shkûn eddâk*; who took you)

Second, by describing the beginning of the party and the consumption of the pleasurable things brought along:

> *nessekru, ndeffigu, kubbu, zidu, mazâl l-Hâl*
> We will be drinking, pour the glass, one more, we have the time (Cheb Khaled and Miloud; *kubbu,kubbu*; pour out, pour out)

> *dhîk T-Twila ya dhîk l-`arîDa, dhîk l gsîra tahder fi l-hwa*
> The tall one, the thick one, the small one, she is intoxicated and talks wildly (Cheb Khaled and Miloud; *kubbu,kubbu*; pour out, pour out)

Ending up with a night in close reunion:

> *t`aânegna f r-remla yâw dâna l-mâ*
> We embraced on the sand of the beach and the water took us away (Cheb Khaled; *aya nSeddu*; come on, lets go)

> *ditha lil l-ghâba w khla`aaha l-dhib*
> I took her to the woods and the wolf [male sex] scared her (Cheb Khaled; *ya Sayâda*; the huntress)

The places for the pleasure parties will always be described as being away from public view. Thus the woods, the beach and the railway tracks stand as a synonym for *basTas* in raï songs, unless the scene depicted takes place in much poorer conditions:

> *baytîn basâta `ala Dâw camiûn*
> We spend the night doing a basTa in the light of a truck (Cheb Khaled; *hây weddi*; oh, my luck)

But the main locations for pleasure parties in the city of Oran are the cabarets. Here you will find women smoking and drinking with men, couples kissing in public or dancing closely. Here men will take women out, talk to them, have fun with them, fondling them, kissing them and, all in all, engaging in an affair that is impossible or unthinkable with their wives (underlined by a popular saying that you should divorce your wife in order to take her out).

Raï music in itself is a central medium for the contact between men and women in these places. People tend to dance individually, but will at the same time use the dance movements in a dialogue with the women present. Working with the pelvis and establishing the same movement will confirm contact between the couple, which can subsequently lead to a private exchange of telephone numbers. Another form of contact is to use the game surrounding the singing, where a man will address a woman by paying for a song that has a title referring to the girl's personality.

These contacts sometimes lead to serious love affairs, couples deciding to get together. But from the man's point of view it is known as being a delicate situation. It would be difficult to marry, the parents would rarely agree to such a relationship, and it is commonly considered that once the woman has tasted the 'free life', going out when she wants, she will have difficulties in settling down as a housewife.

Furthermore, it demands capital to enter a relationship with a *meriûla*, either in order to provide her with an apartment or to entertain her in the public life of 'le milieu'. It is also commonly acknowledged that the women will often play 'several horses'. Thus having a relationship with a 'free girl' requires that a man be able to defend his position either by means of money, but also by means of his capacities in the physical fights taking place in the cabarets.

The raï lines of the early 1980s take us into these problems of maintaining a relationship with free women in the milieu:

> *sahr l-lyâli wa`ar w nti ma`amda*

The nights out are tough and you accepted it (Cheb Khaled;
nsâlfîk; you do concern me)

ma ndireh l-aman, lqitha mbasTa fi l-jenên
I don't trust her, I found her in good company in the garden
(Cheb Khaled; *`alâsh t-twalfîni nebghîk?*; why do you give
me the habit of wanting you?)

And often the road to crime is not far off:

khâfi `aliyya l-vola S `aiba, yek l-barâj fi kull Trîg ki ndîr?
Have fear on behalf of me, the wheel is difficult to handle, there
are barrages all over the road, what shall I do? (Cheb Khaled
and Miloud; *kubbu,kubbu*; pour out, pour out)

Tabu jnâbi `ala s-sîma l-barda
my ribs got pains because of the cold cement (Cheb Khaled;
sheHfîya ana lli bghît; it serves me right, I looked for it)

It is a world of little exotism, as is recognized in the songs
themselves:

r-regba w el-meriûl ana ma yebghîh Hadd
No one wants anything to do with the tough guy and the flirting
woman (Cheb Khaled; *SSobri, SSbri*; have patience, have
patience)

mulêt zûj wulidât fi l-ghâba tabât
Mother of two children and she sleeps in the forest at night
(Cheb Khaled; *Liya, liya*; for me, for me)

Last but not least, it is expressed as a world irreconcilable with the
ideal life of the family:

faDat `ala mwa, kûll yûm njîha `aama
I did many bad things towards my mother, every day I come
home blinded [from drinking] (Cheb Khaled; *nti, nti*; you,
you)

rrây el-ghaddâr teleftli rrây w khlitli dâr
Treacherous raï you made me change my ways, you made me
lose my home (Cheb Khaled; *nti, nti*; you, you)

The world of 'the milieu' is expressed in terms of raï:

sahha rabbi nestahel, yana rrây derli
Thank you my God, I deserve it, the raï did it to me (Cheb
Khaled; *testahel ya galbi*; you deserve it, oh my heart)

rrây shîn, wîn emTal'ani, rrây dûni wîn dayni
Evil raï, where do you lead me; hard raï, where do you take me
(Cheb Khaled; *rrây shîn*; evil raï)

Thus you have a whole range of sentences that grow out of – and evoke – spheres of lust and pleasure in Algerian society. They are spheres where the boundaries between gender roles tend to be altered both by males and females. These changes in female and male behaviour when entering male spheres of pleasure have been noted elsewhere in the Middle East (Jansen 1987; van Nieuwkerk 1992; Stokes 1992). In raï the transgressions are reflected in the voices, where the most appreciated female singers sing in a low pitch, while the men tend to sing an octave above speaking level. When singing duos they will maintain the same pitch.

The lines are meant to touch people, either by amusing or arousing them. Others play on a supposed emotional tension of being in between a 'normal' and 'stigmatized' life. Others play on the emotions that outsiders may get by witnessing people who have 'surrendered' to the spheres of pleasure.

However, the interesting fact is that it was also these sentences, sung by young voices in the orally-based raï form, amplified by Western electric instruments and recorded on the democratic, mobile cassettes, that achieved such a success *outside* the spheres for which they were primarily intended. It appears that a change in gender roles and the notion of leisure time was becoming of acute concern among Algerian youth during that period. At least it was expressed through the relationship between music and sexuality.

But countervalues were also prevalent; a main idea of the rising Islamist movement being the segregation of men and women in public spheres.

THE 'WHERE AND WHEN' OF LISTENING TO RAï

Listening to early raï with the family poses major problems. The simple evocation of the woods, drinking, women that drink, and even of raï music itself, creates embarrassment in many families. It is interesting that the producers in the mid-1980s sought to eliminate topics considered most vulgar from the songs, because early raï posed such problems in numerous Algerian families. They thus created the notion of clean raï (in French, *raï propre*). On one hand they not only implied by this that early raï was 'dirty', they also established a semantic link between raï, the moral organization of the family and at least two other spheres of Algerian society in which sexuality and lust are central: the month of Ramadan and the mosque.

Today, few young men would thus listen to 'dirty' raï in front of their father, nor would they allow their sisters to do so in their presence. But many listen to raï in the presence of their mother (and quite a few in the presence of their brothers).

When asked, most will say they do it out of respect for their family, and thus refer to the notion of *qder* which includes not smoking, drinking alcohol, or evoking sexual or amorous topics within the family. The same elements would be mentioned – without referring to respect – in relation to the mosque and Ramadan.

Young men who profess their faith in Islam and even in the Islamist Party will abstain from praying out of rationalizations as these: 'If I see a woman that excites me on my way to the mosque, I can't go in there.' 'I am weak, I have relationships with women and I drink, I can't pray at the same time.' In the latter case they would stress that Ramadan is not only a month of worshipping and fasting, but also one of rest for the ears and the eyes, where in fact most young men will abstain from entering into any relationships with women. Both are examples of purification in terms of Islam (cf. Boudhiba 1975), and raï music thus seems to belong to a complex in conflict with these states of being.

There is however a significant exception to this pattern. At weddings, people will not decline to dance and listen to raï while other members of the family are present. When asked, people say they lose their head, they blow off steam, and thus do not observe the texts as they otherwise would.

In a sense, the weddings have a close relationship to the raï performances of the cabarets. In both places you find the same competitions and exchange of words for money that accompany raï performances. In both places people 'lose their heads'. Both places also feature sexuality: in cabarets by men's acquaintance with 'free women', at weddings through the consummation of the sexual contract between two families manifested by the man's defloration of the bride on the last wedding night.

Both performances can thus be seen as inversions of moral and sexual norms of daily life, i.e. of turning the world upside-down. But at the same time there are significant differences. In the cabarets, for example, one can frequently hear dedications to women mentioned by name, whereas this is unheard of at weddings. Naming women in public is considered to open up the possibilities of uncontrolled sexuality as well as exhibiting women in public life (cf. Benkheira 1982; Mernissi 1983). Thus, if cabarets are spaces for featuring uncontrolled leisure and lust, where male and female roles are altered, the wedding party features regulated sexuality where male and female roles are confirmed. Bringing raï within situations of everyday life in the family thus seems equal to bringing the danger of uncontrolled sexuality into the sacred, pure realm of the family (symbolized by the role of the father).

All things considered, young men tend to listen to raï in age and gender groups, where the evocation of sexuality does not have the same consequences as in mixed groups. They will do this outside the family, in the streets, in cassette shops, on the beach, in the woods, in vacant sites of the cities, in bars, etc., and – before the rise of the Islamist party – at concerts.

But young people will also sometimes arrange disco parties in rented halls at the end of the week, to which they can bring a girlfriend before she has to return home before dark. It is a common saying among young men that everyone can have a girlfriend if he wants. But questions then arise concerning the status and conditions of these male-female relations, neither taking place within the family nor at pleasure parties. This is what clean raï is about.

CLEAN RAï

If dirty raï takes us into nature, to the woods, the beach, the wild olives, clean raï takes us into the city. Here you find streets, local areas, doors, houses, post offices, telephones and cars. And if dirty raï is populated by drinking and sexually active men and women, in clean raï you will find the father and mother, the cousin and of course the dual relation of 'you and me','me and her' or the triangle of 'you, me and the others'.

You and me (Part 1)

All in all, if dirty raï is intended to arouse or touch people by mentioning spheres of lust, clean raï is based upon the idea that people's deepest concern is *love*, i.e. a man's emotions or tensions when he engages in a relationship to a woman.

kwît gelbi b kiyya m el-meHna[21] *t-tâlya*

My heart was burning because of my latest passion (Cheb Khaled; *ma nemshîsh m'aâk*; I won't go with you)

minha hiyya ma Hlâli n-nûm
Because of her I don't sleep (Cheb Khaled; *ma Hlâli en-nûm*; the sleep doesn't come to me)

In this endeavour it seldom specifies any qualities of the persons involved but gives open-ended descriptions, leaving people to fill in their own gallery of people.[22] And rarely does it describe the conditions, 'the where', 'the when' and 'the how long' of the love meeting, apart from:

bâb 'aend l-bâb w âna f l-'adhâb
Door to door and I am in pain (Cheb Mami; *ana mazâl*; I am always)

khallûni minha kebret m'aâya
Don't mention her anymore, she grew up with me (Mohammed Sghir; *khallûni menha*; don't mention her)

Instead, it often stresses the fact that it can become a serious meeting based on mutuality:

l-mût lli tedîk – tedîni m'aâk
Death that takes you away, will take me away with you (Cheb Khaled and Cheba Zahouania; *ha jedek*; oh grandfather)

lli bik w biya welli Darrek Darrni
What's in you, is in me and what hurts you, hurts me (Cheb Khaled; *mânish minna*; I am not from here)

But it is also a relationship which basically gives great pain to the man involved:

'ala mulât l-khâna râni n-sufri, ha rabbi
I suffer because of the girl with the beauty spot, oh my God (Benchenet; *Helli l-bâb*; open the door)

dokhân w zalamît, ana menha gudît
With cigarettes and matches, I burned of love (Cheb Khaled; *shkûn edâk*; who took you?)

râni mrîD w mejrûH w m l-ghrâm bâyet n-nûH
I am ill and hurt, of love I spent the night crying (Cheb Mami; *FaTma, FaTma*; Fatima, Fatima)

In raï songs the love meeting is very rarely brought to a happy consummation. We seldom find songs or lines praising happy love, about people forming a relationship or getting married. Rather:

> *minni Tellegt anaya ya tzewwjti nti*
> When I divorced, you married (Cheb Khaled; `andi mHeyna`; I have a passion)

> *ma dhennitsh netfarqu min b`aad `ashretna*
> I didn't think we'd divorce after our life together (Cheikh N'aam; *ma dhennitsh netfarqu*; I didn't think we'd divorce)

Thus the raï notion of society is one in which a commercial success is not expected by singing about honeymoons (cf. Carey 1972) or by expressing 'happy love'. It is not manly to exhibit this feeling in public. But still, singing of love meetings is. Most often they are expressed through the well-known metaphor of the eyes (your eyes are like mine, etc.), but some of the sentences also hint at a social environment in which the eyes can be the only medium for contact:

> *`aynik gâluha w fummuk ma hdar*
> Your eyes told it and your mouth doesn't speak (Cheb Khaled; *ghîr dûni l-dârna*; just bring her to our house)

> *`aynik m`aamrîn klâm w fummuk ma hdar*
> Your eyes are plenty of words and your mouth doesn't speak (Cheb Khaled; *Hasdûni fîk*; they were jealous of me because of you)

You and me and the others

In other words, the raï songs take place within the framework of a Muslim city, in the sense of a spatial organization of public and private life and in the sense of a spatial segregation of the sexes. Thus raï sentences never take us into any tension within the sacred place of the family, the house. Rather, they exploit the sentiment of an ideal peace presumed to be found there and the sentiments of the social identity and strength it gives.

> *ma dâm `aandi lumwîma ngeyyel fi Dlâl*
> As long as I have my mother, I sleep in the shade [of our yard] (Cheb Khaled; *dellâli,dellâli*; my guide, my guide)

> *sh-shedda fi allâh w da`awet el-walidin m`aâya*
> I hold on to God and the blessings of my parents are with me. (Cheikh N`aam; *lli bini w binek mât*; what is between you and me is dead)

la mha, la buha, ktafha berdine
No mother, no father and her shoulders [social relations] are
cold (Cheb Khaled; `aTûni kuwaghti`; give me my personal
papers)

Any tension that comes near the family rarely gets close

trîg l-`omri Halwa w dima nfûtha
The road to my life [love] is sweet, I always take that way
(Cheb Khaled; *testaHel ya galbi*; you deserve it, oh my heart)

At least no closer than the door.

Helli l-bâb `aliya wella nheddem
Open the door to me, or I'll break it down (Benchenet; *Helli
l-bâb*; open the door)

Helli l-bâb `aliya, ana manîsh `aadûk
Open the door for me, I am not your enemy (Cheb Khaled;
`alesh Hbîbek tensih`; why do you forget your boyfriend?)

If the lines do admit tensions within the sacred place of an Algerian
family, it is by indirect means and not direct physical contact:

hetreft bîk el bâreH w sm`aatni mma
I dreamt of you yesterday, and my mother heard me (Zargui;
ana ma nwellîsh; I won't come back)

ma t`aeyeTish fi dâr d-de`awa dâje
Don't call home, the situation is dangerous (Cheb Hamid and
Cheba Zohra; `aeyyeT fi Tilifûn`; she called by telephone)

But then everything in the songs also happens as if what could really
threaten the peace of the house and the social base of man is the
development of a relationship between a man and a woman from the
outside. As in dirty raï it is expressed in an irreconcilable split between
the home and life outside and also as in dirty raï, it is primarily
expressed as endangering a man's relationship with his mother:

ma ndîr meHna w ma tkheybini `ala mma w ba`athûri
I won't take this passion, she will not make me deceive my
mother or my roots (Cheb Khaled; *dellâli,dellâli*; my guide,
my guide)

D-Durr liya w SaHHa l-mwimti
The pain is for me, and the well-being for my mother (Cheb
Hasni; *âna ndabbar râsi*; I will manage on my own)

Thus in raï, the boundaries between the notion of unregulated sexuality and the notion of love seem to be diffuse. But clean raï adds to this fact: that what touches people particularly, beyond the evocation of the peaceful site of the home, is the evocation of the relationship between a man and his mother. What moves people is the evocation of the tension between a man and his mother if the former engages in relationships with women outside the home.

It is a noteworthy set-up, because it puts into perspective the fact that hypothetical tensions between two other member categories of the family are left totally unexploited, i.e. the father and the sister (the latter being totally off the record). The mother is the central figure in the parent couple. If the father figure is evoked, it is as the moral guardian of daughters. But it is never the father of the 'storyteller's' home, it is always the father of 'other' daughters or sisters.

> *bûha hlef b-l-imîn w m-dâr majîsh*
> Her father swore by his faith, that she wouldn't come out of the house (Cheb Khaled; *testahel ya galbi*; you deserve it, oh my heart)

> *shûfu l-munkur, bûha w gaTTe`aha l-bHar*
> Look at the injustice, her father made her cross the sea (Cheb Khaled; *`andi mHeyna*; I have a passion)

The emotions exploited here are the ones experienced with other men keeping up the peace and sacredness of their houses, a challenge that requires of a man to be watchful:

> *nerslek mersûli `andi yweSSalni l-xbâr*
> I'll send you my messenger, he will bring me the news (Cheb Hamid; *ana qâsît*; I suffered)

> *zelfeTlak l-mersûl Hatta l-dârkum, haya `omri*
> I sent you a message to your home, oh my 'life' (Zargui; *Dyâf rabbi*; the invited of God)

The most popular choice of contact technique is the telephone:

> *Tilifûn Hrem l-Hitân derrgûh, tekhrej `omri nekri el-busTa*
> The telephone doesn't work, the walls are hiding it, my spirit goes out, I rent the post office (Benchenet; *Tilifûn Hrem*; The telephone doesn't work)

> *fi Tilifûn nessem`aaha w b-`aayni la*
> I hear her on the telephone, but with my eye no (Cheb Hamid and Cheba Zohra; *`aeyyeT fi Tilifûn*; she called by telephone)

Thus raï exploits the supposed tensions in young men's efforts to engage in relationships with women outside their houses. All in all, the lines contain a notion of society in which engaging in relationships with women seems to be an emotional, tense and problematic affair in terms of the family. But in raï you never hear of any clashes between youth and the parental generation. The raï lines follow the same patterns as we found in the 'where' and 'when' of listening to raï. No conflicts with the father are allowed; rather, he is absent. A strong sentimental link to the mother is confirmed, and power over the sisters is upheld by means of hiding them away.

If many love meetings between men and women do take place in raï, they take place in the same moments of the day and the same spaces of the city, where raï tends to be listened to by young men, i.e. outside the home.

In Oran, such meetings actually take place in the institutions of education, if not on the students' way to and from school; others occur in local public areas or in rooms at the backs of shops kept by young men. In the city centre some tea-shops, restaurants or ice-cream bars will allow 'mixed couples' a free space, but otherwise the lovers must go to the places which are associated with the 'dirty' spheres of lust: the beach, the forest, the wild olives or the few parks not reserved 'for families'. Unless of course they possess capital either in terms of money or social relations, i.e. the means for renting a hotel room or a villa (preferably in another town), a vacant apartment or friends who can lend them one, or a car.

The raï sentences play on the fragility of the chances of meeting:

> dîtha rendivû, fi bâli nsât
> I gave an appointment, I really think she forgot it (Cheb Khaled; rrây, ha rrây; raï, oh raï)
>
> qâr`at `ala waHda, thlâta fayta, Hbibti gharatni
> I waited till one o'clock, three hours passed, my love deceived me (Cheb Khaled; rrây, ha rrây; raï, oh raï)

But the tensions found to be most worthwhile exploiting in the meetings outside are caused by a situation similar to the performative context of raï, i.e. that man is never alone, his life is embedded in constant social relationships to other men:

> kull yûm nesme `a hadra lli `asheqtha gâlu dâyra
> Every day I hear talk [gossip] telling that the one I loved has 'done it' (Benchenet; Helli l-bâb; open the door)

kedhbu `aliya gâlu baddâla
They lied to me, they said you were a woman of many men
(Benchenet; *kedhbu `aliya*; they lied to me)

A social life is embedded in competition over a scarce commodity,
the presence of women or relationships with femininity:

gulu l-Sayyad yekhTini Hmamti
Tell the hunter to leave my pigeon alone for me (Cheb
Saharaoui; *Deblet galbi*; torment of my heart)

mnîn gult nerbaH nâdhuli l-`areb
When I said I was winning the Arabs [people] rose against me
(Cheb Hasni; *si pa la pên*; it's not worth it)

Thus in these lines everything happens as if a man, when entering
into a relationship with a woman, comes to possess a rare quality
which – if exposed in public – makes him fragile and brings him into
opposition with his social surroundings that compete for and comment on this same quality. Many raï lines deal with the feelings of
men – possessing this rare quality – in being victims of forces greater
than themselves. They deal with the feeling that these forces will
have an effect on the object in their possesion:

sm`aw l-`aadyân w dâruli kontra
My enemies got the news, they counter attacked me (Cheb
Khaled; *nti, nti*; you, you)

kothra min `aadyâni saknîn Hûmti
Most of my enemies live in my local area (Cheb Khaled; *nti,
nti*; you, you)

l-ghelba t-`aemmer râsha w ma tHî
The subduers fill her head without any scruples (Cheb
Abdelhaq; *ntîya sbâbi*; you are the reason)

derti `ala klâmhum, Allah yekhli klamhum
You followed their words, may God punish [empty] their
sayings (Cheb Khaled; *ma tgûlish râni nebghîk*; don't tell me
I want you)

In solving these problems, it seems that the greatest commercial
value is expected when expressing the act of counter-attack, rather
than introspections into men's personalities. The same idea prevails
in sketching their problems in face-to-face encounters with women.

You and me (Part 2)

We have already seen above that the love encounter can provoke great pain in a man; this pain can become chronic:

> *ma ndîr l-meHna w ma teSbeghli gwaymi*
> I won't take that woman, she will not weaken [paint] my bones
> (Cheb Khaled; *ma derti dâr*; you didn't make a home)

> *mashi gharDi dellâli, ghelbûni sHûr*
> It is not my fault, my guide, the witchcraft won over me (Cheb Abdelhaq; *mashi gharDi*; it's not my fault)

> *l-shîra wellât tesHer w tekmi jmar*
> The girls are now practising witchcraft and burning wood embers (Cheb Mami; *l-bnât hâju*; the girls fly out)

Man might be led into an abnormal state of being when entering into a relationship with femininity.[23] Here we find a notion of a dual society expressed in which the other half, the feminine side, possesses a power, the knowledge of sorcery, which is out of man's control and against which he has no counter power. Meeting the other half might endanger the fragile quality obtained through a love meeting; it might also endanger his social and physical being and it creates suspicion:

> *nxâf ndîrfik kunfianse tekhawnili galbi*
> I am afraid of trusting you, that you steal away my heart (Cheb Khaled; *Hasnû awni*; bring me to sense)

> *`ayish m`aak fi l-amân, nâkra khd`aatih*
> He lives with you in confidence; you, ungrateful, betrayed him (Cheb Khaled; *ashHâl bqatni nuSbur*; how much can I endure?)

Thus the final bricolage theory of raï, in expressing the tensions brought about by men meeting women outside the sacred realms of society – in unaccomplished gender encounters – is one of forces getting out of man's control: the world of women.

> *bnât l-yûm ki Hyût r-remla welli shâdd fihum yrîb*
> The girls of today are like walls of sand, if you lean on them you fall (Cheb Khaled; *S`aeyda b`aîda*; Saïda is far away)

> *Hasbu kullshi sâhel ma bqâsh l-`aqel*
> They think everything is easy, they have lost their knowledge of right and wrong (Cheb Mami; *l-bnât hâju*; the girls fly out)

khûtak murDa w nti fi zunqa
Your brother is ill, and you go around in the streets (Cheb Mami; *l-bnât hâju*; the girls fly out)

lukân Sberti w xemmemti, nHjebti w Hashemmeti
If only you were patient and wise, if only you had veiled [stayed at home] and had kept your shame (Cheikh N`aam; *lli bini w binek mât*; what is between you and me is dead)

Women are not as women ought to be. It is the world of sisters coming out in the open, women seeking male qualities, or what is supposed to be male material power:

tmûti `a- S-Syâgha w jurri Hâykek
You die out of want for jewellery and you drag around your veil (Zargui; *ana ma nwellîsh*; I won't come back)

bent l-`aemm trûH w tji w m`aa lli `aTah rabbi
The cousin comes and goes, with those God has gifted (Cheb Mami; *khellûni nebki*; let me cry)

mûl l-luTu yklaksûni shira jâya tejri
The car owner sounds his horn, the girl comes running (Cheb Mami; *khellûni nebki*; let me cry)

All in all, a material power which is necessary in order to bring a relationship of love *out* of the field of contest and *out* of the 'impure' spheres of society. But the idea of these latter lines are also built on the supposition that the listeners in fact do not possess either the car, the house, or any other material goods women are thought to want.

The lines express the tensions young men feel at not being able to enter 'modern' spheres of leisure, nor to establish themselves as adults on the basis of the idea of the couple. But still, in raï, commercial value is expected when expressing possible relief of the unsolved tensions.

si pa la pên bâsh nwalli lîk
It's not worth it, that I come back to you (Cheb Hasni; *si pa la pên*; it's not worth it)

ana kammelt m`aâk w sheffina kull Hsabêtna
I am all finished with you, all accounts are done (Benchenet; *ana kammelt m`aâk*; I am all finished with you)

One idealized solution to be found in raï is man's repentance and his retreat into the sacred life of the family:

gelbi `aya me tekhmâm, bâghi ntûb se fini
My heart is tired of worrying, I repent, its all over (Cheb Mami; *khellûni nebki*; let me cry)

ndîrha fi yedd l-lâh w rabbi kbir
I put her in the hands of God, and God is great (Cheb Khaled; *SSobri, SSbri*; have patience, have patience)

It is a solution, pleading for the reinstallation of the authority of the father in society, a sacralized father above competitions and strategies:

khâlefti l-`aehd w `aend rabbi nHâsbek
You betrayed the pact, before God I'll ask for accounts (Cheb Hamid; *ana qâsît*; I suffered)

râni msâmHek guddâm rabbi lli ma derti fiyya
I forgive you in front of God, for all you didn't do for me (Benchenet; *ana kammelt m`aâk*; I am all finished with you)

A man who upholds a sharp distinction in gender roles, who seeks to sacralize the public spheres of society and who upholds his power by stigmatizing the sisters for being 'free women':

ana bHar `aliya ya w ntiya la
For me it doesn't matter, for you it does (Cheb Saharaoui; *deblet galbi*; torment of my heart)

TâH qadrek ma bqalak shân
Your honour has fallen, you have lost your rank (Benchenet; *ana kammelt m'aâk*; I am all finished with you)

Another idealized solution is to look elsewhere – outside society – in order to establish a material base for realizing an adult life with women outside the power relations of Algerian society:

ya zina manîsh `alik w râni `ala r-rumiyyât
Oh beauty I am not like you, I go for the European women (Raïna Raï; *zina tdîr l-tey*; beauty, make the tea)

samHaliya zarga m`aak malqît fâida
Excuse me brown-haired girl, with you I didn't find anything of interest (Cheb Hasni; *beiDa mon amour*; my blonde, my love)

A third ideal solution is of course to sway between the former two, and to go on listening to raï ... sometimes joking by turning the world upside-down.

CONCLUSION

Having ended this analysis of the poetics of raï, the obvious must be stated. It presents a generalized view on Algerian male youth which is not to be found in real life. First, the analysis is built solely on youth in 'leisure time activities' and second, it is built on the assumption that our listeners would take in all the lines presented above, which of course is not so.

Raï music is commercial, producing hundreds of songs and phrases, that seek to exploit particularly touchy scenes in the daily life of youth. Of course, everybody is not in love all the time, nor does everyone find lust scenes constantly arousing. Not everyone has a particularly good relationship with his mother, nor a relationship of respect with his father. Not everyone believes in sorcery and avoid women for this reason. And not everyone would agree that women are of another order, that they are to be compared with 'free women', etc. The effect of a raï song will differ according to the individual's life circumstances at the time of the release of the song.

However, I do think an analytical approach to a mass-produced and popular music such as raï – the poetics, the form and style that surround it – does contribute to an understanding of the expressions of youth conditions in Algeria.

On one hand, the breakthrough of the 'electrified raï' (integrating musical formulas from international pop music) in the 1980s and the way in which it is perceived as being modern, and consequently labelled as 'pop raï', 'raï reggae' and 'disco raï', indicates, first, that raï is associated with an image of Western youth culture and leisure time; second, that the notion of leisure time, as expressed in the relationship between music and sexuality, is one of acute concern among Algerian youth; and third, the love themes in raï indicate the need for youth to create a sphere for their concerns, independent of the parent generation.

On the other hand, the negative stereotyping of groups associated with powers of consumption, and the tendency for a positive consideration of the 'islamist style', indicate that consumption of leisure and sexuality is not sought without a critical perception of Western youth. Furthermore, I have found no contest of the basic values structuring the moral organization of the Algerian family, neither in the social organization of listening to raï nor in the lyrics. Consumption of raï and of leisure time activities is generally not valued in opposition to the parent generation, rather it is valued outside the family sphere. In this sense the popularization of cassette technology has not been without significance for the success of raï, due to the possibility it gives in bringing raï listening out in 'family-free' spaces.

The themes of raï point to the fact that the basic concern of youth is the outcome of young men engaging in relationships with the female world and of young women entering the male world, both sides seeking to enter what is perceived as a modern sphere of leisure, or seeking to establish themselves as adults on the basis of the idea of the couple. They are tensions that never come to a resolution in terms of union.

The relationship to the mother, the unquestioned moral authority of the missing father, the hiding away of the sisters in the house, the jealousy of the social surroundings in want of scarce values (relations to women), the non-questioning of the theme of contest for women (also embedded in the raï performance), all create contradictions which remain unsolved.

When facing problems in seeking to create an independent forum for meetings with the opposite sex, the main focus in raï becomes *women* rather than the parent generation. In this sense raï expresses more a common male concern than a generational one (and this is reflected in the fact that the Islamist style of dress is not a mark of youth). Leisure time outside the family home is a matter of gender division in Algeria rather than a generational one. The number of themes related to youth problems in raï has thus rather to do with the numerical importance of young unmarried men as consumers than with a marked gap between generations.

All in all, the problem of the boundaries between gender roles is the central theme in raï. It is found in the dirty raï and the clean raï's critique of women's materialism; and furthermore, it is reflected in the negative stereotyping of male youth seen as having a life-style related to Western consumption capacities. It is a theme, closely related to the notion of the couple and the changes in post-independent Algeria concerning the family structure, the lengthening of the youth period and the arrival of women in the public spheres. Furthermore, it cannot be dissociated from the worsened economic conditions in Algeria throughout the 1980s. Access to material power is needed to create room for the concerns for love meetings of Algerian youth not against the family, but outside the family.

Thus an analysis of raï music, performed by singers from the lower stratas of Algerian society, is one that concerns national political matters in terms of love and women. Rather than isolating youth as an independent social category within Algerian society, it contributes to an understanding of the most manifest expressions of the current crisis in Algerian society: young men's movement towards the mosque on the one hand and their movement towards the West on the other.

NOTES

1 This chapter is based on life in Algeria and Paris between 1990 and 1992. Since that time Algeria has become the arena of a tragic civil war. Today the chapter must be read in the past tense. The fieldwork was financed by The Danish Research Council for the Humanities. Its main purpose was to follow raï music in the different stages from live performance through studio production to its mediatization and consumption. The main site for fieldwork was the city, the music, musicians and male youth of Oran (*Wahran*). Fieldwork conditions did not allow for a quantitative perspective on raï and male youth and claims only qualitative insight. I base my generalizations as to the listeners, appreciation and consumption of raï, on initial structured interviews with twenty-four young men about their musical tastes and with fourteen cassette dealers. Later my fieldwork centred around regular meetings with ten young men, whom I interviewed in depth on their appreciation of a selected repertoire of raï songs (see Schade-Poulsen 1992; 1993b). In addition to this I frequently had the opportunity of discussing raï music informally with numerous men belonging to the large network of friends of my main informants. The vast majority in my 'sample' are unmarried Oranians, 20 to 30 years of age and with few social, economic and educational resources at their disposal.

   I have adopted a simplified transliteration system which is fairly readable by anglophones and which has the advantage of being accessible from a standard word processor keyboard. Commonly printed words are given their usual newspaper spelling. Since I have used capital letters as equivalents of some Arabic letters, a word beginning with a capital is not necessarily a proper noun. Arabic plurals are often irregular, so rather than confusing readers with two forms I follow a word with a non-italicized *s* to indicate a plural.

2 For a review see Bentahar (1989: 12–13) and Tauzin and Virolle-Souibès (1990). Martin Stokes's (1992) book on arabesk music in Turkey is a recent valuable contribution to this field. He does not, however, focus upon the consumer or youth conditions in particular.

3 There were 11,908 million inhabitants in 1966, 23,038 million in 1986. Algeria has witnessed the birth of a new generation of 11,130 million people in a time span of twenty-one years (Sari 1990). Some 31.4 per cent of the population was urbanized in 1966, 49.67 per cent in 1987 (ONS 1988). In 1989 out of 854,000 officially unemployed, 507,000 were 15 to 24 years of age (Sari 1990). In 1992 1.2 million were unemployed (*Le Matin*, 24 August 1992).

4 For a perspective on women and raï, see Virolle-Souibès (1988b).

5 This endeavour is inspired by Bourdieu's (1979) notions of the interlinkage between cultural, social and economic resources and styles of consumption and by Hoggart's (1971) description of the pleasure in – and awareness of – the form of 'low budget' products to be found among its consumers. Finally, Frith (1983) (reflecting on Barthes 1977) and Hennion (1983) stress the fact that popular music should be analysed as an expressive art rather than as a written narrative.

6 In 1966, 18.3 years for women, 23.8 years for men. In 1987, 23.7 years for women and 27.6 for men (Sari 1990: 28).

7 Out of a potential of four million women, only 365,000 were employed in wage labour in 1987. Nevertheless this represents an increase of 164 per cent in ten years with the significant fact that the majority of the female workers are young, unmarried women living in the cities (Sari 1990: 37). In the large cities today 85 per cent of the girls are enrolled in the system of education at primary level (*Horizon*, 11 September 1991). Some 30 per cent of students in Algeria at the secondary level are women (Sari 1990: 45).

8 Raï (*rrây*) means literally an opinion or a point of view.

9 Other sources, however, mention elements which are associated with raï music of today – such as the repetitive musical form, binary rhythms, improper expressions, women entertaining men, games of competition – which indicate that raï as a genre goes back much further in history (Daumas 1869/1983; Gaudefroy-Demombynes 1901; Rouanet 1920).

10 The most well-known groups being Les Students, Les Clarks, La Main, Les Welcomes, playing the music of the Bee Gees, Led Zeppelin, the Beatles, Johnny Halliday, Adamo, Charles Aznavour, etc.

11 The latter being a more sophisticated syncretic style dating from the 1950s from which modern raï has drawn a good deal of its musical inspiration.

12 For example Sahraoui and Fadhela, Kouider Bensaïd, Houari Benchenet, Chèb Hindi, and the most well-known today, Cheb Khaled.

13 Mainly to compete with a commercial Moroccan-based channel, Médi 1, launched in 1982.

14 With a star image and a musical product which have little to do with Algerian raï. See Schade-Poulsen 1993a.

15 Except for some articles in the Algerian press. Even among adherents to the Islamist party with whom I have spoken, the musical part is not the first topic to be put under criticism.

16 A topic which has also been cultivated in the Western press, which stresses that raï should even be seen as expressing an opposition to Islamic values. See Schade-Poulsen 1992; 1993a; 1993b.

17 Cheb Khaled, *Ma derti dâr* (you didn't make a home). For an analysis of this song see Schade-Poulsen 1993b.

18 *gaSba*, a reed flute used together with the hand drum *gellâl*. *Shîkh* is here synonymous with old people.

19 By this I am not implying that conflicts are not expressed.

20 The selection of sentences have been taken from a sample of 120 songs covering the whole period of modern raï, but with a certain emphasis on the most prominent of the singers, Cheb Khaled. The songs have initially been deciphered and translated by Amina Ben Salah. A range of them

have then been discussed in detail with raï consumers in Oran. However, the responsibility for the interpretation of the sentences rests solely with me.

21 MeHna has been translated into 'passion'. However, there is the double connotation of pain as well as pleasure in the expression.

22 For a similar description of French pop music see Hennion 1983.

23 It would take us too far afield to go into the techniques of sorcery (see, for example, Plantade 1988). Sorcery represents a serious problem in Oran today – a symptom of the state of crisis in Algeria (Ouitis 1984). Men who become bewitched are seen to lose their hair, and grow thin and their skin to turn yellow; others suffer from chronic impotency. Some become motionless, sitting passively with their eyes dead. Others avoid the company of their peer group in favour of the woman who is said to have bewitched them. Others again are unable to sleep, wracked at night by physical pain.

REFERENCES

Appadurai, A. (1990) 'Disjuncture and difference in the global cultural economy', in M. Featherstone (ed.) *Global Culture*, London: Sage.

Barth, F. (1989) 'The analysis of culture in complex societies', *Ethnos*, 54, 3–4: 120–143.

Barthes, R. (1977) 'The grain of the voice', in S. Heath (ed.) *Image, Music, Text*, London: Fontana Press.

B'Chir, B. and Zghal, A. (1984) 'Les jeunes et le temps libre: reproduction ou transformation de la société', in *Jeunesse et Changement Social*, Tunis: CERES.

Belkhadem, S.M. and Miliani, H. (1981) 'Les représentations de la femme dans la chanson populaire oranaise dite raî', *G.R.F.A. – Document de Travai* no. 8, ronéotype, Université d'Oran.

Benkheira, H. (1982) *Alcool, religion, sport*, Oran: Université d'Oran.

Bentahar, M. (1989) *La jeunesse arabe à la recherche de son identité*, Rabat: Al Kalam.

Boudhiba, A. (1975) *La sexualité en Islam*, Paris: PUF.

Bourdieu, P. (1979) *La distinction*, Paris: Minuit.

Boutefnouchet, M. (1982) *La famille algérienne*, Alger: SNED.

Bouzar-Kasbadji, N. (1988) *L'emergence artistique algérienne au XXe siècle*, Alger: OPU.

Camilleri, C. (1973) *Jeunesse, famille et développement*, Paris: CNRS.

Carey, J.T. (1972) 'Changing courtship patterns in the popular song', in S. Denisoff and R. Peterson (ed.) *The Sound of Social Change*, Chicago: Rand McNally and Company.

Chebel, M. (1989) 'La bataille du raï', *Le Monde de la Musique*, 119: 104–107.

Daumas, E. (1983 (1869)) *La vie arabe et la société musulmane*, Genève and Paris: Slatkine Reprints.

Davis, S. and Davis, D. (1989) *Adolescence in a Moroccan town*, New Brunswick and London: Rutgers University Press.

Déjeux, J. (1989) *L'image de l'étrangère*, Paris: La Boîte à Documents.
Fabian, J. (1978) 'Popular culture in Africa: findings and conjectures', *Africa*, 48, 4: 315–334.
Fornäs, J., Lindberg, U. and Sernhede, O (1984) *Ungdomskultur: identitet-motstand*, Stockholm: Akademilitteratur.
Frith, S. (1983) *Sound Effects – Youth, Leisure, and the Politics of Rock*, London: Constable.
Gaudefroy-Demombynes, M. (1901) *Les cérémonies du mariage chez les indigènes de l'Algérie*, Paris: Maisonneuve.
Guignard, M. (1975) *Musique, honneur et plaisir au Sahara*, Paris: Geuthner.
Hannerz, U. (1987) 'The world in creolisation', *Africa*, 57: 546–559.
—— (1992) *Cultural Complexity*, New York: Columbia University Press.
Hebdige, D. (1979) *Subculture, the Meaning of Style*, London: Methuen.
Hennion, A. (1983) 'The production of success: an antimusicology of the pop song', in R. Middleton and D. Horn (ed.) *Popular Music* 3, Cambridge, London and New York: Cambridge University Press.
Hoggart, R. (1971) *The Uses of Literacy*, London: Chatto & Windus.
Jansen, W. (1987) *Women Without Men*, Leiden: E.J. Brill.
Lévi-Strauss, C. (1962) *La pensée sauvage*, Paris: Librairie Plon.
Lord, A. (1960) *The Singer of Tales*, Cambridge, Mass.: Harvard University Press.
Manuel, P. (1988) *Popular Musics of the Non-Western World*, New York and Oxford: Oxford University Press.
Marcus, G. and Fischer, M. (1986) *Anthropology as a Cultural Critique*, Chicago and London: University of Chicago Press.
Mazouzi, B. (1990) 'La musique algérienne – et la question raï', *La Revue Musicale*: 418–420.
Merad, A. (1967) *Le réformisme musulman en Algérie*, Paris: Mouton & Co.
Mernissi, F. (1983) *Sexe, idéologie, islam*, Paris: Tièrce.
Messaoudi, A. (1990) 'Chômage et solidarités familiales', *Peuples Méditerranéens*, 52–53: 195–219.
Mezouane, R. (1992) 'Génération raï', *Autrement*, série monde 60: 64–70.
Miliani, H. (1983) 'Culture populaire et contradictions symboliques', *G.R.F.A. – Document de Travail* no.9, Ronéotype, Université d'Oran.
—— (1986) 'Parcours symboliques de la chanson raï', *Internationale de l'Imaginaire*, 5: 17–21.
Mortensen, L.B. (1989) *'At være eller ikke være' – tyrkisk ungdom i København og Ankara*, Kultursociologiske Skrifter no.27, Copenhagen: Akademisk Forlag.
van Nieuwkerk, K. (1992) 'Female entertainers in Egypt: drinking and gender roles', in D. Gefou-Madianou (ed.) *Alcohol, Gender and Culture*, London and New York: Routledge.
Office National des Statistiques (1988) 'Armature urbaine 1987', *Les Collections Statistiques*. Alger.

Ouitis, A. (1984) *Possesion, magie, et prophétie en Algérie*, Paris: L'Arcantère.

Plantade, N. (1988) *La guerre des femmes*, Paris: La Boîte à Documents.

Rouanet, J. (1920) 'La musique arabe dans le Maghreb', *Encyclopédie de la Musique et Dictonnaire du Conservatoire*, Paris: Delagrave.

Sari, D. (1990) 'L'indispensable maîtrise de la croissance démographique en Algérie', *Maghreb-Machrek*, 129: 23–47.

Schade-Poulsen, M. (1992) 'Mit hjertes ulykke – om analysen af algiersk pop', *Tidsskriftet Antropologi*, 26: 59–76.

—— (1993a) 'Ingen relevans for raï', *Information* 14/7/1993.

—— (1993b) 'Essai d'analyse d'une chanson raï – côté hommes', in F. Colonna and Z. Daoud (eds) *Etre marginal au Maghreb*, Paris: CNRS.

Stokes, M. (1992) *The arabesk debate – music and musicians in modern Turkey*, Oxford: Clarendon Press.

Tauzin, A. and Virolle-Souibès, M. (1990) *Femmes, familles, société au Maghreb et en émigration*, Paris: Karthala.

Virolle-Souibés, M. (1988a) 'Ce que chanter rrây veut dire: prélude à d'autres couplets', *Cahiers de Littérature Orale* 23: 177–209.

—— (1988b) 'Le ray, coté femmes', *Peuples Méditerranéens* 44–45: 193–220.

—— (1989) 'Le Raï entre résistance et récupération', Revue du Monde *Musulman et de la Méditerranée* 1, 51: 47–62.

Zghal, A. (1984) 'Note pour un debat sur la jeunesse arabe', in *Jeunesse et Changement Social*, Tunis: CERES.

Chapter 6

The making of a black youth culture*

Lower-class young men of Surinamese origin in Amsterdam

Livio Sansone

Since the late 1960s, when mass immigration from Surinam got under way, there has been a sizeable African-Caribbean presence in the main Dutch cities. Throughout their experience in The Netherlands lower-class African-Caribbean young people of Surinamese origin – the 'Creoles' – have reinterpreted Creole culture from a somewhat provincial Caribbean culture into a new, highly syncretic and complex black subculture which is based on eclecticism and discontinuity.

This reinterpretation relates to developments in mass communication, consumer electronics, the leisure industry and, more generally, the globalization of Western urban culture, all of which impose a certain degree of change and even uniformization upon most cultures of ethnic minorities in Western cities. At the same time these developments offer a number of facilitating conditions for the creation of new ethnic subcultures and certain forms of ethnicity – the celebration of specificity and otherness (see Hannerz 1989; Appadurai 1990). This 'global heterogenization' has thus led to the growth of symbolic exchange between African-Americans on both sides of the Atlantic. On the one hand, this exchange homogenizes the styles and music of young blacks living in different countries – reggae and hip hop have given a further impulse to a process which already started with jazz and blues. On the other hand, this exchange forms the basis for the creation of a new black culture based on estheticization of blackness through highly visible (youth) styles and pop music. To the attractiveness of this new black culture can be added two seemingly contradictory factors. On the one hand, the feeling of being excluded from upward mobility mainly because of racial discrimination. On the other hand, the fact that many young African-Caribbeans, in particular those who have been raised in

Europe, have absorbed the hegemonic views of mobility, self-realization and consumption – that is, in cultural terms their 'integration' has succeeded.

In this chapter I focus on variation and manipulation in the culture and ethnicity of the Creoles in Amsterdam from 1981 to 1991. The emphasis is on the visible features of constructing ethnicity within the domain of public leisure among young lower-class Creoles. Public leisure is that part of leisure time which is spent in public, during which youth styles are created and in which the leisure industry is more active. Young men have been more conspicuous in this aspect of the construction of ethnicity, if only because they are more street-wise and more easily perceived as a threat by outsiders than are girls. Creole girls take a less 'visible' and defiant role in the recreation of Creole ethnicity. Their reinterpretation of Creole cultures and experiments with black ethnicity take place mostly in the classroom and at home, or, rather, in their bedrooms. Like the white working-class girls in England who create a 'bedroom culture' (McRobbie and Garber 1976), lower-class Creole girls get together with a few girlfriends in the cosy secrecy of their bedrooms to comment on (black and white) men, Dutch society, fashion, Creole traditions and being a (teenage) mother. However, Creole girls do not only explore new ways of being black in Dutch society from their homes – for example, by experimenting with new haircuts and clothes. They also support – albeit not unconditionally – the efforts and exploits of young Creole men (often 'their men' – boyfriends and brothers) to achieve status in the leisure time arena (Van Niekerk and Vermeulen 1989; Sansone 1992a: 207–209). Here I limit myself to a conspicuous minority of young black men in the age range 15–30. Attention to this group is important for two reasons. Beginning in the 1970s, popular and media representations of young blacks in Amsterdam have been largely based on street-wise 'loud' young men. In turn, these representations have also had a major influence on the self-image of the less street-wise majority of young Creoles. At school, in youth centres and when looking for work, most young Creoles are confronted time and again with the style and behaviour of that 'loud' minority which sees itself, and is seen by outsiders, as behaving as all black men should. First, I will give a brief outline of my approach to black culture and some background data.

'Black' and 'white' is one particular way of conceptualizing human diversity in multi-ethnic societies (cf. Mintz and Price 1985: 8; Phoenix 1988: 156). If being black is largely defined by white society, the formation of black ideas, values and institutions occurs in a complex interaction with this society (Kilson 1975: 251; Mercer 1990). Today the leisure industry, music industry and mass media – aided by recent developments in consumer electronics – play a key role in the making of what is commonly considered black or white. Hence the creation of subcultures and ethnic identities among lower-class young African-Americans and African-Caribbeans in North American and West European cities has to be studied in the context of developments among young people at large – both in terms of social situation (work, unemployment, etc.) and in terms of taste and style. This is particularly important in Western Europe, where blacks usually live in areas in which white people are the large majority and where, to a large extent, young blacks share schools and leisure facilities with lower-class white youth.

Attention to the wider context and a longitudinal perspective – which might indicate a degree of change – are badly needed for an anthropology of black people that counteracts the deeply seated stereotype which holds that black culture is more genuine, traditional and natural than white culture, and that black ethnicity is given, static or hardly manipulated (Maxwell 1988).[1]

In 1991 the population of Surinamese origin in Amsterdam totalled 55,000 (out of approximately 230,000 in the Netherlands): 35 per cent are in the age group 15–29.[2] In Amsterdam the Creoles account for 60–65 per cent of the Surinamese. In the last ten years a key characteristic of the Surinamese community is a large welfare dependency and very high unemployment rate – reaching over 60 per cent in Amsterdam in 1989 in the age group 25–35 (Sansone 1990). Such percentages are strikingly similar to recent figures of many US black ghettos (Taylor 1990). So, although there are no spatial black ghettos in the Netherlands, the majority of blacks of Surinamese origin live a somehow segregated non-work life. Dramatic changes in the production process have confined the bulk of the immigrants from Surinam and their offspring to the weak and 'flexible' segment of the labour market. In the Netherlands many of theses immigrants have never actually performed regular paid work and are excluded from production altogether; they have been reduced to the role of consumers – with little money to spend (cf. Willis 1986). A large number of Creoles find themselves even while young in long-term unemployment and living on welfare benefits – which are relatively generous if compared to the low wages paid to young unskilled workers.

The marginal position of most Creoles in the labour market has affected the motivation and performance of the younger generations at school – more than a third of my informants dropped out of school before completing compulsory education. This has contributed to a transfusion of energy from the arena of regular work to 'alternative' sources of income such as moonlighting (for example, taxi driver, 'heavy' in a discotheque, sales assistant in a coffee shop) [3] and street-wise hustles (mostly petty pimping and pushing drugs). Another consequence of this marginal position on the labour market is that 'leisure' has become more important. To most lower-class Creole young people leisure time is not simply the non-productive consumption of time. 'Hanging around' and 'going out for fun' in places such as youth and community centres, clubs or discotheques is, in effect, the main if not the only manner in which they can participate in and explore the city, and in which they test the majority white society. In the leisure arena they try by means of distinctive styles and subcultures to bridge the gap between expectations and actual opportunities in the labour market, and to tackle anonymity, undesirable cultural uniformity and social marginality. A series of highly visible ways in which young Creole men have gathered in the streets or in certain leisure time facilities over the last fifteen years in Amsterdam forms the topic of the next section.

FROM STREET CORNERS TO GANGS, YOUTH SUBCULTURES AND STYLES

Within these highly visible ways of young Creole male gatherings can be identified four, successive forms. Each of these forms concerns, by and large, a different group of young Creole men, but a minority of these young men experience more than one form.

The first form can be called the street corner. In the late 1970s in Amsterdam, a few groups of first generation young men attempted to recreate the life-style of the Surinamese 'wakaman' (Biervliet 1975). [4] The wakamans met on certain street corners, usually in front of a bar so that if the weather turned bad there was somewhere to keep warm. These street corners were in the centre of the city and in particular in the red light district where the several Chinese shops reminded them of the Paramaribo corner shops. Their way of killing time and getting together conjured up the 'winkel', the corner shops in Paramaribo which were the regular meeting places of crews of Creole males (cf. Brana-Shute 1979). Their 'effortless sociability' recalls the gatherings of black men on street corners in the US described by Liebow (1967: xii). From these corner bases young men 'looked around' in groups and evaluated the opportunities Dutch society had to offer. They discussed girls, the news in Amsterdam, what was going on among street friends. Surinamese newspapers were read and commented on out loud, and every now and again another young man coming straight from Surinam joined the group and informed everyone about the situation back in Surinam. Hanging around on the corner was not only for fun. While being with friends and acquaintances and enjoying life, one discussed possible sidelines or hustles – and occasionally carried them out. Here in Amsterdam, however, hustling soon acquired a new connotation: the word itself became associated with both quasi-legal and thoroughly illicit practices, especially peddling drugs. Many wakamans became addicted to drugs and kept on dealing only to support their addiction. In the last ten to fifteen years hard drugs have affected the life of the majority of lower-class Creole men in the age group 25 to 45. By approximately 1980 the main meeting places of the wakamans had became the heart of the Amsterdam street-level hard drug scene.

The second form is the 'gang'. Between 1975 and 1980 Creole boys who had already spent a few years in the Netherlands formed twelve to fifteen so-called 'youth gangs' (*jeugbenden*). Such a term was given to these gangs by the youth police and mass media. In reality only a few groups or just a section of the 'gang' had to do with (petty) crime. Rather than gangs in the North American sense of the word, these 'gangs' resembled armoured peer groups, catering to some of the more assertive Creole boys from one particular area or school. Each 'gang' consisted of between twenty and two hundred members who were divided into several smaller peer groups. There was no admission ritual except performing adequately in 'gang' fights or, for some 'gangs', petty crime.

> There were five of us, all Surinamese, without a boss and without uniform. We were not a gang, just normal. We did bad things together, like, mugging, snatching bags and annoying girls on the street. You had to do it, otherwise you did not belong. For example, we wanted to go to the movie and we had no money. Well then, somebody said 'lets snatch a bag so that we have some cash'. You needed guts. That feeling that we were living together and running risks together was nice.
>
> (Stan, 23 years old, 1983)

Each 'gang' had its own territory which defended against other groups and delimited by painting the name or the symbol of the 'gang' on the walls. For example, The Monks had a white counterpart, the Outlaws, but fought against the Black Brothers and the Bijlmer Boys, black 'gangs' from other areas. Sometimes the defence of territory was more important than ethnic solidarity.

> In Slotervaart [a neighbourhood, LS] there are a lot of Surinamese, but I get on only with those who belong to the Monks. The four bosses never really fight . . . just when they have problems with another group of Surinamese, the Black Brothers.
>
> (Guido, 18 years old, 1982)

The Creole youth 'gangs' started to develop the rudiments of a Creole youth style by borrowing symbols from the life-style of the wakaman (often the member of a 'gang' had an older brother who was a wakaman). They also borrowed symbols from karate films and 'black movies' (US-made cops and robbers films with blacks in the main roles), and from the local white working-class youth gangs. The latter, according to the police, had already existed for a long time. The rudiments of a Creole youth style were, for example, the use of distinguishable names (most names were English), the use of graffiti and the wearing of certain clothes (such as a particular hat or bomber jacket). Through the 'gang' the first steps were taken towards getting to know white youth. With white peers these 'gangs' had an ambivalent attitude. On the one hand, they were at odds with white kids, with whom they competed in youth clubs and on the streets. On the other hand, they observed white kids carefully to detect their fashionable trends and expectations. For the Creole youth 'gangs', going out meant going to shopping promenades downtown, Dutch youth clubs and discotheques visited mainly by white youth.

The third form is the youth subculture. From 1981 to 1984 a large number of young Creoles, many of whom had been members of the youth 'gangs', turned to two youth subcultures: the Rastafarians and the more numerous disco freaks. The Rastafari millenarian religion which originated in Jamaica in the 1920s reached Creole youth through the lyrics of reggae music. Reggae music records were on sale in the Amsterdam 'alternative' record shops by the early 1970s. Another source of inspiration were programmes broadcast by British radio stations. The pictures of rastamen on record sleeves and, a few years later, the first reggae films provided suggestions for the rasta style. This style, a new 'African look' combining military surplus clothes and training suits, was a conscious protest against the glamorous, glossy and Westernized look of other Creoles and in particular of many wakamans. These, argued the rastas, were entrapped in a white way of life and in a white outlook.

> I'm not at all happy with the Surinamese community. I mean, it's OK that they like winti and bigi poku, but I cannot stand the way they dress . . . those glamorous suits . . . so European! You can see women with wigs, even blond wigs! Know what I mean, they should be happy with their own hair. Sometimes they put on too much make-up.
>
> (Glenn, 16 years old, 1982)

The Creole rastamen tailored their own version of Rastafarianism as a specific black counterculture,[5] by drawing also on symbols and practices of the white counterculture. For example, eating habits were influenced by the many vegetarian food shops. Clothes were also bought in 'Indian-hippy' shops and soft drugs were easily available in Amsterdam even before the rastas.

The disco freaks, in their turn, created a 'distinguished' black style by drawing on the international symbols of the disco scene. They maintained that in the discotheques nobody is discriminated against on the basis of class and race: in the disco what matters and can discriminate is fashion.

In spite of the fact that rastas and discos saw themselves as the opposite of each other they were similar in both sociological and cultural terms. Both styles used codes and symbols – such as clothes – which meant something only within Dutch youth culture, refused what thus far had been the conventional way of being young in the Creole community and drew selectively from traditional Creole culture. The rastas drew on the Christian and Afro-Surinamese religiosity of their parents.

> Yes, I was stealing until they caught me and put me in the jug. Then I started to believe more in God. I told to myself: I shall not steal. . . . My grandmother used to mention the Bible a lot and the Word of the Lord. She let me read the Bible and explained the whole thing. You can say that the Bible has always been important for me . . .. My mother belongs to the Evangelic Brotherhood [a Surinamese Protestant church, LS], although she does not go to church. She believes in God too, but not in my way.
>
> (Winston, 15 years old, 1982)

The rastas maintained that in the Netherlands only the rastas continued the unspoiled ('deep') tropical life-style which, according to them, characterized black people in Surinam. Also the disco freaks thought of themselves as 'pure Creole Surinamese' and saw in their disco style a positive appreciation of blackness. They traced their aggressive consumerism back to the life orientation of the parent culture. They believed that the expectation of a more affluent life was the main reason for migrating to the Netherlands. The disco freaks were keen on 'action', the modern aspects of Dutch society.

> We should learn from the Dutch, so that when we go back to Surinam we can make of it a modern and rich country, with many new houses. The old shantytowns should be cleared with a bulldozer. In their place we should build the kind of new housing they have over here.
>
> (Mike, 16 years old, 1982)

They stress the need to adjust to Dutch society much more than do the rastas.

> I don't want to be a member of a Surinamese organization. It's a rip off . . . Surinamese organizations keep on insulting the people from here. You know, you can keep on doing it, but they are in their own country. You are not in your own country. You better settle so that they stop talking negatively about you. . . . The Surinamese organizations scream that once we were used as slaves, even though the people who did that died a long time ago. . . . I don't need to say: 'You forced my ancestors to work'. I don't know how it was and, really, don't even need to know.
>
> (Steve, 18 years old, 1983)

The discos maintained, moreover, that a certain flamboyance with which white society regards the black man was in effect a part of Surinamese Creole culture, and that the rastas' pursuit of a 'roots look' was in fact a refusal of traditional Surinamese black fashion and beauty. The disco freaks' appreciation of blackness stressed other aspects than those stressed by the rastas. The former use their blackness to support their interaction with what, in their own opinion, were interesting sections of white youth (in particular, higher-educated young people who were also fashion conscious). The latter sought appreciation of their blackness mainly among Surinamese contemporaries and only indirectly among white youth – in which case they related to countercultural groups, such as neo-hippies, punks and squatters. In their innovation of blackness rastas stressed 'naturality' and disco freaks 'manipulation'. This difference was made explicit in their hair fashion. The rasta dreadlocks were the epitome of the 'untrimmed' hair, had to communicate to the outsiders the 'African difference' and the sorrow of the rastas. The disco hair was greased, trimmed, remodelled time and again, and by adding silver powder or little coloured light bulbs, had to communicate modernity and joy. These two logics of aesthetic stylization are only formally antithetical because they both involve modelling oneself according to metropolitan images of blackness. Also the 'naturality' of the rastas owes more to Western culture than to Africa because it is inspired by Western ecologists' themes and by the Western idea that black people are closer to nature than white people.

In a way we are old-fashioned as we want to go back to how it was . . . Babylon is Europe and what is artificial. Better to be stupid but live in contact with Nature than be clever and live in Hell. In the Western world they are clever but they have polluted everything. We [the black people] have other talents.

(Ital, 21 years old, 1983)

In fact the polarity 'naturality' versus 'manipulation', and the debate between purists and manipulators, have to be seen as basic elements of the discourse of black youth styles and, perhaps, of black culture in general [6].

The fourth form is the black youth style. In the mid-1980s many disco freaks, rastas and a whole group of Surinamese young people who had spent almost all their life in the Netherlands, became attracted to a new improvisation on the theme of youth styles coming from the US: break-dance and electric boogie. These styles became popular among Surinamese youth – and, to a lesser extent, the youth of other ethnic minorities and white youth – almost immediately after its creation in the US.

I was really impressed when I saw it on TV. In America they are much further. Then I thought, I want to learn it too. . . . I do it for the show, because it's so cute. Everybody says so. At parties and at school they always ask me to dance a bit. They all get crazy. That's how I have become popular at school.

(Steven, 17 years old, 1983)

Already in the spring of 1983, groups of teenagers danced

'electrically' in the streets of the town centre with the aid of a 'ghetto blaster', to earn some money or simply because they found it far out: 'I tell you, that rhythm goes through your blood and gets everybody, even some white geezers.' The police did not know what to do and started to prevent the street sessions. But it could not be stopped. By the autumn of 1983 groups of break-dancers performed in some of the trendiest discotheques. By the end of the year a group was invited to appear on the most popular television shows.

Most break-dancers, together with a new generation of young Creoles, created the Amsterdam hip hop around 1987; this still exists today and is hardly any different from the original US version. Young Creoles learn this style from watching well-known US and, to a lesser extent, British hip hoppers playing in – mostly white – venues and by closely studying their video clips. The hip hop style comprises specific music, singing ('rapping'), dancing (a development from break-dancing and electric boogie) and special clothing. One has to look 'rough': requirements are expensive sportswear and trainers (Benetton, Adidas, Puma) which must be worn 'casual', modern haircuts inspired by music magazines and video clips, and particular gestures. These are the 'gorilla walk', a way of greeting each other in public, and a way of stressing certain statements by moving the limbs. The hip hoppers use a lot of Surinamese and English words, but they also invent many new Dutch terms, usually by adding a Dutch ending to an English word. Rapping becomes 'rappen' and rough becomes 'rof'.

Some years ago you had rastas and disco freaks, now you have hip hop. Here in Bijlmer [a neighbourhood, LS] we are all hip hoppers. You don't know anybody who is not a hip hopper, at least on a part-time base. Today you have two styles: kaseko-men [something like wakamans, LS] and us. The kaseko-men wear crocodile-leather shoes and golden arm bands. We come just rough, simply with my plimsolls [expensive Adidas, LS]. No problem at all . . .. Many young Creoles are into hip hop because it begun in America among black people who did it to earn money. It's just street music, life on the street. A kind of blues of today's youth. And blues is black . . . America is a source if inspiration for us. It does not have to be a model. In Amsterdam we've got to develop our own style. We have guts. We are not ashamed. Our ideal is Public Enemy. Actually, I ought to live in the Bronx, but I find it nice over here in Bijmer. America, moreover, has got such name because of films, but I know for sure that if you live there there is not so much difference with here. Those who speak a lot about America, know it only from the comic strips of the Spiderman!

(Group interview with the hip hop group Freeze Five, 1989)

Mass media, modern technology and the entertainment and music industries have a growing influence on the subcultures and styles of young Creoles. Wakamans and the members of the youth gangs drew inspiration from 'black movies' which they saw in groups in so-called 'ethnic cinemas'. The rastas had heard of Rastafarianism for the first time from radio; after a while they also saw it on television. Electric boogie dancers and, even more so, hip hoppers also learned to dance from the television. In recent years video clips, broadcast around the clock on certain television channels, have become an important source of information and inspiration for their style. In the meantime the music of young Creoles – a key ethnic and style marker – has gained acceptance into mainstream white taste. Disco music, reggae and, later, hip hop concerts attract a much larger white audience than the concerts where *bigi poku* (the modern Creole dance music, also known as *kaseko*, which is similar to some versions of the *merengue*) is played. Bigi poku concerts are usually held in venues which are well-known meeting places for the Surinamese. The other kinds of music mentioned previously are usually played in white venues which for the occasion receive also a large black audience.

Between 1981 and 1991 there has been a transformation in the subcultures and styles of young Creole men from more cohesive social forms, oriented towards Surinam and the subculture of the urban lower-class males in its capital Paramaribo, to expressions which are less gang-like and less strictly organized because they require neither total commitment in terms of time nor sophisticated rituals. One can join and quit them easily: they are youth subcultures and styles with an ethnic tinge. A similar development was observed in Britain where over the last two decades young West Indians created different subcultures: the rude boy, the teenybopper, the rasta and, last, the hip hopper (Hebdige 1979; 1987; Pryce 1979: 107–8).

These less hierarchical subcultures and styles have attracted a larger and increasingly younger following, also consisting of girls, white youth and young people from other ethnic minorities who can participate part-time. In 1972–78 there were an estimated 300 wakamans in Amsterdam. In the 1980s there were at least twice as many disco-freaks and rastas and in 1991 in Amsterdam an estimated 2,500 young Creoles had some connection with hip hopping. If for the first generation wakaman the average age in the 1970s was 20–25, for the hip hoppers in 1991 it was 12–16. The larger number of young Creole men involved in these visible subcultures and styles cannot be accounted for only by the increase of the size of the total Surinamese community in Amsterdam – from 40,000 in 1980 to 55,000 in 1991.

Young Creoles in Amsterdam created specific styles and sub-cultures only after 1980–81 (Sansone 1987). In those years the Creole children who had come to the Netherlands on the eve of mass immigration reached adolescence and had already been in the Dutch education system for a number of years. These young Creoles considered themselves different not only from their white peers but also from the young Creole adults who had migrated to the Nether-lands at a more advanced age. In turn young Creole adults considered Creole teenagers to be too Westernized. In the following section I will refer to these two groups respectively as the younger and the older group.

ETHNICITY AND YOUTH CULTURE

Youth culture and the arena of leisure time have been favourable vehicles for the redefinition of the ethnicity of lower-class Creole young men. Throughout the subcultures and styles sketched here ethnicity changes meaning and becomes more complex and extro-vert. That is, for the wakamans, 'action' – street life, visiting leisure facilities and having fun in groups – was primarily meant to boost one's status within the Surinamese community and only secondarily in Dutch society at large. For the youth gangs and the more recent youth styles the 'action' was, and still is, largely meant to impress outsiders and in particular the mostly – white trend-setting groups in youth culture.

For the older group, ethnicity tends to be a matter of fact. It is something based on emotional bonds with people in one's social network which already existed in Surinam. It is 'given' to you and can be used to protect yourself from the outside world but not to confront it or, even less so, to negotiate a symbolic space. For the wakamans, who overwhelmingly belong to the older age group, leisure time tends to be the moment in which to replay in Amsterdam the lower-class, street-wise youth life-style left behind in Paramaribo

– with only slight adjustments to the new social settings and to different climatic conditions. Apart from a few members of this group who are part of the jazz or salsa music scene, they do not visit places frequented by white people but mainly a limited number of coffee shops and bars, Surinamese community centres and self-help organizations, Creole parties and concerts.

The ethnicity of the younger group is a much more complicated phenomenon, and is combined to an increasing extent with other, equally 'lived' identities based on age, gender, peer group, neighbourhood and class. It is a matter of creation and exploration and it is less Surinam-based. Blackness is more relevant than being a Surinamese Creole – physical appearance is more important than, for example, mastering Sranan Tongo. For creating its ethnicity the young age group reinterprets, on the one hand, the parent culture and, on the other hand, the subcultures and styles of certain groups of white youth and, as we see later, black youth in other countries. Young Creoles, moreover, have a less superficial knowledge of certain aspects of Dutch society (e.g. the system of education, access to the labour market, career advisory services, youth work, multiracial leisure activities, etc.). During leisure time, and within the limits of their lower-class position, the members of the younger age group can play with two cultures and decide whether or not, and when, they want to be or to feel Surinam-oriented or simply Dutch. For example, they can choose between Surinamese-based and 'white' leisure facilities, and between languages. They can switch easily from high Dutch to the Amsterdam dialect and from Sranan Tongo to a sort of 'community Surinamese-Dutch'. This is a variety of Dutch used in leisure facilities by young people which borrows many words and even some expressions from Sranan Tongo and from English.[7] Their daily life depends very much on the management of ethnicity. Their ethnicity implies a great deal of self-reliance, skills in the presentation of self in different circumstances and a degree of integration in, and familiarity with, Dutch majority society. In fact, their use of traditions requires both detachment from the parent culture and a particular form of ethnic allegiance (see Roosens 1989: 150).

Fifteen years or more after the period of mass immigration from Surinam, these young black people cannot keep alive an ethnicity based chiefly on commitment to the established organizations of their own ethnic community, tight ethnic cohesion or religious culture. Their participation in the official organizations of the Surinamese community is low. They deem the language of the established

Surinamese media too old-fashioned and consider Surinamese welfare organizations as useful only in the first period of settlement in
the new country. This, however, does not automatically imply a weak
allegiance to their own ethnic community and traditions. Young
Creoles do not simply discard or accept them. There is a complicated
process of evaluation and reinterpretation of one's culture and
traditions. Creole traditions are, as it were, retailored so as to assist
the symbolic negotiation with white peers. The aspects of the
traditions that young Creoles turn down – or confine to home – are
usually those which they believe cannot be repackaged in a language
understandable within youth culture in general. Other aspects of
traditions, in particular with regard to recreational roles and the
management of physical appearance, are enhanced and rediscovered.
In fact, established ethnic markers and forms of participation in the
ethnic community are replaced by markers and forms which are more
in accordance with the need to participate in the social life of the
modern city and to cope with the disadvantaged position of most
Creoles in Dutch society.

The black ethnicity of the younger group shows similarities with
what Gans (1979), in defining the resurgence of interest in ethnic
origins among third and fourth generation white ethnics in the US,
has called 'symbolic ethnicity', and Alba (1981) the 'twilight of
ethnicity'. It is mostly a leisure time activity which does not require
close-knit communities or networks and it can be associated with
other social identities. It is the product of people who have some
choice about when and how to play with ethnic roles, and who are
more concerned with creating and maintaining ethnic borders than
with actually practising a different culture. This applies less to the
wakamans of the older group; for the younger group ethnicity must
be understood 'in response to current needs rather than only as
departure from past traditions' (Gans 1979:3), and mostly refers to
a perception of diversity within unity. There are, however, major
differences compared with the situation described by Gans. The
long-standing relative dependence of Creole culture on Dutch
metropolitan culture, the close relationship of young Creoles with
general youth culture and with the symbols of international black
culture have speeded up the process by which Creole-black ethnicity
has become symbolic – not after three or four generations but after
only fifteen or twenty years in the Netherlands. Another difference
is that the ethnicity of young Creoles, and black ethnicity in general,
is created by people who cannot deliberately choose to assimilate

and disappear into white society, as can be the case of fourth generation white ethnics – for example, the 'hyphenated Americans': Irish-Americans, Polish-Americans or Italo-Americans. For young Creoles, being black – and therefore visible – is not subject to choice, even though they can choose to stress or play down certain aspects of blackness, for example, by using a particular haircut and 'streetwise' posture (Mercer 1990).

Has the creation of new styles and ethnicity led to a better negotiating position for Credes in Dutch society? Many young Creoles would have liked to turn their ability with styles and fashions and their knowledge of white taste into a spectacular career; for example, in show business or professional sport. Only a few succeeded. The active role played by young Creoles in the leisure time arena, and their ability in manipulating traditions and creating new styles, has led, however, to a situation in which lower-class young Creoles are more integrated and enjoy a higher status in (sections of) the leisure arena than at school or in the workplace. Many of their white peers do accept the opinion of young blacks that they, not the whites, are the 'rulers' of the dance floor and that young black males have developed a fashionable street style. This ephemeral success, in turn, adds to the importance of body care and fashion for black culture. One of the dogmas of this culture is that black people are more elegant and attractive than white people. It also strengthens the belief of many young black people that the only way up is through typical 'ghetto outlets' such as fashion, professional sport and crime. In such a way, participating in this black culture can lead to self-exclusion from the (limited) job prospects available to poorly educated young blacks (Sansone 1992a).

Such creativity in youth styles and the development of a more 'extrovert' black-Creole ethnicity are related to several factors. On the one hand, they are related to the life cycle, to being young. By the time most young Creoles leave or drop out of school and reach the age of 18 to 20 they become less interested in the white-dominated youth culture, spend more of their leisure in Creole clubs and, in general, mix less with non-Creoles. Their leisure pattern will then resemble that of their older brothers. Such a 'retreat' in the immediate social network after completion of education seems to be common also among white working-class boys (Willmott 1966; Hazenkamp 1980) On the other hand, there is a progressive trend – the syncretism of today's black youth will bear on their adult life and on the next generation.

First, although in 1991 the wakaman's life-style still has significance for the adult (ex) rastas and (ex) discos, today there are fewer
'traditional' wakamans than ten years ago. The wakamans I referred
to before are nowadays 35 to 45 years old. After so many years of
hanging around and street hustling – with its dangers but also
excitements and rewards – many of them try to get a job. But on the
competitive Dutch labour market the only jobs available to them –
for example, as a cleaner – pay little and have a low status. Most first
generation wakamans are condemned to idleness. Little by little even
the street corner is precluded to them – because they are ridiculed
by the new generation of more 'Dutchified' street corner men, many
of whom were once rastas, disco freaks or hip hoppers. Many
first generation wakamans have visibly failed in achieving a better
position 'fast' through street hustling (in particular peddling hard
drugs). Many have become conspicuous drug addicts. For these
reasons, in the last ten years the term wakaman has acquired a more
negative connotation, being used nowadays mainly in jokes or with
the same meaning as 'hosselaar' (hustler). These are also the main
reasons why the new generations of young Creoles have looked for
something different from the Surinam-oriented style and street life
of the first generation street corner men which they consider
inadequate in Dutch society. Today, the young Creoles who have
grown up in the Netherlands and turn to hustling do it in new ways
which owe more to the techniques of the Dutch underworld than to
Caribbean street-wise entrepreneurship. They try to set up a coffee
shop, an escort service, a pornographic phone line or a cocaine ring.
Second, leisure patterns and social life during leisure time have
changed for all young people over the last few years. Many of the
established leisure organizations of white working-class youth are
also in a crisis (e.g. in Amsterdam football supporters' clubs have
lost much of their membership). Third, during and just after their
adolescence young Creoles learn a lot about the fashion, taste and
style of white people as well as about the management of ethnicity.
Their familiarity with Dutch ways, however, is combined with
marginalization in Dutch society. This makes them more alert to
racial discrimination and social disadvantage, and will certainly
influence their adult life. Fourth, the exploration of Dutch ways in
the arena of leisure, which over the last ten years has involved masses
of young Creoles, has produced a collective historic memory, a
'youth style tradition'. Most of the styles and subcultures created by
young Creoles are short-lived and fade away after a few years, but

the newer styles and subcultures that follow inherit some of the elements and symbols from the former ones. The break-dancers drew upon the experience of the disco freaks and the break-dancers, in their turn, heavily influenced the hip hoppers. The creation of a new style is in fact an act of quotation of former styles as much as an invention of something original. Nothing is created completely anew and nothing vanishes completely. Beside these factors, largely associated with the youth condition, such creativity in youth styles and the development of a new black ethnicity can be considered as a new stage in the creolization of the Surinamese-Creole culture – a process which has been accelerated by the new living conditions in the Netherlands.

FROM CREOLE TO BLACK

The term 'Creole' is often used by scholars to refer to new syncretisms arising in the life-styles of New World people, including New World blacks (Whitten and Szwed 1970: 38). In Surinam, the term 'Creole' refers both to the culture and the phenotypes of a large part of the urban population: the blacks or those who show in their phenotype some degree of African origin.[8] In the Netherlands, the Surinamese-Creole culture is instead the expression of a relatively small immigrant minority, but it forms the core[9] of a new ethnic culture, a black culture with international links. Black culture is 'the great subculture at our door' (Whitten and Szwed 1970: 31), the specific subculture of the people of African-American origin in a society which is in its majority white. As well as Creole cultures, black culture is by definition syncretic: 'The glory of Afro-American culture . . . has depended upon creativity and innovation, far more than upon the indelibility of particular culture contents' (Mintz 1970: 9–14). Although black culture has mainly got a connotation of a lower-class creative adaptation to social disadvantage, it differs on a number of points from other expressions of the lower classes, such as white working-class subculture. Belonging to black culture is largely based on the management of physical appearance in the context of a prevailing somatic norm which places the Negroid at the bottom, or near it. Another specific binding force of black culture is the feeling of a common past as slaves and the underprivileged. Black culture is also different from most other ethnic subcultures in Western cities because of its higher degree of interdependence with Western urban culture. For their relative intimacy with Western urban culture black people have to pay a price: their culture does not usually enjoy the official recognition of other 'established foreign cultures' such as the Arabic-Moroccan, the Turkish or the Italian (e.g. in the Netherlands there is no supplementary education in Sranan Tongo). As a consequence they have more problems than most other ethnic minorities with expressing themselves as a community and capitalizing on ethnicity. It is mainly white negrophobia, and the perception of racial discrimination, which on occasion can be the basis for black pressure groups.

As well as black culture in other countries, the version of black culture created by young Creoles in the Netherlands is highly syncretic, and able to monitor white taste and anticipate white expectations as to the exotic and the sensual. It is thus swiftly incorporating aspects of other urban subcultures – in particular, other ethnic subcultures, youth subcultures and subcultures relating to professional groups or long-term unemployment – and is adjusting rapidly to the demise of the prospect of remigration to Surinam by refocusing on what life in the Netherlands means for black people. The other important characteristics of the black culture created by young Creoles are, first, the international orientation on Afro-America which is combined with a pan-black discourse that plays down differences among blacks from different countries, and, second, the relativization of work together with a specific view of leisure time as the focus of conspicuous consumption and as the moment in which black physical appearance can be turned into 'capital'. These were also the characteristics of the black culture created by black Britons one or two decades ago (Gilroy 1987 and 1993; Hebdige 1979). In the following section we see how this international orientation relates to a process of globalization of black culture.

GLOBAL BLACK CULTURE

Black cultures exist in the Caribbean, most Spanish-speaking countries in central and South America, and the two countries with the largest black communities in the New World (Brazil and the US). In more recent times black cultures have developed out of Creole cultures within the Caribbean diaspora to the colonial 'mother countries': France, Great Britain and the Netherlands. Each black community in the New World and in the Caribbean Diaspora in Europe produces a specific black culture. Relatively specific to the black culture which has been recently developed by lower-class young Creoles in the Netherlands are, on the one hand, the very low labour participation of the Creoles and their dependence on welfare cheques and, on the other hand, the vitality, in particular among first generation Creoles, of certain African-Surinamese traditions (such as the *winti* religion). This latter aspect is largely due to the fact that Creole mass immigration to the Netherlands only took off twenty-two years ago. Yet, these specific black cultures are increasingly becoming versions of one single modern global black culture. The emergence of such black culture is the result of both white stereotypes and black choice.

Black people from different countries develop a similar culture partly because white people from different countries develop a similar culture and a similar way of looking at black people. White images about black people are distributed world-wide and are globalized by, among others, the music industry, the fashion industry and television. These images, such as the idea that blacks are the most sensual and natural people in our society, which had been developed in a specific area with a particular history of colonialism and slavery, reach and permeate different countries.[10] This is in particular the case of images and terminology created within the polarized nature of the black-white relations in the US. The internationalization of black culture is also the product of the growing convergence of certain determining structural factors in the environment of black people on both shores of the Atlantic (see, among others, Patterson 1973: 237). In American and Western European societies black people tend to be over-represented among the poor and, more specifically, among those who are portrayed by the media or by some welfare agencies as the 'undeserving' poor.

The creation of a global black culture is also the product of the action of black people themselves. Small black elites from different countries have had contacts for a long period of time. Possibly the first international 'agora' for English-speaking black artists and intellectuals existed in New York in the 1920s during the Harlem Renaissance. In the 1930s, there originated in Paris another black 'agora' around the notion of negritude (Lowenthal 1972: 282). Over the last few decades the actual exchange between black people from different countries has involved, besides the intellectuals, much larger numbers of black people. This has to do, in the first place, with mass migration and the creation of large black communities, particularly in Great Britain, France and the Netherlands. The exchange among black people from different countries has also been influenced by the development of more rapid means of communication at lower cost and mass media. Television, cinema, home video, the music industry, advertising and so forth, bring information and symbols from far away (black) cultures also amidst the less well educated. Other vehicles for the globalization of black culture have been academic networks (particularly those of Black Studies), exchange programmes of black policy workers and youth workers (these are quite intensive between Great Britain and the Netherlands), the networks of black militants, television programmes such as the epic series *Roots*, the situation comedy *The Cosby Show* and educational series on black people in the world broadcast by the BBC. To these vehicles must be added the growing number of black consciousness tour operators, who bring considerable numbers of US blacks to visit some historical places of the black diaspora in Western Africa and, more recently, Bahia in Brazil. One of the results of this exchange of black symbols and white images of blacks world-wide is that the term 'black' has been taken over by some black intellectuals in Germany and France. However, the globalization of black culture has occurred particularly among English-speaking blacks in the US, the Caribbean and the black community in Great Britain (Gilroy 1987: 153–222 and 1993: 72–110). Soul music, black militancy, rastafarianism and recently hip hop are examples of this process – the cultural exchange being made easier by the same language [11] and by the cultural and (neo)colonial ties between these countries. US blacks, thanks also to the central position of the US in the world system of culture, are historically at the giving end of the symbolic and economic exchange leading to the internationalization of English-speaking black culture (Patterson 1973: 221). That is, most products and symbols at the basis of this culture come from the US: from the paraphernalia of black nationalism to black beauty products and the models used in black hair salons. Many of its ideals have also originated in the US and have later spread through the black communities of other countries. A classic example is the notion 'black is beautiful'. Two more recent examples in this sense are 'positive action' – also 'positive discrimination' – and '(black) empowerment'. More recently, the West Indian community in Great Britain, particularly Jamaican reggae and the rasta movement, have patterned English-speaking black culture.

In Surinam some black people started relating to English-speaking black culture; for example, in terms of music taste, soon after the Second World War, when US troops were stationed in Surinam. The influence of the English-speaking black culture has increased ever since. Emigration to the Netherlands has multiplied the opportunities of 'direct' contacts with different black subcultures from all over the world and the US in particular. The Netherlands is better connected than Surinam with the international media, leisure and music industry. In the Netherlands the mythical achievement of many 'super blacks' from the United States becomes a key source of inspiration for the life-style of many Creoles who want to be 'modern', but wish in the meantime to differentiate themselves from white Dutch people. The conspicuous use of symbols which are commonly associated with North American culture can be a way to increase the prestige of ethnic subculture (Schlesinger 1987; Appadurai 1990). One of the results of this is that, in particular for the Creoles who have grown up in the Netherlands, English-speaking Afro-America is becoming one of the cultural points of reference.

Besides these cultural contacts with English-speaking Afro-America, a large group of first generation Creoles have maintained close social and cultural ties with Surinam. A part of this group has actually developed a transnational life-style by 'commuting' between Surinam and the Netherlands (Sansone 1992b). In effect, the orientation to Afro-America and Surinam tend to complement rather than to combat each other. This adds to the complexity of Creole-black culture in Holland – where locals and cosmopolitans coexist, together with different degrees of Surinam-ness, ethnic allegiances and cultural influences.

CENTRALITY OF LEISURE

For the centrality of leisure in their present life, young Creoles themselves provide two kinds of justification. On the one hand, it is said to be the logical follow-up of the tropical street-wise hedonistic life-style which, according to these young people, distinguishes the life of all young people in Paramaribo. It also has to do with their view that black people have it in their blood to have fun and enjoy life. On the other hand, they say that the leisure time arena offers black people more opportunities for the attainment of status, and even for spectacular careers, than education and regular work. In addition, many young blacks are convinced that the places where they can be noticed and can 'score' with their blackness – and thus capitalize on ethnic origin – are 'showbiz', professional sport or fashion. Even less respectable careers such as the occasional (black) gigolo or drug peddler, which also take place in and around the leisure arena, are often seen as potential economic niches for Creole men. In fact, from our point of view, the emphasis on leisure and pleasure has to do only in part with the reinterpretation of Surinamese traditions. Certainly, an important factor for this emphasis is the tradition of street-wise socialization of young men (which in Paramaribo culminated in the subculture of the corner shop described by Brana-Shute 1979). To an extent, this tradition lives on in the lifestyle of the wakaman. Most explanations, however, relate to Dutch society and to Western urban culture. There is the marginal position of most Creoles on the Dutch labour market and a form of cultural division of labour in many Western societies which assigns to young blacks the 'task' of entertainers and 'sexualizers' of white urban society. There is also a series of developments in Dutch society and in Western urban culture in general (Reitz 1980) which facilitates the creation of new forms of (black) ethnicity centred on leisure. These conditions make it easier to be a rastaman or a hip hopper today than it was ten or twenty years ago.

First, specifically in Amsterdam, the presence of many ethnic groups and cultures, and the central place of this city in the history of post-war youth subcultures and counterculture in Europe has turned Amsterdam into a large 'symbol bank'. From this 'bank' symbols can be borrowed for the construction of new, and more complicated, youth styles and ethnicities. For example, the Creole Rastamen drew symbols and slogans also from hippies, the green movement and the squatter movement.

Second, the way in which the state and local authorities in the Netherlands provide financial support to initiatives catering for specific ethnic groups and sections therein (like Surinamese young people and women) forces ethnic communities to keep alive a number of conspicuous differentiating boundaries based on ethnic origin, age and gender. Ethnic communities receive funding very much on the grounds of visible difference, and sometimes the extent to which their social problems are visible to outsiders they get media coverage.

Third, more generally, the growth of the leisure industry in the modern city creates new places for specific socio-cultural groups and age groups. For example, an increasing number of music venues, discotheques, coffee shops and youth clubs specialize, as it were, in one specific youth style and subgroup. Together with the leisure industry, mass media and new leisure technologies (e.g. ghetto blasters and home video)[12] can facilitate the redefinition of social and ethnic identities in the modern and multi-ethnic city. Commercialization can make certain ethnic symbols accessible to a wide audience and can give status to a style. Today, mass media and leisure industry adjust, more than ever before, to some of the expectations of young blacks – they scout and invent new black talents, incorporate certain symbols of blackness and black culture in their message and eventually make trendy and fashionable a certain way of being young, gifted and black. The symbols of this fashionable blackness, in particular the music and paraphernalia of a style (rasta, hip hop, etc.), are distributed internationally through the mass media and advertising. The advertising campaigns of Adidas or Benetton portray black kids as hip hoppers (of course wearing the right track shoes and T-shirts).

In this process of diffusion through the media and new technologies certain aspects of black culture tend to lose their local specificity and become genuinely international. The cheap computerized drum machines, produced by multinationals in the Far East, and which are used by hip hoppers on both sides of the Atlantic, contain the same pre-programmed 'African beats'. Clothes in 'African style' are now on sale, and specialized magazines and television programmes give tips on the 'roots style'. Nowadays there is increasingly less difference between the look and the music of the highly visible styles created by young black people in New York or Philadelphia and those created by young black people in London or Amsterdam (see Hall 1989).

It still needs to be studied why this process of unequal exchange between leisure industry and black culture does not occur to the same extent with other ethnic subcultures. The answer may dwell in the interdependence of black culture and Western urban culture, the fact that many whites feel attracted to certain aspects of the esthetics of blacks and their culture (body motion, complexion, dance, music and even speech) and the central place those black elements take in Western leisure. Other reasons are the more thorough separation of blacks from production and the common understanding among (too) many whites but also blacks that the latter are the ideal 'leisure people'.

CONCLUSION

As several authors have pointed out (Reitz 1980:16; Cohen 1985;

Hannerz 1980:247–261), in the modern cities the 'quest for community', the survival of ethnic groups and the creation of ethnicities are both the result of common need or interest and of the new 'facilitating conditions' which are offered by Western urban society. In particular, mass media, leisure industry and new leisure technology allow the act of quoting, imitating and inventing traditions (Hobsbawm 1983) – those of one's own groups and of other groups – to develop with few limitations. There is, as such, no conflict between social and technical innovation, a high degree of participation in certain aspects of Western society, and the survival of ethnic groups and the development of new ethnicities. In many ways, global black culture and ethnicity have developed within modernity and 'postmodernity' (cf. Gilroy 1993: ix) – even though their discourses are often in opposition to modernity and to the eclecticism of 'postmodernity'. Certain ethnicities can actually foster the development of a world system of culture, other ethnicities can grow with it. Ethnic revival, the rediscovery of the specific, and the development of a world system of culture, the generalization of the specific, need not be antithetical.

The main conclusion of this chapter is that in general these new facilitating conditions do not simply preserve ethnic groups and boundaries but help to replace one ethnicity with another. The relationship between mass media, the leisure industry and new technologies and the new ethnicity of lower-class young Creoles in Amsterdam is that between the world system of culture and local cultures, which 'rather than creating massive cultural homogeneity on a global scale, is replacing one diversity with another' (Hannerz 1987: 555). Among these young Creoles new 'facilitating conditions' are contributing to the transformation of Creole culture into a black subculture centred on the estheticization of blackness, which combines Creole traditions with a close relationship to both white youth culture and global black culture.

Within this new and complicated relationship between black culture, advertising and the leisure industry, the creation of ethnicity is also an exercise in monitoring media and advertising. The creation and maintenance of a new black ethnicity, in the context of these 'facilitating' conditions, requires many new cultural skills – together with the preservation of contacts within the ethnic group. One has to be aware of fashion, white taste, television programmes, the plight of black people in other countries, and so forth. In a way, the management of this new black ethnicity shows a considerable degree of participation in white society and integration in Western urban culture. This points to the paradox of black culture today. Mainstream urban culture is incorporating many black symbols. Even more black symbols are to be found in white-dominated youth culture. Participating in youth culture requires from white young people a considerable knowledge of 'black ways' of walking, talking, dancing, singing and in general creating style (cf. Hewitt 1986; Hebdige 1987). In the meantime black people are marginal to the centres of production and power.

The black culture and ethnicity created by lower-class young black people of Surinamese origin in Amsterdam are highly complex and eclectic – cacofonic rather than symphonic. They are combined with other equally lived social identities, such as those relating to age, class and gender. Moreover, they are created, and make sense, within a modern multi-ethnic and multi-cultural city, from which ethnicities, subcultures and styles can draw upon for inspiration as if the city were a symbol bank – their black culture can use a great variety of symbols. Many new symbols are made available by the increasingly transnational character of black culture, and its close relationship to mass media and the leisure and music industries. Further complexity results from the fact that these young black people are at the same time experiencing integration in Western urban culture and marginalization. Last but not least, these young Creoles are not the noble savage of modern urban society, nor black avengers. They send contradictory messages to Western urban culture and society – ranging from self-exclusion and protest against disadvantage and stigma to negotiation of a cultural space and even the outright wish for participation.

Acknowledging such a complexity of black culture is necessary if we are to dismantle modern racist ideologies and the binary system of representation and 'impossible boundaries' which they create.

NOTES

* This chapter results from a postgraduate longitudinal research, from 1981 to 1991, on the survival strategies of lower-class Creole young people in Amsterdam in the arenas of regular work, informal and criminal economy, and leisure time (Sansone 1992a). Parts of the chapter were first published in *Critique of Anthropology* 14(2): 173–98 (1994).
1 Projecting black culture on to the past and considering it intrinsically different is not only an exercise in exoticism but has implications for

social policy. For example, assuming that the main influence on the work ethic of young Creoles is the pre-industrial and hedonistic work ethos allegedly rooted in their traditions or considering young black males as intrinsically antagonistic to white males has often been used by policy makers to account for the marginalization of black youth – in this view a straightforward self-exclusion.

2 Sources are the Dutch Central Bureau for Statistics and Council of Amsterdam.

3 The term 'coffee shop' refers here to an unlicensed though tolerated establishment which is usually owned by an (informal) entrepreneur and run by a group of young people. Coffee shops revolve around the sale and use of soft drugs and in a sense function like self-help small-scale youth clubs. Coffee shops of this kind started opening in 1981. Their number has grown ever since, reaching, according to estimations, approximately 300 in 1991. During these years the coffee shops have undergone commercialization.

4 A word in the Creole language of Surinam, Sranan Tongo, for the smart and swinging street corner men who are self-proclaimed exploiters of women.

5 A counterculture is a specific subculture with an alternative view of the world. If a counterculture has a particular style – such as the hippie counterculture had, to whom this terms generally refers – this is a means to provoke and carries a (quasi) political message. For most youth subcultures instead, the creation of a style, and abiding by its conventions, is an end as such. A style, for example, a youth style, can be more or less spectacular and consists of a specific use of rituals, clothes, hair, language and music by which one group can be distinguished and differentiates itself from outsiders (Clarke 1976: 52–54).

6 The importance of such polarity for black youth styles has been stressed by Mercer (1990) and Gomes da Cunha (1993) with reference, respectively, to the United States and Brazil.

7 The term 'community language' is borrowed from Hewitt (1986) who created it to refer to the variety of English spoken by ethnically mixed peer groups in the youth clubs of an English city. On the 'microculture' of ethnically mixed peer groups see Wulff (1988).

8 In Surinam, Creole culture has developed on the basis of a precarious compromise between what was assumed to be 'African' (often identified in the paria culture of the Bush Negroes) and Dutch culture: it is in many respects a 'catch all culture' which has produced Sranan Tongo (the Creole language which has become the lingua franca of Surinam) and brings together urban African-Caribbeans, people of mixed blood and even native Americans and Hindustanis who do not fit into their own community.

9 In the Netherlands there are also much smaller black communities: Antilleans, Capo Verdians (in Rotterdam) and Africans (in Amsterdam: mainly Ghanaians). Some young Antilleans and Capo Verdians have participated in the black subcultures described above.

10 Post-war black immigrants met with popular and elite images of black people among the Europeans, which had already been formed prior to

their arrival and from a distance. An interesting case of a sophisticated set of images of blacks, which was developed in the 1920s, was the 'negrophilia' of the French avant-garde. While pursuing the exotic, the sensual and the regenerating naturality of the African, many modernists created myths such as the 'universal negro soul' (Gendron 1990: 153). The relevance of French avant-garde for the highbrow Western culture of the interbellum meant that 'negrophilia' had an homogenizing effect on how blacks were perceived – at least among artists.

11 Different languages have been a major obstacle for the globalization of the symbols of English-speaking black culture among French, Spanish and Portuguese speaking blacks in the Caribbean, South America and Europe. In those regions cultural exchange with English-speaking black people was restricted to intellectuals until not so long ago. Among black people speaking the same language, usually from countries which were linked by colonial ties, cultural exchange has recently greatly increased. For example, black people from the French Antilles and from French-speaking Africa have influenced each other's pop music. However, aided by the growth of the music industry, certain symbols of English-speaking black culture, such as soul music, reggae music and the rasta parapher-nalia, have over the last two decades reached and influenced large numbers of black people in the French Antilles (Giraud and Marie 1987) and Brazil (Barcelar 1989; Sansone 1993). A different process of modern 'creolization' is also going on in certain areas of Africa (Hannerz 1987).

12 Developments in mass communication and technology can both maintain and transform ethnicities. Relatively cheap air fares, telephones, home video and television programmes in the immigrants' mother tongue have dramatically changed the relationship with the country of origin. Through home video, for example, the immigrant communities which come from countries with a film industry can keep in touch with the official language of their country. Hindustani Surinamese have learnt to speak or at least understand official Hindi or Punjabi through the video cassettes coming directly from India and Pakistan. In Amsterdam a probable majority of immigrant families has a video player at home. Setting up a video rent shop for one's own ethnic community has become by now a popular and relatively easy form of ethnic entrepreneurship. The result is that by 1991 there were video shops in Punjabi, Hindi, Turkish, Arabic and several other 'immigrant languages'. Alas, there are no films in Sranan Tongo available on video cassette. Two articles of which I am aware on the function of home video among ethnic minorities in Europe are on Turks in Germany (Klitzke 1981) and on the audio-visual culture among South Asian families in London (Gillespie 1989). Very recently some immigrant groups, such as Italians and Turks, in the Netherlands, Belgium, France and parts of Germany, can watch their national television channels because these countries have been admitted to television cable systems. Spanish and Moroccan television are to follow. Developments in consumer electronics have also influenced the creation of ethnicity. Creole youth styles – and many other youth styles – have benefited from the increasing availability of 'portable music'

(from transistor radios, portable 45rpm record-players, portable cassette recorders, and recently the powerful portable cassette recorders known as 'ghetto blasters') (Hebdige 1979; Gilroy 1987). Music has always been a core ethnic and life-style marker in post-war youth subcultures. Cheap recorded music and 'portable music' have made it possible to play your own music on the streets and to have your music with you all the time. Ghetto blasters and the like make it possible to take the struggle for music hegemony from the discotheques into the streets. Break-dance and hip hop could not have existed without them.

REFERENCES

Alba, R. (1981) 'The twilight of ethnicity among American Catholics of European ancestry', *Annals AAPPS*, 454: 86–97.

Appadurai, A. (1990) 'Disjuncture and difference in the global cultural economy', in M. Featherstone (ed.) *Global Culture. Nationalism, globalisation and modernity*. A Theory and Society Special Issue, London: Sage.

Barcelar, J. (1989) *Etnicidade. Ser negro em Salvador*, Salvador (Brazil): Ianama.

Biervliet, W.E. (1975) 'The hustler culture of young unemployed Surinamers', in H. Lamur and J. Speckmann (eds) *Adaptation of Migrants from the Caribbean in the European and American Metropolis*, Amsterdam and Leiden: ASC-KITVL.

Brana-Shute, G. (1979) *On the Corner, Male Social Life in a Paramaribo Creole Neighbourhood*, Assen: Van Gorcum.

Cohen, A.P. (1985) *The Symbolic Construction of Community*, London: Tavistock.

Clarke, J. (1976) 'Style', in S. Hall and T. Jefferson (eds) *Resistance Through Rituals*, London: Hutchinson.

Gans, H. (1979) 'Symbolic ethnicity: the future of ethnic groups and cultures in America', *Ethnic and Racial Studies*, 1 (2): 1–20.

Gendron, B. (1990) 'Fetishes and motorcars: negrophilia in French Modernism', *Cultural Studies*, 4 (4): 141–155.

Gillespie, M. (1989) 'Technology and tradition', *Cultural Studies*, 3 (2): 226–239.

Gilroy, P. (1987) *There Ain't no Black in the Union Jack*, London: Hutchinson.

—— (1993) *The Black Atlantic. Modernity and Double Consciousness*, London: Verso.

Giraud, M. and Marie, C.V. (1987) 'Insertion et gestion socio-politique de l'identité culturelle: le cas des Antillais en France', *Revue Europeenne des Migrations Internationales*, 3 (3): 31–47.

Gomes da Cunha, O.M. (1993) 'Fazendo a 'coisa certa': reggae, rastas e pentecostais em Salvador', *Revista Brasileira de Cincias Sociais*, 8, (23): 120–135.

Hall, S. (1989) 'Cultural identity and cinematic representation', *Framework*, 36: 68–81.

Hannerz, U. (1980) *Exploring the City*, New York: Columbia University Press.

—— (1987) 'The world in creolisation', *Africa* 57(4): 546–559.
—— (1989) 'Culture between center and periphery: toward a macro-anthropology', *Ethnos*, 54: 200–216.
Hazenkamp, J. (1980) *Arbeidersjongeren*, Meppel: Boom.
Hebdige, D. (1979) *The Meaning of Style*, London: Methuen.
—— (1987) *Cut 'n' Mix*, London: Comedia.
Hewitt, R. (1986) *White Talk, Black Talk. Inter-racial Friendship and Communication Amongst Adolescents*, Cambridge: Cambridge University Press.
Hobsbawm, E. (1983) 'Introduction: inventing traditions', in E. Hobsbawm and T. Ranger (eds) *The Invention of Tradition*, Cambridge: Cambridge University Press.
Kilson, M. (1975) 'Blacks and neo-ethnicity in American political life', in N. Glazer and D. Monyhan (eds) *Ethnicity. Theory and experience*, Cambridge, Mass.: Harvard University Press.
Klitzke, D. (1981) 'Türkee video kasetler – oder das Geschäft mit dem mangelhaften Programmaangebot', *Migration*, 1 (1): 95–102.
Lowenthal, D. (1972) *West Indian Societies*, London: Oxford University Press.
Liebow, E. (1967) *Tally's Corner*, Boston, Mass.: Little, Brown.
McRobbie, A. and Garber, J. (1976) 'Girls and subcultures. An exploration', in S. Hall and T. Jefferson (eds), *Resistance Through Rituals*, London: Hutchinson.
Maxwell, A. (1988) 'The anthropology of poverty in black communities: a critique and systems alternatives', *Urban Anthropology*, 2–3: 171–192.
Mercer, K. (1990) 'Black hair/style politics', in R. Ferguson (ed.) *Out There: Marginalization and Contemporary Cultures*, Cambridge, Mass.: MIT Press.
Mintz, S. (1970) 'Foreword', in N. Whitten and J. Szwed (eds) *Afro-American Anthropology*, New York: The Free Press.
Mintz, S. and Price, S. (1985) 'Introduction', in S. Mintz and S. Price (eds) *Caribbean contours*, Baltimore, Maryland: The Johns Hopkins University Press.
van Niekerk, M. and Vermeulen, H. (1989) 'Ethnicity and leisure time: Surinamese girls in Amsterdam' in J. Boissevain and J. Verrips (eds) *Dutch Dilemmas*, Assen: Van Gorcum.
Patterson, O. (1973) 'Reflections on the fate of blacks in the Americas', in L.Rainwater (ed.) *Black Experience: Soul*, New Brunswick: Transaction Books.
Phoenix, A. (1988) 'Narrow definitions of culture: the case of early motherhood', in S. Westwood and P. Bhachu (eds) *Enterprising Women. Ethnicity. Economy and Gender Relations*, London: Routledge.
Pryce, K. (1979) *Endless Pressure. A Study of West Indian Life Styles in Bristol*, Harmondsworth: Penguin.
Reitz, J. (1980) *The Survival of Ethnic Groups*, Toronto: Mac Grow.
Roosens, E. (1989) *Creating Ethnicity. The Process of Ethnogenesis*, London: Sage.
Sansone, L. (1987) 'Ethnicity and leisure time among Surinamese adoles-

cents and young men in Amsterdam', *Migracijske Teme* (Zagreb), 3 (1): 75–84.

—— (1990) *Lasi boto. Over Surinaamse jongeren, werk en werkloosheid*, Amersfoort and Leuven: Acco.

—— (1992a) *Schitteren in de schaduw. Overlevingsstrategieen, subcultuur en etniciteit van Creoolse jongeren uit de lagere klasse in Amsterdam 1981–1991*, Amsterdam: Het Spinhuis.

—— (1992b) *Hangen boven de oceaan. Werken, hosselen of emigreren onder Creoolse jongeren in Paramaribo*, Amsterdam: Het Spinhuis.

—— (1993) Negro parents, black children: work, ethnicity and generational difference in Bahia, Brazil. Paper presented at the International Conference on The Anthropology of Ethnicity, 15–18 December 1993, Amsterdam.

Schlesinger, P. (1987) 'On national identity: some conceptions and misconceptions criticised', *Social Science Information*, 2 (26): 219–264.

Taylor, R. (1990) 'Black youth. The endangered generation', *Youth and society*, 22 (1): 4–11.

Whitten, N. and Szwed, J. (1970) 'Introduction', in N. Whitten and J. Szwed (eds.) *Afro-American Anthropology*, New York: The Free Press.

Willis, P. (1986) 'Unemployment, the final inequality', *British Journal of Sociology of Education*, 7 (2): 155–169.

Willmott, P. (1966) *Adolescent Boys of East London*, Harmondsworth: Pelican.

Wulff, H. (1988) *Twenty Girls. Growing Up, Ethnicity and Excitement in a South London Microculture*, Stockholm: Studies in Social Anthropology 21, University of Stockholm.

Chapter 7

The waltz of sociability

Intimacy, dislocation and friendship in a Quebec high school[1]

Vered Amit-Talai

The world, Arjun Appadurai observed, is increasingly in transit with more people contending with the reality or the hope of moving than ever before (1990: 297). An aspect of that increased mobility, Roger Keesing once noted, is that fewer and fewer people live out their adulthood with their childhood friends. What, Keesing wondered, was the consequence of that radical dislocation of social relations?[2] In this chapter I contend that in Western industrialized countries, this kind of disjunction has come to be viewed as a routine aspect of friendship. This 'terminal' view of friendship (Paine 1974) has, in turn, affected the construction of adolescence. Continuity of friendships in the passage from adolescence to adulthood is neither commonly expected nor facilitated.

'Adolescence is a period of the life course involving extensive change', Petersen *et al.* tell us (1991: 93). Transition and impermanence are the most consistently defining characteristics of adolescence in scholarly and popular constructions. Adolescence is associated with a shift in cognitive development, social roles, institutions, attachments, concerns and stress. Liminality has become such a well-rehearsed identifier of adolescence that its very familiarity can anaesthetize us to certain key assumptions which are often associated with it.

This chapter is concerned with the relationships among a small, largely female, group of students in their last year at a Montreal high school. When I first embarked on a consideration of the dynamics of friendship among these youths I, like many of the other authors in this volume, felt frustrated by a tendency for anthropologists and sociologists to treat the construction of peer relations as a footnote to problems of socialization (Schlegal and Barry 1991) and class reproduction (Clarke *et al.* 1976; Willis 1981). While the intensity and importance of adolescent peer relations has often been observed (du Bois 1974: 23; Larson and Asmussen, 1991; Schlegal and Barry 1991: 68), as Goodwin (1990) has noted, few studies focus on the structure of these relations in their own right rather than as an aspect of life cycle development. This failure to problematize the organization of the peer group, it seemed to me, closed off consideration of an especially intriguing aspect of adolescence. How and why do these generally short-term affiliations generate such high levels of emotional concern? The more I examined this question, however, the more I realized that I had uncritically adopted two contentious assumptions: that the peer relations established by teenagers are likely to be temporary, and that friendship takes on an extraordinary and distinctive importance in adolescence.

These suppositions are hardly mine alone, recurring in much of the social science literature on adolescence. They also permeate the institutional organization of adolescence through school and residential arrangements which compress and repeatedly disrupt youth peer relations. There is, as we shall see in the following, an element of self-fulfilling prophecy in the responses of at least one group of Montreal youth to this relentless shuffle. Disjunction and distinction are, however, less the outcomes of teenage peer relations than the conditions in which North American youth cultures often develop. My question about adolescence and friendship therefore needs to be rephrased to ask: What are the cultural implications of the presumption of impermanence and intensity in youth peer relations?

FRIENDSHIP AND ADOLESCENCE

The study of youth peer relations, limited as it is, seems veritably cornucopic beside the scarcity of sociological and anthropological studies of friendship in general (Jerrome 1984; Allan 1989). Like adolescence, this is a field which we have largely deferred to our colleagues in psychology. At first pause, this absence seems puzzling given anthropology's concern with interpersonal relationships. Twenty-five years ago, Robert Paine already noted this anomaly.

One supposes social anthropologists themselves live lives in which friendship is every bit as problematic as kinship, and probably a good deal more problematic to handle; in our professional writings about the cultures of the world, however, we dwell at length upon kinship and have much less to say about friendship.
(1969, 1974: 117)

In the 1990s we dwell much less upon kinship but the gap between our personal lived experiences and our professional indifference to friendship is, if anything, even greater. This scholarly disinterest is due, however, to the persistence of an asocial view of friendship which ironically received one of its most emphatic expressions in Paine's own rendition.

Specifically drawing his observations from Western, middle-class culture, Paine viewed friendship as a dyadic, confidential and personal relationship (Paine 1974). Friendship in this account stands as the purest antithesis to bureaucracy and the corporate group . It is private while the bureaucracy is public; personal where the bureaucracy is impersonal; voluntary and equal, rather than hierarchical and prescriptive (Schwartz 1974).

In conceptualizing friendship as the alter ego of the corporation, Paine also rendered it by definition asocial. Friendship stands outside and apart from other relationships, beyond social control (1974: 128–129). Disconnected and isolated, Western, middle-class friendship becomes a marginal wonder, a 'sociological luxury' not easily afforded in other cultures (ibid.: 127). While arguing for more anthropological attention to friendship, Paine ironically provided a rationale, for a discipline that has concerned itself with cross-cultural comparisons and social groups, to vacate the field.

Such a rendition of friendship has proved stubbornly persistent in subsequent social science literature. For Dorothy Jerrome, friendship in Western societies is voluntary and not subject to cultural prescription (1984). In a survey of personal networks among Californian adults, Claude Fischer distinguishes a special category of 'just friends'. Just friends are the 'purest' form of friendships, voluntary and operating outside of any specific context, with no structural or cultural supports (1982: 108). As in Paine's earlier account, friendship continues to be identified in terms of its separation from other social roles. It is therefore hardly coincidental that the literature on friendship has tended to focus on friendships among the young and the elderly (Duck and Gilmour 1981; Jerrome 1984; Allan 1989), i.e. those populations regarded as most likely to be unmarried and outside the paid labour force. Friendship, Dorothy Jerrome argues, 'assumes special importance at times of relative rolelessness' (1984: 698). With significance varying at different stages, a certain measure of contingency and impermanence become intrinsic elements in this life cycle reading of friendship. A friendship, according to Robert

Bell, is unlikely to last throughout the life cycle: 'New friends are added and old friends drop off' as different needs arise (1981: 21).

The emphasis on friendship as private and personal has therefore been associated with its treble marginalization: (1) as peripheral to the central, theoretical concerns of anthropology and sociology with social and cultural organization; (2) as marginal to economic and social production; (3) as of greatest significance to relatively marginalized populations. It also, as Graham Allan has pointed out, incorporates a quite uncritical adoption of conventional and idealized representations of friendship (1989: 2).

Adolescence is commonly defined as a stage in which peer relationships assume their peak importance, intervening between integration into the natal family and establishment of a new family and social network (Dickens and Perlman 1981; 107; Schlegal and Barry 1991). As the analysis of friendship totters precariously on the verge of cliché, the conceptualization of adolescence, conceived as a stage of friendship, tends to follow accordingly. Adolescence and friendship become incorporated into a tautology of personal relationships which obscures the structure and circumstances of adolescent peer relationships. In the following section I want to deconstruct this relationship by reassessing four features commonly attributed to it as they bear on a group of high school leavers in Montreal: (1) that true friendships are private, free-floating relationships; (2) that adolescents have more time for developing such friendships and fewer competing commitments; (3) that friendship takes on a special intensity in adolescence; (4) that adolescent friendships are necessarily transient as a function of life cycle changes.

ROYAL HAVEN SCHOOL

This group of approximately forty students were enrolled in secondary V (grade 11) at Royal Haven School. On the fringes of Montreal's inner city, Royal Haven was situated in a working-class district which has, until recently, served as an important reception area for newly arrived immigrants. The composition of Royal Haven's student population was ethnically very diverse but with a preponderance of youths with origins in the Southern European countries of Italy, Greece and Portugal. Household incomes tended to be low.

In 1987/88, the year during which this research was conducted, Royal Haven School had a total enrolment of 1043 students of which 283 were in secondary V. The Quebec government is presently engaged in organizing a shift from a confessional to a linguistic based public school system. Royal Haven, however, was still a public Catholic school with English as the language of instruction. Physically, Royal Haven was a rather grim edifice, designed for economy rather than beauty or comfort. With its concrete, window-less walls, asphalt paved yard and fluorescent lit corridors, the occasional references of the students to school as a prison from which they were soon escaping through graduation seemed not altogether fanciful (Amit-Talai and Foley 1990).

Research in Royal Haven formed part of my larger study of English-speaking youth in Quebec. Qualitative fieldwork was also conducted during the same period at Park School which is situated in Western Quebec and was preceded the previous spring by a province-wide survey of secondary V students in twenty-nine Quebec schools (Amit-Talai and Foley 1990; Amit-Talai 1993; Amit-Talai 1994). The two case studies involved a small team working under my direction with two full-time research assistants, Kathleen Foley and Kevin Barclay based respectively at Royal Haven and Park Schools. Fieldwork combined participant observation and open-ended interviews with a focus in Royal Haven on female students. This focus was however complemented by interviews, observations and discussions with male students as well as teachers and administrators.

Time

In their survey of 186 pre-industrial societies, Schlegal and Barry point out that the large majority of adolescents in these settings work (1991: 173). In industrialized societies such as Britain or Canada, however, adolescence has often been associated with a privileged access to leisure, a special freedom from the future limitations of family and work (Clarke *et al.* 1976; Willis 1981; Frith quoted in Brake 1985: 189). This relationship has been underscored and 'fetishized' (Clarke *et al.* 1976:50) by the development of a mass leisure market oriented towards youthful consumers (Brake 1985). The Western youth/leisure equation however obscures two critical features. First, even while European and North American adoles-cents are not working, the majority spend nearly as much daily time in an activity as highly structured, hierarchical and subject to alienation and coercion, namely, school. Adolescents who are not at work do not necessarily have more 'free time' as a result. Second, consumer pressures on youth are more likely to limit leisure time than extend it. As Clarke *et al.* cogently note, working-class youth need money to spend on these commodities and activities (1976: 55). In Paul Willis's 1970s study of the counter-school culture of a group of high school students, the 'lads', as they called themselves, were constantly in search of part-time jobs to support their leisure pursuits: dances, pubs, dating, clothes and clubs. Sometimes, they held more than one job and over ten hours a week of work was not unusual (Willis 1981: 39)

In Quebec, the rates of labour force participation among full-time students aged 15 to 19 more than doubled between 1975 and 1989, rising steadily from 15.8 per cent to 36.3 per cent (Langlois *et al.* 1990: 187). In my own more age-specific 1987 survey of 1295 full-time English high school students in their final year of high school, I found that 51 per cent had part-time jobs. Among a comparison group of 492 secondary V students in French schools, 59 per cent had part-time jobs (Amit-Talai 1994). The combination of full-time school and part-time work suggests that youth in an industrialized society such as Quebec, probably if anything, have less leisure time than do their counterparts in pre-industrial societies. They may even have less leisure time than their parents.

In Royal Haven, most students were either working part-time after school, had just recently left such a job or were in search of one. They rarely worked less than twenty hours and in some cases as much as thirty hours a week. Like the 'lads', they used the cash to pay for clothes, music equipment and discs, graduation tickets and dresses, cigarettes, movies and other leisure activities. But Bonnie also purchased savings bonds. Georgina was saving the money she was earning as a coat checker to pay for her post-secondary education. She had opened a savings account into which her wages were directly deposited. Sally used the money she earned baby-sitting to buy school books, supplies, and even spectacles. For a while, Mark was living on his own. He was being supervised by a social worker, under a social services programme designed to help teenagers who had severe problems at home. Mark received some financial aid under this arrangement but it was not enough to cover all his basic expenses, so he worked the evening shift at McDonald's. The conflict with his parents and the late hours had taken their toll on his school performance. The wages of Royal Haven students therefore sometimes covered their basic expenses as well as more expendable commodities. While no one reported having to hand over their wages to their parents, the earnings of some Royal Haveners supplemented the family income by providing for expenses such as school supplies which their parents would otherwise have been hard-pressed to cover.

The Royal Haven youths held jobs, attended school full-time, sometimes took care of their younger siblings, and had obligations to their parents and other family members. They spent an average of fifty hours a week in structured work and school activities even before taking into consideration homework assignments, extra-curricular activities or domestic tasks. Rolelessness and a privileged access to leisure hardly seems an accurate description of their situation or many other similarly employed Quebec students. A liberal supply of time will therefore not explain friendships among Royal Haveners. Instead we will have to look to both the structure of the activities in which they are engaged and the presumptions that operate and arise from these activities.

Compression and Informal Contacts

Like most high schools in Quebec, Royal Haven housed five principal grades, secondary I to V, (7 to 11), with the majority of students ranging in age from 12 to 17 years old. Royal Haven also housed several special programmes including one for older youths returning to school after a break in their education, another for students who appeared to be at risk of dropping out of school, and finally one for handicapped pupils. Courses were organized by grade. Students therefore moved from one class to another in cohorts of one-year age spans. This institutional age grading was extended by the students themselves to freer spaces during the school day such as lunch hour or recess where, overwhelmingly, they continued to congregate with peers from the same grade. Grade and age differences were regarded as glaringly obvious.

On a fall day, a group of secondary fives were gathered in front of a window watching people arrive for the day. The arrival of one teacher prompted a discussion. 'You know, she's really weird', commented John, 'she keeps making mistakes about people's grade'. 'Yeah', agreed Sheila. 'you know what: she thought I was a secondary three, last week!' The comment was greeted with a chorus of laughter. The tone of insult in Sheila's voice rose a notch. ' I mean, look at me: do you think that I look like I'm fourteen years old?'

Displacement from the grade cohort could be an uncomfortable and unsettling experience. Matt, a secondary V student, had been unable to graduate with his fellow grade mates the year before. He had to return to Royal Haven to complete two outstanding course requirements while his friends moved on to college. Matt felt out of place and distanced from this new cohort, concentrating his efforts on maintaining extra school contacts with his previous Royal Haven companions. Meanwhile his fellow secondary V students tried to socialize with each other after school.

As I have described elsewhere (Amit-Talai and Foley 1990; Amit-Talai 1994), their efforts at doing so were not always successful. Among youths with South European origins, tightly restrictive parental supervision was quite common and directed with special protectiveness towards girls.[3] Girls like Isabelle, Georgina, Sally, Gina or Kathie frequently encountered difficulties in getting permission to stay out late or sometimes until just after dark, go out unaccompanied by an older sibling or cousin, attend a friend's party or host their own. Only a small number of students, of either gender, regularly invited their friends into their homes. They might go with a friend for a walk around their residential block, meet just outside the front door and go on to a movie together but they did not often venture inside the home. If they did invite friends over, they tried to do so when their parents were not there. Home and friends did not easily mix while the varying and often conflicting hours of part-time jobs created scheduling problems as well as limiting spare time altogether. The organization of a get-together after school could therefore take time to co-ordinate, require a certain amount of determination and be the source of frustration, as planning was impeded by competing obligations and constraints.

These limitations on the availability and use of leisure time rendered school an even more critical site for peer contacts. School interaction was, however, tightly compressed by the strictures of the school day and a constant subtext of adult apprehensions. So long as students remained on school property, they were subject to supervision. Staff monitored the halls, bathrooms, cafeterias and school grounds during recess and lunch-time as well as during class periods, a monitoring edged with an undertone of anticipating suspicion.

Lunch-time presented an ongoing contest between the determination of students to cluster and the equal determination of staff to disperse them. Pupils were not allowed to linger too long in the cafeteria. Once they had finished eating, it did not take much time before the teacher on duty came by to hasten them out. The daily washroom gatherings of girls as they attended to their hair and make-up, conversed, smoked or munched a slice of cold pizza were regularly interrupted by the arrival of a teacher who would usher them out. Theresa and Melanie went off to the school library only to discover that they could not linger over the magazines. On this occasion the librarian had decided to allow only students completing homework to use the library over the lunch-hour. And so the adolescent/adult waltz danced on, with students in pursuit of space and privacy leading through the building, and staff, sniffing out potential trouble, following.

It was a waltz that was regarded by board officials, school administrators, teachers and sometimes even by exasperated students as part of a Royal Haven success story. Here is one teacher's version of the narrative:

> Well, you know about ten years ago, this place was awful but things are different now. We really have a good bunch of students and I suppose the person who has really made the difference is the woman upstairs. She's real tough and she really cleaned up this place a lot and is making it into a really good school.

Other versions recounted Royal Haven's earlier well-deserved reputation for being a school with more than its fair share of violence, drugs and troublemakers 'cleaned up' by a new principal who had instituted strict controls over student attendance and behaviour. Such accounts provided legitimating rationales for strict supervision and continuing vigilance, suggesting that without this regimen the school might become 'awful' again. Among the symbols of this 'strict' regimen was the bouncer who, in 1987/88, still patrolled the hallways to ensure that outsiders did not enter the school, unlocked the locker rooms in time for the recess and lunch periods and interceded in the event of fights. While a bouncer was a rather unusual presence for a Quebec high school, the constant struggle to control student movement and informal interaction was not. Our study of Park School, a suburban institution in Western Quebec, revealed very similar monitoring even without the accompanying narrative of transformation (Amit-Talai 1994).

For Paul Willis, the zone of the informal is the province of a minority counter-school culture and oppositional style.

> The informal group is the basic unit of this culture, the funda-mental and elemental source of its resistance. It locates and makes

possible all other elements of the culture, and its presence
decisively distinguishes 'the lads' from the 'ear'oles'
[the school conformists]. (1981: 23)

Rather than identifying this opposition in terms of distinct student
camps and styles as Willis does, the formal/informal tension can
more fruitfully be viewed as a more general contradiction embedded
in a particular institutional treatment of adolescence. Peer contacts
among Royal Haveners were subject to successive compression:
focused in the school day by competing obligations and worried
parents concerned to protect their daughters, concentrated by ped-
agogical structures into narrow age grades and hemmed in by
supervision conducted in continual anticipation of trouble. On the
one hand then, for a sizeable portion of the week, adolescents, –
Royal Haveners, 'ear'oles' and 'lads' alike – are segregated and
intensively concentrated in age specific school groupings. These
divisions are also often reproduced in other structured activities for
children and youths: sports, summer camps, or clubs. This form of
organization, as a number of authors have noted (du Bois 1974;
Clarke *et al.* 1976; Schlegal and Barry 1991) compresses and hence
intensifies adolescent peer interaction. It is hard to avoid other
adolescents if you are surrounded by them for six hours a day, five
days a week. On the other hand, the identification and potential
solidarity which this intensive contact engenders is treated with
suspicion as subversive of bureaucratic order and adult authority.

These contradictions are inescapable for any youth implicated in
this institutionalized adolescence, although there can be very different styles of responses. For some of the secondary V students in
Miss Devlin's art class, the formal/informal tension was handled
through accommodation. Miss Devlin had split a large group of
students into two small classrooms. The 'good' students were
allowed to work unsupervised in one of these rooms. That left a
whole class period for chatting informally about parents, television
programmes, radio, the weekend's activities, plans for the summer
and so on. And as they chatted, Mike and Mark, Isabelle, Marina and
their mates confirmed their reputation for reliability and ensured
continuing freedom from supervision by completing their art assignments. It was in this environment that Melanie and Georgina initiated
their friendship. As the friendship developed, they began eating
lunch together at the café down the street and a few weeks later they
met for the first time after school to go to a movie.

Challenge and confrontation were the response of four secondary V girls in Miss Rona's class. The girls sat at the back of the classroom, talking to one another about their families, Julie complaining frankly about her family and her brother in particular.

You know, I hate my fuckin family. They are all crazy. My brother's just going crazy. He's a madman. Last night he comes home and he starts screaming and shouting at us all. My dad told him to shut up but he just wouldn't. You know what he [the brother] did? He started lacing after me. He chased me all over the house. I thought he was going to kill me. I had to lock myself in the bathroom.

Julie and her friends were talking loudly, making no effort to whisper. The teacher allowed this to go on for a while but finally interrupted the lesson to chastise them. When she asked them why they were talking, Julie defiantly replied: 'We were not talking. I am working so you should just get on with what you were saying.' Miss. Rona looked less than pleased but she continued the lesson.

Accommodation or confrontation, divergent as these responses are, they both construct sociability through management of key institutional dialectics. It is a construction of sociability which works to bridge distinctions between private and public, personal and bureaucratic, formal and informal, which can never be fully reconciled, but equally cannot be allowed to remain truly separate. The person who cannot manipulate these distinctions, who cannot transform a schoolmate into a friend or a lesson into an opportunity for informal exchange risks being publicly judged as socially incompetent. For the compression of peer relations makes anonymity and social distance, at least among one's grade-mates, extremely difficult to maintain. Even Matt, who had reluctantly returned to school after his cohort graduated, ran for and was elected to student office during that year.

Intimacy

In this context therefore, youth peer relations were constituted by a series of partial, tactical (de Certeau 1984) transformations shaped through but also pressing against institutional constraints. Key catalysts effecting these transformations were disclosures and activities. Both disclosures and activities were used to criss-cross social roles/zones and drove the process of friendship. Indeed, I want to argue generally that rather than relegating friendship to a segregated zone of privacy, the generative capacity of 'making friends' derives from its blurring of boundaries between social roles and spheres. By that logic however, the attempt to identify 'pure' categories of friends which recurs through much of the literature on friendship misses the point. It not only disregards the transmuting blurring of this form of affiliation but it also treats friendship as classification rather than process. It demands that people dissect relationships which are continually being constituted into finished categorical products. At what point did Melanie and Georgina, the art class-mates, become friends: when they met, started to converse in class, ate lunch together or went to a movie after school? Little wonder then that studies which rely on measurements of friendship such as number of friends or amount of interaction quickly become en-tangled in the difficulties of accounting for the categories being enumerated (Dickens and Perlman 1981; Solano 1986). Rather than trying to distinguish between achieved categories of Royal Haven peer relations such as acquaintances, friends or mates (Allan 1989), I have therefore focused on the liminality of making friends.

Friends, as the case of Melanie and Georgina indicates, were made by extending the range of opportunities for interaction. The develop-ment of friendship was commemorated and deepened by sharing recess and lunch-hour time and in most cases by getting together after school. To what extent, however, friends owed each other this time could be a source of constant tension in relationships. Isabelle, Francesca, Marina and Marsha had become friends during secondary V. Most lunch-hours would find these four together in the cafeteria or the washroom. While they were frequently joined by other students, the question of obligation was usually raised in respect to a member of the foursome. Thus when one day, Francesca left the cafeteria early in the lunch period without telling Isabelle or 'anybody else' at the table where she was going or inviting them to come along or meet her later, Isabelle experienced the departure as a violation of the obligations of friendship. 'Some good friend she is!', she exclaimed sarcastically before storming off to the bathroom. On another occasion however, when Isabelle was preoccupied with a friend she had known in another school, it was Francesca's turn to feel abandoned. When Isabelle did not join her, Marina and Marsha for lunch, Francesca began to complain about her friend's behaviour. 'I can't believe', she exclaimed, 'that [Isabelle] would behave in this way when someone new comes into the school. I can't believe that she would ignore us all and act as if she didn't even know us. ' Had the shoe been on the other foot, Francesca argued, Isabelle would have been furious with her and would not have spoken to her for weeks. Francesca, Marsha and Isabelle also regularly made an effort to see each other outside school as well. Marina however rarely socialized with them outside Royal Haven, a choice that she knew infuriated Isabelle.

Friends were supposed to spend time with each other, but which time, i.e. how much, when and where was a matter for ongoing, and often uneasy, negotiation of expectations and limitations. Isabelle who was particularly demanding of her friends' attention and time was, however, the most constrained in extra school activities. Her parents' protectiveness and restrictions on visits to friends' homes were infamous among a number of Isabelle's Royal Haven associates. The extra contacts which friendship entails could thus yield special information about the persons concerned, their households, boyfriends and, perhaps most importantly, their behaviour in other contexts.

More intentional disclosures however were also made to deepen the intimacy of friendship. Friends deliberately divulged material that would not otherwise be readily available through school interaction. Sally told Francesca and Kathleen Foley – my research assistant – about her parents' arranged marriage, her fear that if she did not go along on a trip to Portugal, her mother, still bitterly unhappy in Canada after twenty years, might not return. She told them that up until two years earlier, her father used to hit her with the edge of his belt buckle, that he only made $20,000 a year with four children to support, that she hoped to study medicine and expected to eventually leave Quebec. It took some time however before Sally would divulge to her friends that she was romantically involved with a black man ten years her senior. Later, it was to Kathleen Foley rather than her friends that she revealed the relationship was faltering. Most of all, it was to Kathleen Foley alone that she confided hurt and bewilderment over her parents' disinterest in her studies and college aspirations, their disappointment over her lack of femininity, her mother's distrust and tendency to assume the worst. 'Sometimes I feel so lost', she despaired.

Friendship thus posed a delicate see-saw between concealment and revelation. To effect the transformation of acquaintance into friend, the intimacy provided by contacts and mutual disclosure *beyond* school was critical. But the information consequently revealed posed serious risks to the impression a Royal Havener strived and was expected to convey in school. Isabelle was none too pleased to discover that news of her drunkenness at a New Year's Eve party had been passed on in school by Francesca who had also attended. 'I hear you got really drunk at New Year's', greeted Marina at lunch time. 'I hate [Francesca] Isabelle exclaimed, 'she's always telling people about me.' Sally was one of the best-known and well-liked students in secondary V. She had successfully been elected to student office. She performed well in scholastic requirements and was an accomplished and committed athlete. She was known for her liveliness, humour and self-sufficiency. Her domestic and romantic difficulties posed a vulnerability which could certainly have altered this image. Knowledge of that vulnerability would not only have been surprising to her friends and associates, self-exposure might also have been viewed as an inappropriate expression of emotions or views.

Like a number of the other students, Gina had transferred from Mount School in her penultimate year of high school. The transfer had been very difficult for Gina. She had been unable to establish new friendships and many of her old Mount School friends had moved on to other relationships. Gina was lonely and unhappy and she did not mind telling people like Georgina, Melanie and Kathleen Foley about her misery. As she described her constant crying, how Georgina, her 'best friend' at Mount School had established new friendships, her strict and restrictive parents, their constant fighting, Georgina and Melanie alternated between embarrassed silence and repeated attempts to change the subject into less emotionally charged terrain such as a movie outing or a school assignment. Not a word of acknowledgment of or comfort for Gina's unhappiness was forthcoming.

For Mike, there was no question about the necessity of watching what you said to friends at school. Mike had participated in a retreat organized by the Royal Haven chaplain for students from several high schools. Approximately forty students were divided up into seven discussion groups and left to talk among themselves. Over the course of several hours, they discussed such topics as Aids, drug abuse, sexual promiscuity, God, friendship and loyalty. At the end of the day as the youths reviewed the day with Father Martin, Mike talked about how much he had enjoyed the retreat. He said that he did not get much time in which he could really be himself and say what he wanted to say. At school, Mike felt, you couldn't really talk about these things with your friends because they would just laugh at you. At the retreat, he didn't feel scared that people would laugh at him. Everybody listened to what you had to say.

Anthony Giddens defines intimacy as 'the disclosure of emotions and actions which the individual is unlikely to hold up to a wider public gaze' (1992: 138). Personal relations between Royal Haveners developed within a hierarchical, institutional context but through activities and disclosures that moved friendships beyond this milieu. The blurring of roles and domains which was thus entailed in the push towards intimacy could create significant ambiguities in what Goffman called the 'interactional modus vivendi' (1959: 11). When a group of Royal Haveners gathered in the corridors, bathroom or even in class, definitions of the situation could alternate between a private conversation between friends, a public gathering, a formal lesson, a display of comic talent, sometimes in the space of seconds, sometimes between simultaneous interpretations. Intimacy was thus refracted through rather than protected from the public gaze, transforming the latter but also heightening the risks entailed in the former. Intimacy, Anthony Giddens argues, always involves a gamble on the integrity of a confidant (1992: 138). Making friends was so important that most Royal Haveners insisted on taking the gamble. They also, however, tried to limit the hazards of intimacy by drawing an invisible line between safe and risky disclosures. That boundary occupied such a wide range, from Julie's loud outburst in class about her 'fuckin family' to Mike's hesitations about expressing general views to his friends, that the variety of interpretations could easily produce conflict, embarrassment and confusion. Peer pressure therefore derived not so much from the onus towards conformity to a collective standard as from the indeterminacy of that standard.

Disjunction

A working understanding was rendered all the more precarious by the constant institutional – domestic as well as educational – dislocation of peer relationships. For a few minutes every hour, class doors burst open and students flooded the hallways on their way to another course, another teacher, another classroom and another set of students. Every year, students were assigned or chose a new set of courses with a corresponding shift in locations, teachers and classmates. For a significant group of secondary five students at Royal Haven, the annual organizational shuffle the year before had been especially traumatic. For the first three years of high school, they had been enrolled at another institution. When Mount school shifted its orientation from a comprehensive to a fine arts programme, the general students were required to enrol elsewhere. Most moved on to Royal Haven, although some of their classmates and friends were sent to other schools. On a smaller scale, individuals frequently had to change schools as their families moved house and neighbourhood.

With each shuffle came a new set of associations and friendships. That at least some friendships would emerge as people made the acquaintance of new class- and schoolmates is hardly very surprising. What is more interesting is the frequency with which new friendships displaced previous relationships. At the start of the school year, Melanie had spent her free time going around with Theresa and Karen. As her friendship developed with Georgina, the frequency with which she circulated with Theresa and Karen gradually declined. A photograph of the guests at Francesca's sweet 16 party revealed a very different sets of friends from less than a year earlier. Marsha, Marina and Isabelle, her most constant companions in secondary five, had not been present. In other words, Royal Haveners did not add friends so much as change friends in response to institutional restructuring.

To try and understand why this would be so, we need to remind ourselves of the way in which free period circulation served to construct and signify friendships. If Melanie was going to use lunch and recess periods to develop her new relationship with Georgina, there would be less time available for her previous friends. Of course, she could always try to incorporate Georgina into her existing circle of friends, meeting both her old and new friends for lunch. Melanie did in fact attempt to do this on one occasion but Georgina was clearly very uncomfortable in joining a group with whom she had no independent affiliation. The attempt was not repeated and gradually one friendship displaced another. Using a similar line of logic, Georgina advised Gina to stop hanging around with Bonnie if she wanted to make new friends.

Friends could also see each other outside school even when they had no occasion for socializing in school. Sally especially enjoyed visiting Angela's house even though she made no special effort to see her at lunch-time or recess. Sally's lunch-time routine was, however, quite unusual in that she did not circulate with any particular friends. She would camp out on the benches in front of the girls' locker room and talk to whoever happened to pass by. Her behaviour could not therefore be construed as choosing one friend over another.

Spending lunch-time or recess with a friend was not simply a logistical consideration. As we saw earlier in Isabelle and Francesca's mutual recriminations, 'free-time' sociability could take on highly charged associations. Interaction during these periods became markers of friendship. In an environment in which peer association is both highly compressed and subject to continual bureaucratic realignments, friendships were prized as well as unpredictable. Lunch-time hanging out became a critical gauge of the daily status of friendship sets, confirming, at least for the moment, a continued commitment. Friendships might not be forever but lunch-time buddies reassured for today. When a friend was not available during these breaks, it could be that she was busy or preoccupied but it could also be a sign that the friendship was on the wane. Hence Isabelle's anxiety whenever she couldn't find Francesca or Marsha during these free periods. The overtones of preference, attachment and rejection associated with this form of congregation thus tended to reduce individual room for manoeuvre and increased the possibility that new friendships would displace, rather than complement, existing relationships. The intensity of free period sociability underscored the precariousness of friendships, ironically sometimes in the very pursuit of commitment.

There were other forms of resistance to the discontinuities regularly imposed on peer relations. Bonnie and Cynthia continued to attend Royal Haven even after they relocated residentially at some distance from it. They commuted two hours a day rather than attend schools in their new neighbourhoods. On the other hand, some individuals maintained contact with friends who had moved to another district. It was not uncommon to find students who had graduated from Royal Haven paying return visits to their Alma Mater. As graduation approached some students tried to reassure themselves and each other that their high school friendships would persevere through the transition (Amit-Talai and Foley 1990).

Most of their friends, however, didn't believe that such continuity was possible. As much as they dreaded yet another institutional dislocation, they expected high school friendships to give way before the new affiliations of college or work. Mike was sure that once summer ended and college began, his friends would no longer see each other (ibid.). Everything would be different in college.

Well, college is where you will find everyone from all different schools and they get together and you see how they are different from each other. You get to see how they act and everything. And in that way you are seeing a totally new change, you know. Everything that you do is going to change. Your social life is going to change. Your behavior is going to change. It is all going to change once you go to college, that's what I think.

Discontinuity of peer relations might be resented and feared, but by the end of high school it had come to be seen as an inevitable and natural outcome of institutional passages.

CONCLUSION

As a small group of Royal Haven students looked forward to the excitement of graduation, they prepared to say goodbye to their high school friends. They were not saying goodbye because they did not like their friends or because friendship was of minor importance. On the contrary, they had invested a great deal of effort, reflection and concern in these relationships and viewed the approaching rupture with apprehension and some sadness.

The expectation that institutional and life cycle transitions prompt an inevitable recomposition of personal networks as well as changes in social roles is hardly peculiar to this group of teenagers. It reflects a more general rendering of friendship as a desirable but ultimately expendable luxury. Friendship from this perspective must adjust to the constraints of other more essential affiliations of work, family and romance, and not vice versa.

This construction of friendship as outside social roles combines with a view of youth as a period of relative rolelessness to provide a circular 'explanation' of peer relations among adolescents. Adolescents, it is presumed, temporarily and unusually, have a special time and freedom from competing affiliations to cater to friendship. Youth and friendship thus share an asocial limbo. A diverse range of anthropology, sociology and psychology literature has been curiously and persistently accepting of this view, more commonly reproducing it than subjecting it to critical analysis (Allan 1989: 2). But the association of adolescence and friendship with marginality and impermanence is not quite so self-evident as might appear in this conventional rendition.

Such a depiction obscures the productive contributions of youth including their increasing participation in the service sector of industrialized societies. It disregards the continuity of relationships which can characterize some local groupings. In a sample of 186 pre-industrial societies surveyed by Schlegal and Barry, adolescence marked a stage in the ongoing development of long-term relationships, a 'time during which the ground is prepared for adult social relations with the same people who are currently one's peers' (1991: 43). The reconstitution of peer relations is not an inevitable element in adolescent transitions; it is an aspect of a very particular construction of adolescence.

'There is no room for passion in the routinized settings which provide us with security in modern social life. Yet who can live without passion . . .', Anthony Giddens wonders (1992: 201). There seems little room for friendship in a capitalist labour market oriented towards mobility and disposability but an industry of talk shows, soap operas, magazine articles and 'how to' books (Allan 1989: 1) attests to our unwillingness to live without it. What the market disposes of with one hand, it seems very willing to exploit with the other. Treating friendship as a private, expendable relationship requires that we ignore this contradiction and take on board only one side of this very public treatment of personal relationships.

These kinds of contradictions are embedded in organizational structures which bring people together in close and daily proximity but also attempt to confine sociability to tidy, controllable compartments of the work or school day: coffee break, recess, lunch-time. In Royal Haven the struggle over sociability involved a cat and mouse game in which adults policed and students sought to create some personal space through accommodation, confrontation or evasion. Interaction in school corridors and classes was a blur of private confidences, public displays of friendship links, classroom discipline, whispered (or not so whispered) conversations, and a perpetual reconstitution of personal networks. Friendship and sociability were never fully private or neatly compartmentalized.

I opened this chapter with Roger Keesing's musing on the severance of social relations as a consequence of increasing mobility. This study has suggested however that dislocation of personal relationships can be structured as routine practice without the antecedent necessities of movement. This kind of disruption is not an incidental outcome of some other activity. It is remarkably stable, planned and institutionalized. There are, as I have noted, elements of control in the deliberate attempt at dispersing and unsettling informal relations. But perhaps its most insidious aspect is the extent to which it convinces young people that intimacy is a prelude to loss.

NOTES

1 This study was made possible by a grant from the Quebec Ministry of Education. As a means of preserving the confidentiality of participants in this study, aliases have been used for the names of individuals as well as schools.
2 Roger Keesing made this remark on 8 March, 1993, at Concordia University in response to a public lecture by Ulf Hannerz on the globalization of culture.
3 In a study of second generation young Greeks living in Montreal, Spyridoula Xenocastas (1991) similarly reported that parents of second generation Montreal Greeks in their early twenties were very concerned about their children's social activities, how late they stayed out, where they went and with whom. Women felt that they were more restricted than their brothers.

REFERENCES

Allan, G. (1989) *Friendship: Developing a Sociological Perspective*, New York: Harvester Wheatsheaf.
Amit-Talai, V. (1993) 'Will they go?: a study of intentions regarding migration among secondary students in Quebec', *Canadian Ethnic Studies*, XXV: 50–61.
—— (1994) 'Urban pathways: the logistics of youth peer relations', in V. Amit-Talai and H. Lustiger-Thaler (eds) *Urban Lives: Routine and Fragmentation*, Toronto: MacLelland & Stewart.
Amit-Talai, V. and Foley, K. (1990) 'Community for now: an analysis of contingent communality among urban high school students in Quebec', *Urban Anthropology*, 19: 233–253.
Appadurai, A. (1990) 'Disjuncture and difference in the global culture economy', in M. Featherstone (ed.) *Global Culture: Nationalism, Globalization and Modernity. A Theory, Culture and Society*, special issue, London: Sage Publications.
Bell, R. R. (1981) *Worlds of Friendship*, Beverly Hills and London: Sage Publications.
Brake, M. (1985) *Comparative Youth Culture: The Sociology of Youth Culture and Youth Subcultures in America, Britain and Canada*, London: Routledge & Kegan Paul.
Clarke, J., Hall, S., Jefferson, T. and Roberts, B. (1976) 'Subcultures, cultures and class' in S. Hall and T. Jefferson (eds) *Resistance through Rituals: Youth Subcultures in Post-War Britain*, London: Hutchinson.
de Certeau, M. (1984) *The Practice of Everyday Life*, Berkeley, LA and London: University of California Press.

Dickens, W. J. and Perlman, D. (1981). 'Friendship over the life-cycle', in S. Duck and R. Gilmour (eds) *Personal Relationships. 2: Developing Personal Relationships*, London and New York: Academic Press.

du Bois, C. (1974) 'The gratuitous act: an introduction to the comparative study of friendship patterns', in E. Leyton (ed.) *The Compact: Selected Dimensions of Friendship*, Newfoundland Social and Economic Papers, No. 3, St. John's, Newfoundland: ISER, Memorial University of Newfoundland.

Duck, S. and Gilmour, R. (eds.) (1981) Preface to *Personal Relationships. 2: Developing Personal Relationships*, London and New York: Academic Press.

Fischer, C. (1982) *To Dwell Among Friends: Personal Networks in Town and City*, Chicago and London: University of Chicago Press.

Giddens, A. (1992) *The Transformation of Intimacy: Sexuality, Love and Eroticism in Modern Societies*, Cambridge, UK: Polity Press.

Goffman, E. (1959) *The Presentation of Self in Everyday Life*, New York: Doubleday.

Goodwin, M.H. (1990) *He-Said-She-Said: Talk as Social Organization Among Black Children*, Bloomington and Indianapolis: Indiana University Press.

Jerrome, D. (1984) 'Good company: 'the sociological implications of friendship', *Sociological Review*, 3: 696–718.

Langlois, S., Baillargeon, J.P., Caldwell, G., Fréchet, G., Gauthier, M. and Simard J.P. (1990) *La société québécoise en tendances 1960–1990*, Québec: Institut Québécois de Recherche sur la Culture.

Larson, R. and Asmussen, L. (1991) 'Anger, worry and hurt in early adolescence: an enlarging world of negative emotions', in M. E. Colten and S. Gore (eds) *Adolescent Stress: Causes and Consequences*, New York: Aldine de Gruyter.

Paine, R. (1974) 'An exploratory analysis in "middle-class" culture' in E. Leyton (ed.) *The Compact: Selected Dimensions of Friendship*, New-Foundland Social and Economic Papers, No. 3, St. John's, Newfoundland: ISER, Memorial University of Newfoundland

Petersen, A. C., Kennedy, R. E. and Sullivan, P. (1991) 'Coping with adolescence', in E. Colten and S. Gore (eds) *Adolescent Stress: Causes and Consequences*, New York: Aldine de Gruyter.

Schlegal, A. and Barry, H. III (1991) *Adolescence: An Anthropological Inquiry*, New York: The Free Press.

Schwartz, R. (1974) 'The crowd: friendship groups in a Newfoundland outport', in E. Leyton (ed.) *The Compact: Selected Dimensions of Friendship*, Newfoundland Social and Economic Papers, No. 3, St. John's Newfoundland: ISER, Memorial University of Newfoundland.

Solano, C. H. (1986) 'People without friends: loneliness and its alternatives', in V. J. Derlega and B. A. Winstead *Friendship and Social Interaction*, New York and Berlin: Springer-Verlag.

Willis, P. (1981) *Learning to Labor: How Working Class Kids Get Working Class Jobs*, New York: Columbia University Press.

Xenocastas, S. (1991) 'Familial obligation: ideal models of behaviour for second generation Greek youths in Montreal', in S. P. Sharma, A. M. Ervin and D. Meintel (eds) *Immigrants and Refugees in Canada: A National Perspective on Ethnicity, Multiculturalism and Cross-Cultural Adjustment*, Saskatoon: University of Saskatchewan.

Chapter 8

Media, markets and modernization

Youth identities and the experience of modernity in Kathmandu, Nepal

Mark Liechty

INTRODUCTION

> The difference is that now in Nepal we have an open society. We have seen the life of the outside. We have heard the new ideas, we have seen the new technology. You know, I still remember in my childhood; I would see things with my own eyes and then I would ask my father for explanations. One day I flatly said 'No' [to my father]. Look at my house. Do you see my father living here?
>
> 40-year-old Newar man

For this man, and even more so for his children's generation, everyday experiences of reality and identity are increasingly inflected by 'the life of the outside'. Kathmandu is a city undergoing a speedy initiation into the late twentieth-century world of international aid, global trade, mass tourism and electronic mass media. Before 1951 public education and all communications (travel, trade, books, cinema, etc.) between Kathmandu and 'the outside' were either banned or the exclusive privilege of local elites. Yet in the 1990s Kathmandu has become one of South Asia's busiest air transportation hubs hosting close to a quarter of a million tourists a year; fashionable shops are jammed with imported electronic consumer goods making Kathmandu 'the Hong Kong of South Asia'; televisions and VCRs have become standard features of urban middle-class homes.[1]

In this chapter I explore some of what it means for young people to grow up in a world radically different from that of their parents. What happens when perceptions of reality are in flux, when identities and imagined lives are no longer confined within local frames of reference, when a multiplicity of meaning systems vie for the status of 'common sense', when local socializing mechanisms no longer enjoy an unquestioned, hegemonic authority? Based on the experiences of hundreds of young people and adults that my co-workers and I interacted with,[2] this chapter examines what it means for youth to live in a present whose past provides few seemingly relevant role models but whose future they can only perceive as an unknown.

IDENTITY AND CULTURAL TRANSFORMATION

Identity formation occurs within communities but in the late twentieth century the factors that shape identities increasingly transcend the boundaries of locale. As I use the term, identity refers to a person's sense of inclusion in (or exclusion from) a range of social roles and ways of being, both 'real' (those derived from lived experience) and 'imagined' (those encountered in realms beyond the everyday: tales, religious epics, mass media, etc.). As a person's frame of reference expands beyond the boundaries of his/her own lived experience, via such avenues as education, travel and consumption of mass media, categories of being multiply into a plethora of 'possible lives' (Appadurai 1990a: 9) – desirable and abhorrent, attainable and out of reach.

Rather than seeing identity as a 'thing' I prefer a model in which a person may have many identities encompassing many ways of being, within and between which there is no *necessary* consistency or logic. Identities may be claimed or ascribed and hence can change depending on the extent of an individual's authority in any given social context. Identities may be lived or imagined; while some identities are manifested daily in such things as labour and gender roles, other identities may never be actualized yet exist in the imagination as potentialities or desired ways of being. Identity formations are never stable; they constantly change as people move through life cycles or through cultural landscapes in which they encounter (and must learn to function in) institutions and social relations based on a variety of social values and epistemic frames.[3] Identity formation is a process and identity formations are always 'in the making' as subjects move through time and space (cf. Fox 1985).[4]

Since the eighteenth century, but especially since 1951, Kathmandu's society has gone from one in which identities were derived from the cultural contrasts found in a relatively stable, contained universe of known roles and ways of being, to a society whose frames of reference and contrastive awareness are of literally global dimensions. For many in Kathmandu, features of an earlier urban culture continue to shape identity: the physical layout of the old city with its relatively homogenous caste communities, traditional occupations associated with family and caste, or minutely defined ritual tasks given to specific family and caste groups in communal festivals (Lewis 1984).

Yet for members of these communities, and even more so for the tens of thousands of residents who arrived in the city only in the last decades, this traditional social fabric is enveloped by layer upon layer of new meaning systems: new patterns of wage labour and cash economies; new ideologies of education, development and change; new arenas of public display and expressive culture; new residential configurations and built environments; and a new universe of material goods.[5] Through repeated enactment, embodiment, and growing relevance to daily life, these new systems of meaning form a slowly hardening structure around and within communities in the city, binding people together in new relationships (e.g. class) without necessarily contesting earlier systems of social meaning (e.g. caste).[6] In Kathmandu the fabric of an earlier pattern of sociality still exists, some strands maintaining remarkable strength. Yet other strands slowly disintegrate, leaving the structures of 'modernity' to increasingly bear the weight of social transactions.

MEANINGS OF MODERNITY

In this chapter I distinguish between three broad categories of 'modern'. First is 'state modernism', the term I use to describe a state ideology of progress, modernization and development, or *bikas* as it is known in Nepal (cf. Pigg 1990; 1992). Here I am less concerned with the macro-economic or political implications of these international relations[7] than with 'development' as a state doctrine and the implications this modernist ideology has for processes of identity formation. *Bikas* promotes a national identity: it seeks to provide people with a sense of *Nepaliness*, an awareness of self as member of a nation. As an ideology, *bikas* creates a national identity for Nepal based on an *external* referent. From infancy Nepalis have etched into their minds the notion that Nepal is a, if not *the*, 'Least Developed Country' (LDC). The ideology of *bikas* asks Nepalis to imagine themselves *as a nation vis-à-vis* other nations in contrast with which Nepal ranks as possessing the 'least' of some quantifiable new value known as 'development'.[8]

The second 'modern' category is 'consumer modernity', a commercially generated 'modernity-as-commodity'. Consumer modernity is a capitalist discourse that privileges the material as 'real'. It is an ideology proposing that reality and value reside in things. Consumer modernity is the commodity form of the transnational capitalist public sphere and as an ideological discourse it is the vehicle for a new kind of post-colonial imperialism; a colonization of the mind via the commoditization of identities. The logic of consumer modernity promotes a material conception of self such that persons are encouraged to purchase their identities in the form of consumer goods. The 'ideal' modern consumer is one who, imagining the self as an object, lives life as a never ending, addictive quest to consume possible selves.[9]

I will argue that these two rhetorical currents, 'state modernism' and 'consumer modernity', coalesce to promote a logic that constructs modernity, and ultimately self, as quantifiable material conditions. Both posit 'ideal states' attainable only through commodity transactions. By this logic, just as the state's modernity is measured in health posts, hydroelectric projects and kilometres of roads, when the self is a thing, the more material goods one appropriates the more 'self' one has. In 'least developed' countries like Nepal, the official discourses of modernity are material discourses that promote consumer logics and transnational relations of dependence.

Finally, the third 'modern' category is what I will describe as the 'experience of modernity'. I will speak of the experience of modernity as the lived experience of people at the point where state modernism and consumer modernity intersect with both old and new patterns of social organization and opportunities on the one hand, and the realities of limited resources and unequal power on the other. When dealing with late twentieth-century consumer capitalism one must not mistake the reality of its 'totalizing discourse' for the reality of lived experience, or, in literary terms, assume the identity of text and subject (cf. Rodowick 1988). Global consumer capitalism *does* form a mutually referencing and reinforcing sphere of images and ideologies and, to the extent that it is internally coherent and compelling, it is a totalizing discourse. But it depends on an imagined realm of 'modernity': a commodity realm which, like fashion, is 'real' only to the degree that any person or group accepts the terms of its discourse. In distinguishing the 'experience of modernity' from the discourses of modernism and commercial modernity, I suggest that while the latter are potent, very real forces in everyday life, they do not constitute it.

THE CONSTRUCTION OF 'MODERN YOUTH'

In this chapter I consider what it means to be a modern youth in Kathmandu: (1) from the perspective of commercial media interests who would compose the category in material terms, and (2) through the voices and experiences of middle-class parents and youth themselves who must live out the contradictions between ideologies of progress and mediated images of abundance on the one hand, and the real world of scarcity and precarious claims to social standing on the other. Part I revolves around the 'teen' in Kathmandu. Via a discussion of a Kathmandu youth magazine I describe one mechanism by which local commercial interests coalesce to constitute a youth market by promoting new, modern youth identities built around the consumption of a host of transnational 'pop' images, as well as specific local goods and services. I also show how parents and youth turn this new consumer discourse back on itself in potent critiques of 'teenage' consumers. In Part II I relate the stories of two young men who, through their personal histories and perspectives, begin to portray something of the experience of modernity for urban middle-class youth in Kathmandu who must navigate the gaps between ideologies of state modernism and consumer modernity, and the particular realities of person and place. I conclude by focusing on the intersection of media, modernity and the imagination; a space in which youth work to envision their own *Nepali* futures.

PART I: YOUTH, MEDIA, AND CONSUMER MODERNITY

'Teenagers' and *Teens* in Kathmandu

Looking at the contents, commercial backers and target audience of a popular Kathmandu youth magazine called *Teens* brings into particularly sharp focus the ways in which local, regional and global market forces intersect in the construction/imagination of the modern youth-as-consumer. The words 'teen' and 'teenager' (as they are used by Nepalis both in English and in colloquial Nepali) designate a new cultural space that is still being created and genuinely contested between young people, parents and commercial interests.

It is in this new space that middle-class youth are debating what it means to be Nepali, young and modern – all categories that are themselves new and open.

Teens, the magazine

Part of my daily routine in Kathmandu was to peruse the offerings at any of the hundreds of sidewalk magazine vendors and shop-front bookshops that I encountered on my rounds about the city. These dealers offer hundreds of publications to the reading public ranging from Hindi murder mystery/detective magazines and dozens of film magazines in Hindi, English and Nepali, to speciality magazines for women, children, sportsmen, etc., as well as dozens of newspapers: the government-produced Nepali and English dailies, English and Hindi daylies from India, and a proliferation of vernacular weeklies representing all the shades of Nepal's vibrant political spectrum. On one such day I noticed a title I had never seen before. Because it was printed on rather low-grade stock with a simple two-colour cover, I guessed that *Teens* magazine, although in English, was probably a local publication.

A few days later I had the first of several long talks with the editors and owners of *Teens*. The two editor–publishers, an early middle-aged married couple whom I will call Diane and Gopal, were from ethnic communities with roots in Nepal, though they themselves had each grown up in India and South East Asia where their 'Gurkha' fathers were stationed with the British army. Both had Master's degrees and had 'returned' to Nepal as adults to forge their futures. Their first publishing venture had been a non-profit monthly devoted to development issues in Nepal. Before long their hopes were frustrated by the fact that while enough people were willing to contribute material to the new magazine, few were willing to pay the subscription fee needed to buy print-stock and pay a small staff. Eventually they turned to soliciting advertisements to help defer production costs. Yet their struggle to get a handful of local businesses to put up money for advertisements was only greeted with criticism by readers who accused them of commercializing the magazine.

Still hoping to keep the magazine alive, Diane and Gopal hit upon a novel marketing scheme. They offered business people free advertising space in their magazine if those businesses would agree to provide sales discounts to magazine subscribers. The idea was to encourage people to subscribe by offering them reduced rates on a variety of local goods and services. Much to the editors' surprise, within months subscriptions had soared, even though relatively few new subscribers were actually interested in the development content of the magazine. Diane and Gopal realized they had stumbled upon an enormously promising commercial opportunity and by early 1991 were considering phasing out the magazine to focus completely on a consumer's club scheme. As Gopal exclaimed, 'Our marketing strategy is stronger than the product itself!'

Not long after they had initiated their new marketing scheme, Diane and Gopal heard that the sons and daughters of subscribers were also eagerly using the membership/discount cards. Gradually they conceived of a whole new marketing and publishing thrust that would target a particular youth market via a subscription magazine for young people. The magazine would link local youth with a range of local businesses that had particular interests in a youthful clientele. In this way *Teens* magazine was conceived of as first and foremost a marketing scheme aimed at upper middle-class youth and designed to move them on to a track leading to membership in the adult consumer club.

Before launching the new magazine, the publishers researched the market and targeted an audience. 'Who is our customer? was the main question', explained Gopal. They decided to focus on upper middle-class youth in their late teens. 'They haven't left the school, and haven't entered into work. They're somewhere in between', Gopal said. Diane went on to explain their target audience in more specific terms:

> Our target group is teenagers coming from boarding schools, English boarding schools. Nowadays, Hindi is fast fading, except for public school teenagers – maybe they still like to see it. But boarding school kids, if they want to *be* English, they have to read English magazines, listen to English music, watch English videos, I mean *everything*. That's who we're going for.

When I asked why the English boarding school students only, Diane replied, 'They are the ones who have the purchasing power, or at least their parents do.' Diane and Gopal estimated the market to be about 6,000 young people between the ages of 10 and 21. The publishers had identified an audience of upper middle-class youth who were pioneering the newly opened modern space – the 'teen' years – between child- and adulthood. Their aim was to also move into this 'in between' space of 'teen' ambiguity with a product that would provide youth with answers to questions about what it means to be modern, 'to *be* English'. From the outset they envisioned a magazine that would provide youth with a blueprint for what it means to be a modern 'teen'.

As with their earlier adult-oriented development magazine, *Teens* made money by publishing free advertisements in a magazine format, and distributing this magazine to members who paid substantial fees in return for a membership card which entitled them to discounts at a growing number of local 'member establishments'. Concerning the *Teens* club, Diane explained:

> When we chose our member establishments, we took into account like, what are the facilities that our teen members would like to use. So we said, like, they'll go to teen joints, they'll go for physical fitness, to, say, stationery [greeting card and poster] shops, ice-cream shops, jeans places, all this kind of thing. We just asked which is the best place for these kinds of things.

The first issue of *Teens* included advertisements for twenty-eight local businesses hoping to cater to upper middle-class youth. These included audio cassette shops and video rental stores, beauty parlours and body-building clubs, computer and foreign language training schools, photo studios and sporting goods stores, stationers and bookshops, yoga centres and discos, and a range of snack and fast-food restaurants. Five months later the number of advertising 'member establishments' had risen to forty-six including some new categories such as a driving school, a pharmacy, and a music and acting school that encouraged readers to 'Be A Film Star! Be an accomplished musician!' Each of these establishments offered *Teens* members discounts on a range of products and services for 'teens'.

Because it brings together a host of business ventures all interested in creating and servicing a youth market, *Teens* magazine is an ideal window on to a new commercial 'youth culture'. The youth culture promoted in the advertisements and articles of *Teens* is an 'ideal world' of youth, leisure and goods presented as naturally desirable, and waiting to be consumed, embodied, enacted. Yet perhaps more important than the actual contents of this universe is the way in which the constituent parts interact. From restaurants to driving schools, beauty parlours to fitness clubs, photo studios and tailors to video and cassette shops, *Teens* member establishments form a mutually reinforcing, self-referencing sphere in which leisure, images and public appearances are constantly promoted. Although diverse, the 'parts' of this world share a common logic of public display, or the display of a public, material 'self' through consumption. In its constant references to transnational consumer modernity in the forms of film, video, pop music, stars and fashion, *Teens* participates in a kind of seamless, global, intertextual media assemblage[10] that constructs its own privileged world of reality-in-images. It is on to this transnational public sphere, the media-assembled space of imagination, that local merchants project their dreams of a local 'youth culture'.

Although conceived of as a marketing vehicle, *Teens* magazine offered its readers more than just advertisements. The magazine featured competitions, comic strips, Nepali folk-tales and Greek mythology, short stories, popular science articles, 'believe-it-or-not' stories, puzzles, contests and games. Yet from the first issue on there was another category of article that blurred the line between entertainment and advertisement. These ranged from articles on sports heroes such as Pelé, Diego Maradona, and Gabriela Sabatini ('the glamour doll of tennis') that could be seen as promoting certain mediated spectator sports or commoditized sporting activities, to more explicitly consumer-oriented articles. From the first issue, *Teens* carried pages devoted to pop song heroes and heroines (from Debbie Gibson and 'New Kids on the Block' to Jim Morrison and Robert Plant) including bio-data and lyrics to popular songs. Starting with the second issue, the music pages were accompanied by a listing of the 'top ten [English language] albums of the month' provided 'courtesy of' a *Teens* member establishment dealing in imported pop cassettes. Recent English language video releases were also featured from the first issue and by issue 5 the magazine included a 'video top ten' column courtesy of a member video rental store. Although the publishers themselves did not view these music and video features as advertisements, the participation of particular 'member establishments' in the magazine indicates the commercial implications of *Teens*' content.

The same link between information/entertainment and commercial interests also existed on a more programmatic level. One of the most consistent consumer themes in *Teens* magazine had to do with fashion and the promotion of a fashion consciousness. From the first issue, *Teens* featured a regular column entitled 'Kathmandu Goes the Fashion Way' provided courtesy of a local 'fashion wear' boutique. In the first issue readers were informed that 'each individual has a

personality + a style of their own' [sic]. Women are then advised
that 'this summer' certain items of clothing give 'an extra chic look'
including culottes which are 'so very in'. For men, 'the look'
includes baggy trousers but they are warned, 'collars this season are
slightly broader'. In the second issue 'Young Fashion steals the
spotlight' while in the third the writer concludes with the admonish-
ment, 'So youngsters, don't wait for that heady feeling of confidence
which comes from knowing that you're looking great. Go for it!! and
be a real head turner' [sic].

The fashion feature in the fifth issue, entitled 'Clothing – The
Silent Language', told readers:

> Appearance says a great deal about a person before a word is
> spoken. When you look at someone, 80 to 90 percent of what you
> see is the persons [sic] apparel. It is the most important signal that
> attracts or warns people away in an initial contact. Does putting
> this much emphasis on dressing strike you as shallow? . . . Well,
> that's the way of our hep [sic] world. Clothing and grooming
> draws an instant reaction because it demands speedy conclusions.
> 'Eat what you want, but dress up for others' is the motto of the
> modern time.

Furthermore, readers are told to 'deal with the realities of your
face and figure', and 'learn to recognize your short-comings and
learn to minimize them'. After all, 'Fashion can be fun and is not
something to resist'. The article concludes with a reassuring synopsis:

> Consciously dressing to gain positive reaction of others is not a
> dishonest action. It is a way to encourage people to regard you
> with interest. It is an invitation to explore the interesting and
> dynamic person that is behind a well presented visual image.

All of these fashion articles contain a number of underlying
themes. First is the insistent association of reality with materiality:
one's 'face and figure' are 'realities' with 'short-comings' that must
be 'dealt with'; a person *is* what you *see*; *feeling good* is the
equivalent of *looking good*. Significantly, the writers are constantly
aware that their local readers will likely see such equations as
'shallow' or even 'dishonest' but repeatedly soothe reader apprehensions through assurances that such behaviour is 'hep', part of 'the
modern times', unavoidable, and will encourage people to 'regard
you with interest'. All of these fashion articles construct modernity
as a material discourse that privileges the material as real, equates

people with objects, and pleasure/emotion with material conditions. Readers are instructed that this new type of *common sense* is 'not something to resist'.

A second theme is the tension between, on the one hand, messages that fashion is about personal style and is expressive of characteristics unique to the presumably unchanging essence of the individual and, on the other hand, messages describing the constant changes in hem-lines, collars, patterns and other aspects of what it means to be young, confident and 'in'. These simultaneous messages exemplify the conflicting 'dreams of identity' and 'dreams of otherness' that Barthes suggests the 'fashion industry' promotes to encourage the never ending pursuit of a fashioned self (1983: 255–6).

A third theme is 'clothing as language' which follows a line of thought found in Western socio-cultural theory starting as far back as Georg Simmel's 1903 essay 'The metropolis and mental life' (1950). According to Simmel, because the metropolitan 'modern man' lives in an intensely monetized cash-based socio-economic setting, he must constantly fight the tendency by which his personal meaning is reduced to a quantitative, monetary value. This he does by seizing upon the 'qualitative differentiation' offered him in commoditized forms of adornment, dress and bodily disposition. No longer able to enjoy the 'frequent and prolonged association [which] assures the personality of an unambiguous image of himself in the eyes of others', the modern man must 'appear "to the point," to appear concentrated and strikingly characteristic . . . [within the] brief metropolitan contacts' that comprise his daily relations (Simmel 1950: 420–421). The *Teens* article on clothing as language takes a Simmelesque world of alienation as given, and celebrates the 'modern' necessity of 'dressing to gain positive reaction'.

Underlying all of these themes is an ongoing discussion of what it means to be a 'teen'. In *Teens* 'teen' is a natural category, desirable and of unquestioned value. Inside the front cover of the first issue is a cartoon of a young boy lying on his stomach, his head propped up in his hands. Above his pensive visage appears a bubble caption with the words, 'God, when am I going to be a teenager?' Scattered about the cartoon boy, as though appearing in his mind, are a range of images: boys playing tennis and soccer, a guitar player, people laughing, a cartoon cowboy with a gun, stylish girls, mystery gift packages, jet planes and planets, and boys and girls sitting around a canopied table at an outside restaurant. When I asked Diane what they saw as the meaning of these images, she replied:

Oh, on the first page we show that every child who's 10 wants to be a teen. And anyone who's 24 still wants to be called a teen. You know, they don't want to say that they are old already! 21, 22, 23, they still want to be teenagers!

Diane's remarks seem to sum up much of the intended meaning of *Teens* magazine. Its aim is to constitute 'teenage' not so much as an age category, but as a kind of desired condition, a way of life that can be achieved through a range of consumer behaviours. In these pages 'teen' is an identity waiting to be subscribed to (pun intended), embodied, and lived out in a series of commercial transactions. As a marketing vehicle in search of a market, *Teens* helps teens to imagine themselves as 'teens'.[11]

But what about the *Teens* target group, those 6,000 upper middle-class boarding school youth? During my last meeting with Diane and Gopal I found that things were not going as their membership projections had predicted. About six months into their new venture the publishers were coming to the unsettling conclusion that even though membership numbers looked good, they might in fact be missing their target audience. As Gopal explained, it was becoming clear that a sizeable number of readers and subscribers were *not* upper middle-class youth. Rather, these were middle- and even lower middle-class kids: their clothing, photo demeanour, English usage and the schools they attended gave them away as less than the type of reader/member the publishers had hoped for. The intention had been for *Teens* to take root among the upper strata and then spread down. 'But if *Teens* gets associated with these lower groups, we'll never have the upper ones', lamented Gopal.

Although unfortunate for the publishers of *Teens*, the fact that the magazine attracted youth from across the middle class is significant for two reasons. First, it indicates that a wide variety of young people are attracted to the concept of *teen-ness*. The publishers had guessed correctly that youth in this 'in between' space – between child- and adulthood, high and low class, desire and fulfilment – would turn to them for answers to questions about meaning and identity that their ambiguous positions pushed to the fore. Yet they misjudged the extent, how far 'down' into the middle class, these feelings of ambiguity and longing extended.

Second, judging by names on the long lists of game and contest winners published in the magazine, *Teens* readers form a *self-associating group* that could never have been imagined in Nepal even a generation ago. From Brahmans, Chhetris and high-caste Hindu and Buddhist Newars, through a range of mid- and low-level Newar caste members, to a variety of ethnic communities including Tibetans, Sherpas, Rais and Gurungs, and (not insignificantly) a smattering of Euro-American expatriates, *Teens* readers are young people brought together by an incredibly complex, thoroughly modern set of factors. A concatenation of local, national and transnational emerging realities, ranging from Nepal's new place in global commodity markets (as consumer/importers as well as produ-cers of cash commodities such as handmade carpets); transnational mercenary labour; global mass tourism; mass poverty and inter-national development aid; and the rise of a centralized state apparatus in Kathmandu: all of these factors have led to the contemporary urban experience of emerging class formations and new cultural logics.

It is this turbulent mix of people and forces from across Nepal and around the world that a product such as *Teens* seeks to refractionate. In *Teens* we see an effort by dozens of local businesses to channel this social torrent into the profit-generating streams of consumer identities.[12] *Teens* unites youth from the new middle class in the common experience of a consumer public (cf. Caughey 1984; Custen 1987), but also offers them a new *language*: in the words of the *Teens* fashion article, a 'silent language' of images, consumer goods and services. Regardless of whether young people wish, or are able, to *use* the new language of commodities, they learn to *understand* it and its logic.[13] It is a language that constructs consumer identities for youth, even if for many young people this new identity is only a space of longing, a sense of deprivation or an unfulfilable 'dream of otherness'.

'Teenagers' in Kathmandu

One remark that I heard early on in my research period struck me as significant, and often returned to my mind as I spent more time with young people in Kathmandu. In the course of a conversation, a Brahman small businessman in his early fifties described, often with exasperation, his experiences as the father of three sons, two of whom were still in their teens. He spoke of how so often these days children will pressure their parents into making a wide variety of purchases. Wanting to probe his sense of how things had changed, I asked, 'Is this something different from thirty years ago?' 'Oh yes!' he replied:

> In those days children were not that much provocative. They could not expect much even from their parents. I mean that then their interests were very much limited. They didn't know about so many things, and even if they did, they had no influence over their parents.

When I asked, 'What has changed?' he went on to explain:

> Twenty or thirty years ago there was no idea of this middle group, these teenagers. I mean then they went from being boys to being adults. In between there was not this type of stage.[14]

With time, I realized that this man's use of the word 'teenager' to denote a new 'in between stage' was significant. For him some 'in between' experience was probably not totally unfamiliar, but the nature of that experience had changed and it was to some new type of 'middle group' that he attached the word 'teenage'.

I found that, like this man, many other Kathmandu residents used the English word 'teenager' (whether speaking in English or Nepali) to designate a new category of youth. What people meant by 'teen' or 'teenager' was not entirely consistent but uniformly the words were used to distinguish one type or group of youth from other young people, not youth as a category from other age groups. Also, 'teenagers' were always *modern consumers*: of drugs and pornography for some, and as a welcome business clientele for others. It is these mixed, often intensely negative meanings associated with the word 'teen' that stand in such sharp contrast to meanings promoted in commercial media.

'Teens' as consumers

To my surprise, few of the scores of young men who my co-workers and I interviewed used the English word 'teenager' to describe themselves. More typically they used the Nepali terms 'boy' [*keTA*][15] or the more inclusive 'boys and girls' [*keTAkeTIharu*]. However, one of the more interesting uses of 'teenager' by a young man to describe himself came from an 18-year-old Sherpa student, a long time resident of Kathmandu. In an interview conducted by a co-worker, this young man explained why he liked Hindi 'love story' films the best:

> Listen, our age is *teenage*,[16] isn't that right? In this age we're

usually interested in doing *love* [*love* *garne*]. These are the
things, no? Like, *how to love*, what to do, how can we do *love*
at first, how to get girls, and all of these angles. These things you
must be able to do yourself so that's why I usually like to watch
the *love stories*.

This young man's remarks seem to capture much of the ambiguity,
tenuousness and anxiety that many middle-class youth feel in
negotiating new identities. His comments about what it means to be
'teenage' seemed to be as much a series of questions as confident
assertions. While his tastes in film and interest in 'doing *love*'
were extremely common among middle-class young people in
Kathmandu, few so explicitly identified mass media as a source of
tutorial guidance in the meaning and behaviours of *teen-ness*.

Others in Kathmandu also saw a relationship between the concept
of 'teenager' and particular media. This came through with ex-
ceptional clarity in a series of interviews I conducted with retail
merchants in Kathmandu who specialized in the sale of cassette
audio tapes. With surprising consistency the middle-aged proprietors
of these cassette shops associated 'teenagers' with tastes in imported,
Western 'English' music. Typical were the comments of one merchant whose shop was located on a back street near the Chetrapati
section of Kathmandu. Here the proprietor, a Newar man in his late
thirties, explained to me why Hindi cassettes were his biggest sellers:

Here Hindi films have had a really big impact. In the cinemas, from
the *videos*, a really big influence. Therefore, those films that are
showing in the theatres, or on *video*, people come here immediately to buy the music *cassettes*.

He explained that most of his customers were high school students
or recent graduates from a range of caste, ethnic and class backgrounds. Hence I was surprised at his answer when I asked who
bought the Western pop music cassettes that accounted for perhaps
a third of his stock:

It's the *teenagers*. They go for the *rock, heavy metal*, and now
rap music is picking up in popularity. We have some of that here
too. I mean some of them also like the modern Nepali songs,
but these modern *teenagers* have been mostly influenced by
Western music and they don't go for the [Nepali] folk songs.
Here the *teenagers* only really go for the *latest* songs. Those
songs are really for the *teenagers*.

The point is that for this man the word '*teenager*' was less a word that distinguished one age group from another, than one consumer group from another. For him, '*teenagers*' were those who bought not just '*Western*' music, but the '*latest*' imported pop songs. They were the ones who were always asking for what was new.

'Teen' addiction: critique of consumer modernity

To my surprise, the words 'teen' and 'teenager', when used by adult men and women and even several teenage girls, were almost always used to describe young unmarried males who were considered unruly or corrupt. For example, after describing how young people these days are often intractable, one young woman (an 18-year-old Chhetri born and raised in Kathmandu) went on to explain:

> Usually I've found that kids [keTAkeTIharu] are good but some people have very bad behaviour, like when they become *teenagers*. These days in Nepal people are using a lot of *smack*.[17] They don't listen to their parents. All they do is hang out with friends and if they don't get what they want, they just argue. Mostly it's the boys who do this.

For this young woman, most kids are good but some become 'teenagers'. For her, 'teenagers' are disobedient, likely to take drugs, and usually boys.

Even more than drugs, the subject that most often elicited use of the English word '*teenager*' as opposed to assorted Nepali words for youth was that of 'blue' (pornographic) film viewing. Typical were the comments of one 35-year-old Magar woman, born in India of Nepali parents and now the owner of her own small business in Kathmandu:

> *Have you ever seen a *blue* film?*
> No, [my husband and I] never watched that kind of film. I guess our thought on that matter is like the old people's thought. We don't like it. I think those that do a lot of *sex*, those who want a lot of entertainment [manoranjan], those who want a *free* life, they watch this kind of film. Like the young, unmarried boys, they watch.

> *Why do people want to watch this?*
> It's especially the *teenagers* who watch these. Because they haven't gotten any experience with this, so they want to know what it is like! Then if they watch once, they want to watch again, and

again. I mean the boys [keTAharu] who haven't watched aren't so interested [in sex] as those who have watched. It's the *teenagers* who like it.

Aside from expressing her moral indignation, in her last two sentences this woman makes the interesting distinction between 'boys' who do not watch pornographic films, and '*teenagers*' who do.

Finally, another interesting usage of '*teenager*' came in the course of a conversation with an upper-caste Newar woman in her forties, the mother of a 17-year-old son. Speaking of drug use in Kathmandu, she explained:

There are so many drug-addicted people who have spoiled everything, even their whole families. The parents are just crying. Oh, how sad this is! I think it's the *teenagers* usually who use [drugs]. This is the age [umer] for spoiling one's life. It is the unmarried ones who take drugs.

Later, when the subject had shifted to films, and finally 'blue' films, the woman continued on the theme of 'teenagers':

Well, it is said that people watch these films, but I feel disgusted just from hearing about them. I don't know who it is that watches these. Maybe some married people, . . . [pause] but mostly *teenagers*. Yes, I think it is the *teenagers* who don't have any common sense [buddhi]. Like my son, he doesn't watch that stuff. He watches only 'Sunday Pop' [a television programme] in which there are only English songs [pop music videos].

The irony is that this woman could speak of drug-taking, 'blue' film-watching 'teenagers,' and then contrast these undesirable young males with her own 17-year-old son. This comment, and others like it, led me again to the conclusion that the term 'teenage' in colloquial Nepali usage was often less a designation of age and more an indicator of a certain social type. For these men and women (including many teenage women), 'teenager' was a category of antisocial, vulgar and potentially violent young males.

Representation and resistance

In the debate over teen-ness we see the forces of consumer modernity at work in the newly opened 'in between' spaces being pioneered by middle-class youth in Kathmandu; forces which seek to define modernity in material terms and construct identities around commodities. Yet while commercial interests populate this new landscape with beatific images of leisure, pleasure, progress, glamour, and beauty, another perspective in the debate counters with the image of the 'teen' as a drug or pornography addict. This critical take links consumer modernity with the seduction and corruption of youth, *not* some longed-for 'teen' epiphany. In the counter-representation of 'teen'-as-consumer-addict lies an indictment of a commercially sponsored material reductionism that encourages people to imagine themselves as objects and then set out on a never ending, addictive quest to find identity in consumption, to purchase reality and meaning, again and again. The battle for the territory of 'modern youth' is one facet of the experience of modernity in Kathmandu, an experience of engagement, experimentation and critique that is lived at the interface between consumer modernity, state modernism and the realities of everyday life.

PART II: MODERNITY, IDENTITY AND PLACE

I conclude this chapter with the stories of two young men. Both stories relate experiences encountered by thousands of other young people in the city, yet the lives of these two men represent the logical extremes – the ultimate consequences – of forces and trends that other youths experience only in part or in diluted form. These stories illustrate some of the anxieties and aspirations, perspectives and values, opportunities and impediments that constitute the experience of modernity for young people in Kathmandu.

These stories are important in that they offer glimpses of the worlds of imagination that young people construct in order to make sense of their lives in the present. It is within these imaginary worlds that the dual discourses of state and consumer modernity mesh with the particularities of local culture and individual life histories. As both stories illustrate, though these worlds of imagination are cluttered with mediated images and meanings, it is never to the exclusion of an awareness that grows from lives lived in contradiction.

'Out here in Kathmandu': anxiety and peripheral consciousness

I had not seen Ramesh for over a year when I glimpsed him out of the corner of my eye while riding my bike down a crowded, narrow

Kathmandu street one chilly spring morning in 1991. Ramesh looked considerably more gaunt and bedraggled than I remembered him from our earlier acquaintance when he was a regular at a drug-free youth centre set up for recovering addicts. I had heard from others that Ramesh had relapsed into his heroin habit and the jittery but probing look in his eyes when I hailed him made me think twice about the wisdom of re-establishing this relationship.

When we met later that day in the garden of a Thamel restaurant, Ramesh gave me one of what turned out to be many lessons in the nature of street life in Kathmandu. Through his narration, the people and places of Kathmandu, and especially the liminal zone of the Thamel tourist district, took on entirely new meanings. In the next hour-and-a-half, in a restaurant I had visited regularly during time spent in Nepal over the previous five years, Ramesh made suddenly *visible* several drug transactions, undercover police surveillance and harassment, kids drinking codeine cough syrup, and a junkie tottering out of the washroom, his face flushed from retching, unable to keep down any food. I began to perceive an entire dimension of reality transpiring around me that I had never before seen.

At 21, Ramesh was living life close to the edge though seven or eight years earlier no one would have predicted the rough times that lay ahead. Ramesh's parents had moved to Kathmandu from an Eastern hill district when he was in his early teens. He had attended a respected English medium high school in the valley and learned to speak competent, colloquial English. He had first tried heroin as a high school student but over the course of a few years, during which his mother died and his father married a woman with several sons, Ramesh developed a habit which grew out of control. Through a combination of mistrust between him and family members, a slow-burning resentment over his father's remarriage, and an increasingly disruptive heroin addiction, Ramesh began to spend more and more time living with friends and eventually, on the streets. The previous year, having gone through a detoxification programme, his good English had landed him a coveted (though typically low-paying) sales job in a retail shop catering to tourists. He swore to me that he had stayed clean and would still be working had not someone told the manager that he was a former junkie. (Others claimed that he had been caught trying to sell drugs to tourists.) By early 1991 he had been in and out of drug rehabilitation seven times and had little more than the clothes on his back and a few rupees in his pocket. He lived by his wits day to day, hustling tourists, taking profits on petty commodity transactions and running a variety of scams such as sewing foreign labels into locally produced garments.

Sitting in the restaurant that afternoon over tea and Danish pastries, Ramesh meandered through stories from his past, sometimes with fists clenched in anger, sometimes close to tears. Ramesh was the *one-in-ten*, a living example of what could go wrong, a reference point that both peers and parents looked to in horror, recognizing so much of themselves or their sons in Ramesh's life. I found that Ramesh's attitudes and opinions rarely differed in *content* from those of his middle-class peers, only in intensity. A member of a middle-class family, the product of an English medium high school, a heavy consumer of Hindi and English mass media from videos to detective novels, Ramesh had much more in common with his peers than many were willing to acknowledge.

Like many others, Ramesh was acutely, painfully aware of his life as a Nepali, a life that he compared to lives lived in distant power centres. Ramesh constantly evaluated his Nepaliness through his awareness of life in the West and Far East, even though he himself had never travelled further than North India. Perhaps because of me, he repeatedly brought up images of 'America' compared to which he found his own life one of extreme deprivation:

> Out here young people like me, we want a *fast* life, not this slow life.

What do you mean a 'fast' life?
I mean like in the States where you can stay out all night until you drop. Here there's nothing, no [late-night] bars, and we can't even go anywhere to play video games.

When I asked how he knew about American bars and video games he explained that he had learned all about these things from films and novels.

Indeed, Ramesh was a special connoisseur of films, books, magazine articles – anything he could find – having to do with America, and particularly New York City. He knew all the city's boroughs and landmarks but he was especially intrigued by 'the Bronx', a place he brought up again and again in our conversations. From dozens of tough-guy films and gangster or mafia novels, Ramesh had constructed a detailed image of a New York City street culture full of drugs, thugs and gangs. He frequently compared Kathmandu's street life with that of New York, as when he explained how Kathmandu street gangs take 'tabs' (specific combinations of prescription drug tablets) before going to a fight, 'just like in the Bronx'. Ramesh could quote lines from Mafioso novels and he frequently spoke of how one's face should never show feeling, a lesson he learned from *The Godfather*. Ramesh's ultimate goal was to move to 'the States' and live in New York City. He often spoke in vague terms of a cousin living in Seattle who might help him get there.

Ironically, it seemed sometimes as though Ramesh already lived in New York. 'The Bronx' in particular seemed to be a kind of shadow universe where his mind roamed while his body navigated the streets of Kathmandu. 'The Bronx' – with its street-smarts and anti-heroic codes of valour – was often the standard of reality against which he measured his own existence. For Ramesh, 'the Bronx' seemed to offer a way of understanding his own life, a life that he hated, yet which he could link with a way of existence at the modern metropole. Ramesh's vision of 'the Bronx' allowed him to identify his own existence as at least some version of modernity, even if it lacked the late night bars, video games and a host of other modern accoutrements that he had never seen in more than two dimensions.

The mediated images in Ramesh's imagination also had important implications for his perception of place. Like many other young adults I met in Kathmandu, when speaking in English Ramesh constantly referred to the place where he had spent most of his life as 'out here'. 'Out here in Kathmandu' prefaced so many of his comments that in the course of time the words barely registered in my mind. This persistent self-peripheralization is almost unimaginable outside the context of global media and a host of other marginalizing transnational cultural forces including tourism and commodity imports. Mass media (but also tourists and foreign goods) are like windows on to modern places that are distant in both time and space.[18] But if the video screen is like a window, it is one with bars that keep viewers like Ramesh outside, 'out here' looking in. The same effect is reproduced in the windows of tour buses and tourist hotels. Young people gaze into these hermetically-sealed wonder boxes to glimpse the modern future, like animals receiving a lesson in evolution and power in some cultural 'wildlife safari park'.

But media and tourism only work in conjunction with the Nepali state and its ideology of progress (*bikas*) and modernization. By assuming the role of recipient and dependent in the global development aid economy the Nepali state also languishes in this 'out here', self-peripheralizing mentality in which modernity is essentially a foreign commodity. Hence in schools and in the government-run media young people are frequently reminded of Nepal's status as a 'Least Developed Country'. Relative poverty and backwardness are among the primary components of a Nepali identity, or a sense of *Nepaliness*, for young people in Kathmandu. By almost all the standards that their education teaches them to value, whether via formal school education, or through consumption of commercial mass media, Nepali conditions are deemed inferior in an evolutionary sense. The rhetoric of backwardness, development, foreign aid and education collapses time and space such that Nepali youth learn to situate themselves on the margins of a meaningful universe as consumers of an externally generated material modernity (cf. Fabian 1983).

This sensibility struck me like a brick in one of Ramesh's comments. Having described his education, problems and knowledge of life abroad (via foreign media), Ramesh slouched in his chair, looked skyward and sighed:

> You know, now I know sooooo much. [pause] Being a frog in a pond isn't a bad life, but being a frog in an ocean is like hell. Look at this. Out here in Kathmandu there is nothing. We have nothing. We even have to stand in line for kerosene.

Ramesh's perspective is only the logical extreme of a vision shared by thousands of other middle-class Nepali young people. A combination of personal misfortune and susceptibility to substance addiction led Ramesh to an uncommon level of despair and marginalization, but many others were also caught in this wasteland between two worlds: the lived experience of 'out here', and the dream of modernity. As a Nepali psychologist who had spent years working with young people in Kathmandu put it, the biggest contradiction that young people face is 'the incongruence between their expectations and their real life'.

As I have suggested above, this is a systemic incongruence borne of modernism and dependence as a state rhetoric, education, commercial interests, global mass media, tourism and the fantastic interconnections of all of these factors. These interests and processes converge to provide an 'education' for young people that is *alienating* to the extent that it instills a self-peripheralizing consciousness. Yet Ramesh's *ocean of alienation* is not simply an enormous mass of knowledge. It is a particular kind of knowledge that explodes his frames of reference, and successfully marginalizes his own lived experience in a discourse of modernization and desire. Much of this knowledge/education comes from interactions with mass media. Like Ramesh, many youth use media to make sense of their own lives, and to imagine what Arjun Appadurai calls other 'possible lives'. Appadurai emphasizes how mass media and other trans-national cultural processes 'deterritorialize' local experience by multiplying the 'imaginative resources' that people use to make sense of their lives (1991:196). Yet while forces such as mass media now guarantee that local experience almost anywhere will be permeated by transnational cultural processes, we should recognize that this same cultural 'deterritorialization' has a very real 'terri-torializing' effect on the minds of people like Ramesh. The rhetoric of modernization, progress and development wafts into the image worlds of media to give people like Ramesh an acute sense of marginality.

'This nowhere place': life in the consumer present

Youth, peers, and fear of the future

I first met Suman one late summer evening in 1991 in a Thamel bar where I had gone to meet a European friend. It was only after my friend left, as I sat writing out some ideas in a notebook, that the young Nepali man who had been sitting next to me for the past hour introduced himself. Suman was a 22-year-old Brahman who had lived in the city since boyhood when his father had moved from central Nepal to Kathmandu to set up a business with a group of relatives. At the time when his father took a second wife, Suman and his mother established a separate residence. Here they led a precar-ious middle-class existence, combining resources from his father, his mother's low-paying office job, and, since Suman had finished high school, his own low-paying job at a relative's Kathmandu travel agency.

Suman was one of the few young people I met for whom experiences of misfortune and anxiety had led to introspection and a growing sense of critical self-awareness. More than anything else, Suman helped me gain some understanding of what the past, present and future meant for middle-class youth like himself. Suman repre-sented an extreme version of sentiments that I often encountered when young people spoke about the future. Especially for these 'first

generation modern' youth – those who were the first in their extended
families to have grown up in a cosmopolitan setting with sustained
formal education and a variety of other powerful extra-familial
socializing influences – the future was often an uncharted void. In
school and at home young people learn that they are responsible for
their own modern future. Yet for most youth, not only are there
extremely few 'modern' role models, those examples of 'successful'
adults around them are often repugnant, as for Suman.

Like so many others I met, Suman found himself in a position
where the past (as embodied in his father, relatives and their village
background), if not actively devalued in the state rhetoric of
progress, was simply irrelevant to his efforts to imagine and
implement his own future. Without a valued past and carrying a
concept of the future as something, like modernity, that arrives pre-
assembled from foreign places, Suman was left in an extremely
nebulous and vulnerable position. On several occasions he told me,
'I don't have any place to stand. I don't know where I stand. I'm in
this nowhere place.' What he lacked was a sense of continuity, a
sense of 'place' in a meaningful sequence from past to future.

Suman had spent his early childhood in a hill village, his teen years
in a Kathmandu English language boarding school, and the last five
years in almost daily contact with foreigners. Once he had actually
accompanied foreign tourists to his natal village, an experience that
was the cause for some painful soul-searching. Suman had been
unprepared for the experience of viewing his 'past' – embodied in
relatives who could just as easily have been himself – through the
eyes of foreign tourists. For Suman, like many thousands of other
Kathmandu residents who grew up on the 'village-side', one's natal
village and rustic cousins are unsettling reminders of a personal past
that the state devalues, consumer modernity negates, and foreign
tourists consume as an exotic commodity. Wedged in this spatio-
temporal in between space – between the future as distant foreign
commodity, and the past as commodity for distant foreigners – it is
not surprising that young urban Nepalis have trouble identifying a
place for identity, or in Suman's words, a 'place to stand'.

For many middle-class young people the only place left to stand
is with peers on the shifting grounds of day-to-day existence, the
'nowhere place' of the present. Youth are in a position where they
are terrified at the prospect of being left behind in the poverty and
backwardness of the past, and terrified by the seeming impossibility
of a modern future that society expects them to construct. It is for

these people that peer groups become extraordinarily important. Young males especially turn to these groups, with sometimes almost desperate attachment.[19] Yet more often than not these groups permit members to evade their individual futures by allowing them to focus their attentions, as a group, on the present. Peer groups allow young people to abandon themselves in the utter banality of a day-to-day material existence, consciously avoiding the future by living for each other in the present.

Suman was one of the few young people I met who had reflected on the experience of peer dependence. He described how over the course of his high school years, and continuing after graduation, he had become extraordinarily dependent on a circle of friends, and only recently realized how for years he had lived in terror of losing these affiliations. Self and group had become so intermeshed that even the thought of jeopardizing these relationships had been tantamount to threatening the only valued sense of social identity that he had. He told of how he had once been willing to do almost anything to please his friends, avoid their disapproval, and often conform to the wishes of others, even when they went against his own sense of propriety. For Suman and others, group identity revolved mostly around conformity to group-dictated standards of taste in dress and other consumer goods like food and music, to one nearly disastrous brush with heroin addiction. Yet the price of falling away is being left behind, Suman explained, which makes people cling even tighter to their peer circles.

Living in the present, with insecure senses of identity based on peer affiliation, I believe that young people are often extremely susceptible to commercial interests clambering to provide youth with commoditized means of imagining themselves as members of groups.[20] Like *Teens* magazine and its host of commercial backers, businesses are only too eager to fill the space of the present with the trappings of a material modernity. Often desperate to claim modern identities, middle-class youth themselves appropriate these commercial offerings; with 'fashions', haircuts, fitness programmes, and modern foods, young people can become modern to the extent that they can purchase their own modern bodies. But like the ice-cream advertised in magazines and sold on Kathmandu street corners, apparently solid commodities soon melt away in the anxious heat of the present, leaving young people to again confront their own futures. Life in the consumer present is like an addiction: as Suman found in trying to break away from his peer dependence, an identity built on consumer goods is one that needs to be purchased again and again. Yet this is the price middle-class youth pay to distance themselves from the past and forestall a future that seems to preclude them.

Youth, agency, and 'youth culture'

For youth in Kathmandu, life in the present is the experience of modernity. It is a life in the 'in between' space: between expectations and reality; between past and future; between village and an external, modern metropole; between child- and adulthood; between high and low class; between education and meaningful employment. The experiences of youth like Ramesh and Suman are strongly inflected by the marginalizing and mediated forces of modernity, though their lives are far from the sublime images of youth offered in the pages of *Teens*. Media and education stake claims in their imaginations, though the possible futures they offer rarely seem to fit the realities of Nepal. Kathmandu's high school and college campuses produce graduates far in excess of the already bloated service and business sector's ability to provide meaningful employment. Even if a young person is employed, wages barely pay for minimal subsistence, not to mention the consumer life-styles they imagine. While the children of the elite typically expect *their* modern futures to be in *foreign places*, middle-class youth are left to reconcile the foreign images of a modern future with the realities of Nepal.

What then *is* 'youth culture' in a place like Kathmandu – where to a considerable extent 'youth' as a distinctive phase between child- and adulthood did not really exist in most social sectors a generation or two ago? Is all youth activity now *de facto* 'youth culture' or are some aspects of young people's lives better seen as part of cultural traditions in which they are expected to assume adult roles? Without suggesting that young people (or anyone else) move between autonomous spheres of existence – that the values and rationales from one set of experiences do not spill over into, inform or frame other experiences – I would contend that the cultural spaces encountered by young people in Kathmandu are not homologous. From school to shopping arcade, to cinema, to temple, to market place, to home, young people move between cultural spaces which, although their boundaries are not always clear,[21] enclose certain expectations, certain valued ways of being, certain 'epistemological styles' (Appadurai 1990b:207) that are sometimes conflicting and contradictory. While the co-existence of these modes in the local cultural economy is not necessarily new, what *is* new is the relative power of the epistemological style that I have associated with the forces of modernity. Thus what might be most meaningfully called 'youth culture' in Kathmandu is the public cultural practice that emerges from this modern mode of being.

To the extent that young people in Kathmandu find themselves in a new 'in between' domain of 'youth' that opens up at the intersection of new patterns of education, labour, and class formation, it is clear that these youth are themselves actively engaged in constructing this new cultural space, marking it off as their own, and imagining themselves as its inhabitants. From the young men who appropriate certain items of 'ethnic Nepali' clothing (produced for the tourist trade) as part of their own uniforms as modern youth (Hepburn 1993), to the local rock band whose members recorded an all-original Nepali language album in the style of the Beatles, examples abound of new forms of youth expression that are clearly local, 'youthful' and modern. So too is the life-style of young middle-class men hanging out on street corners or in tea-shops, exchanging gossip and small talk, slinging jibes at girls passing by, and forming hierarchies within and between groups[22] in processes that occasionally erupt into '*gang fights*' where local 'heroes' try out their martial arts skills, or even weapons. It is in these groups where local youth fashions are negotiated, whether in clothing, music, hairstyles, videos or slang. Within and between these peer groups, styles and behaviours take on meanings that are locally determined, even if they are often deployed in commercially mediated images, ideas, practices and other consumer goods. Young people as groups of peers assemble the components of a youth identity with which they seek to mark off the new cultural space in which modernity has deposited them.

Thus 'youth culture' in Kathmandu is that distinctive public practice through which young people mobilize resources that give shape to the space of 'youth' that they are forced to pioneer. Because this new cultural space has few roles (aside from 'student') to anchor it into social practice, it tends to be a highly expressive culture, one in which distinction is unusually dependent on images and image-bearing goods and services. As I have tried to show in this chapter, 'youth culture' is a contested space: a variety of forces – from the state through education, to commercial interests like *Teens* and its 'member establishments,' to society-at-large where critical voices emerge – compete to 'assist' young people in their project of imagining themselves as 'modern youth'.

The agency of young people in constructing 'youth culture' has to be seen in this light. Choices exist for youth, but they are not unlimited choices.[23] To return to a spatial metaphor, if 'youth' is a newly opened space, there are many interests with vast resources scrambling to develop that space. Commercial and state 'developers' invest heavily in lavish new structures of imagination for 'youth', constructing sparkling mansions and then offering for a price the 'furnishings' or goods needed to inhabit and enjoy these spaces. For many middle-class young people[24] choices often occur within these 'ready-made' structures of imagination, for few have the resources, confidence and cultural authority to construct their own alternative, non-mediated visions of valued, modern and Nepali selves. In the rush to claim the newly opened space of 'youth culture', young people are key actors but their agency can never be unravelled from the actions of other interests also seeking to colonize the space of 'modern youth'.

CONCLUSION: YOUTH, CLASS AND MODERNITY

As Kathmandu's middle class situates itself in the global political economy at the terminus of the 'development aid' pipeline it simultaneously secures itself a local position of class dominance (based on its control of local resources), *and* locks itself into a position of dependence and marginality *vis-à-vis* an external cultural metropole. Herein lies the irony of 'affluence' in the 'developing world': the paradox of the experience of modernity in a place like Kathmandu. The new middle class builds a position of *local* power by entering into the ultimately dependent discourses of state modernism (progress and development) and commercial modernity.

These discourses are a kind of 'mode of representation', a system of meaning production that constructs a valued, privileged and powerful domain of material or commoditizable forms (ranging from education to electricity to film heroes) with which the middle class experiments as it imagines itself as a new social entity, and distinguishes itself as a class. The middle class can also invest in the new 'means of representation', especially mass media, which serve as effective vehicles for promoting a class-privileging ideology of material reality and consumer subjectivity. By adopting this mode and means of representation, local interests can produce local 'authentic' forms of *consumer modernity* as well as tap into transnational forms. From the 'teen' magazines and interactive radio shows of Kathmandu, to the electronics factories of Japan or Taiwan, to the pirate cassette mills of Singapore or Bangkok, to the film studios of Bombay or Hollywood, the 'modern' mode of representation links the industry of consumer modernity as it functions at all levels by joining political economies, from local to global, in symbiotic relationships.

In Kathmandu, as elsewhere, to experience modernity is to encounter this modern metropole and its space of imagination. The experience of modernity lies in the meeting of one's own imagination with the explosion of 'imaginative resources' (Appadurai 1991: 196) that are offered *for a price* in the market place. This is where the structural realities of power and control of resources come into play. The experience of modernity is to engage both the space of imagination, with its commoditized logic, and the realities of power. Almost by definition, middle-class youth in Kathmandu are those who have invested in these new 'imaginative resources', those who have embraced the discourse of modernism, those who envision/ imagine themselves in the image mirror of a mass-mediated consumer modernity. For middle-class youth like Ramesh and Suman, the experience of modernity is in the ever growing gap between imagination and reality, becoming and being.

My point is that to experience modernity is to engage in some way – even if only in reaction or as a sense of longing – the cultural economy of the transnational public sphere. At least since the nineteenth century, when 'to modernize' became synonymous with 'to improve', and 'progress' became a linear law of history (Williams 1985), and especially since the rise of mass commodity production (including images) in this century, modernity has never been more than an imagined condition, a longing, an aching desire. Thus from Kansas City to Kathmandu, the experience of modernity is always the same, yet always different. It shares a longing and restlessness for change and a dream of becoming, but those dreams and longings are as numerous as the minds that engage them. Like subjectivity itself, these dreams always occur where local and personal histories intersect with lived realities of cultural and economic processes of increasingly global dimensions. Thus the experience of modernity is not a derivative experience; it is never simply a reliving of someone else's life, or the enactment of some commoditized script. Rather, it grows out of the particularities of person and place, culture and history, as these converge with larger, ultimately global, political and cultural economies.

Suman's dream

One of the most powerful memories I have of Suman concerns the story he told me of his feelings upon watching the American film *One Flew Over the Cuckoo's Nest*. Suman regularly went to friends' homes to watch Hindi video films but also made a point of seeing Western films both for entertainment and to improve his English. Yet, according to Suman, before he had watched *One Flew . . .* several nights earlier, no other film had ever affected him in the same way.

> After seeing it at my friend's house I just wanted to go out and scream. I wanted to start hitting someone. It was all I could do to keep from hitting my friend.

Trying to imagine why he would have reacted this way, I asked if he meant that he empathized with the main character, perhaps feeling like a sane person surrounded by lunatics. At this he gave me a puzzled look and replied that this was not really what he meant. He seemed to have trouble articulating his feelings about the film but said that he had mainly been shocked, even terrified, to think that something like this could happen in 'America'.

While trying to explain his feelings and reactions, Suman brought up the dream he had dreamed that night after watching *One Flew. . .*:

> In the dream I was a street vendor sitting by the side of the road selling some small things, when a big three-wheeler[25] completely full with people came by and covered me with dirty water from a big puddle by the road.

> The next thing I remember was seeing someone – he was a friend of mine – riding on a bicycle, peddling as fast as he could, trying to go away from something. Then the three-wheeler that was already full went after him and with a big mechanical arm grabbed him by the head and pulled him inside.

Although I am not one to say that dreams have intrinsic meaning, I believe that dreamers can assign them meaning. In this case both Suman's remembering of this dream and his conscious association of it with the film, make it an experience worth exploring.

Youth in Kathmandu often view Western films as tales of modernity – a modernity that is virtually always depicted as an *object* of desire. What was so shocking to Suman about *One Flew* . . . was that here was a picture of modernity's dark side, a picture he had perhaps never before seen in a Western film. But what made the picture of modernity in *One Flew* . . . doubly terrifying was that, probably for the first time in his experience, this horrifying image matched a vision of modernity he himself had already intuited in his experience as a Nepali youth. The powerlessness of the mental patient 'hero' in *One Flew* . . . and his ultimate domestication and total subjugation to the irresistible will of the 'modern' institution, seemed to resonate *powerfully* with a dark premonition that Suman harboured of his own Nepali future. The vivid dream images of the three-wheeler hurtling like a juggernaut, drenching in filth a petty street merchant crouched by the roadside selling trinkets, and finally pursuing a young man on a bicycle only to grab him by the head and stuff him into its maw – all are authentically Nepali images that Suman self-consciously linked with the film.

Suman seemed to equate the dreamed three-wheeler with the filmed mental hospital. Both were images of modernity gone wrong, technologies that turned on their makers. Perhaps not insignificantly, Suman's three-wheeler seemed to distinguish, or even produce, two kinds of people: the petty vendor of baubles left behind, defiled and sputtering in its toxic wake; and the young man, fleeing but eventually forcefully co-opted on to its course. In a sense, these two fates are the 'options' that a 'modernization' paradigm seems to offer the new Nepali middle class: either to be left behind wallowing in the noxious effluent of 'progress', or to be appropriated by some inhuman, mechanistic monster of modernity.

In many ways this dream vision encapsulates both the terrors that lie at the heart of the experience of modernity for young people (where life confronts the material ideologies of modernism) and a powerful critique of consumer capitalism as it exists on the Third World periphery. The challenge for people like Suman is to envision alternative modernities, to construct (and enact) futures that are not already appropriated by the state or the forces of consumer modernity. They must acquire the 'imaginative resources' to erect an alternative modernity that transcends, or diverges from, the unilinear path of 'modernization' *projected* on to the future by global structures of transnational state modernism/dependence, and commodity markets. I stress the verb 'project' to emphasize the fact that images, as representations of and for life, are 'real' only to the extent that they can successfully compel. In this chapter I have explored some of the factors in the lives of young people that make these images compelling, but I have also suggested that their influence is never total.

NOTES

1 Due to lack of space I am able only to hint at the complex socio-cultural and political dynamics of nineteenth- and early twentieth-century Nepali history. As I show elsewhere (Liechty, 1994), pre-1951 Kathmandu was not some pristine functionalist dreamland, yet only after the fall of the Ranas in 1951 did the *rate* and *intensity* of change increase dramatically as the city began to overcome the effects of geography and centuries of extreme isolationist rule.

2 This research was conducted during sixteen months between 1988 and 1991 with the help of the Departments of Anthropology and South Asia Regional Studies of the University of Pennsylvania, and a Fulbright-Hays Doctoral Dissertation Award. Special thanks go to Som Raj Ghimire, Krishna and Ganu Pradhan, Ang Tshering Sherpa and Surendra Bajracharya.

3 In such a model of multiple identities, the 'self' is an inner dialogue between one or many identities (and their associated interests) on the one hand, and the individual's immediate context on the other. Such a model emphasizes the shifting nature of self, the possibility (even likelihood) of contradictory outlooks, and the link between self-expression and context.

4 For a more detailed discussion of 'identity', see Liechty (1994).

5 Space permits only a few pertinent statistics. Well into the twentieth century agriculture and craft production were the dominant occupational categories in Kathmandu, yet by the 1980s as much as two-thirds of the urban labour force was engaged in wage-based service and professional activities (Shrestha *et al.* 1986: 89–95; Sharma 1989: 89–93). Between 1971 and 1985 over one-third of Kathmandu's (mostly middle-class) residents moved from the densely packed urban core of the old city to the concrete homes and walled compounds of the suburbs (Shrestha *et al.* 1986:132). Between 1951 and 1980 the number of secondary schools in Kathmandu *alone* rose from a tiny handful to forty-eight and by 1990 that number again tripled to almost 150 (in addition to almost 700 primary and lower secondary schools (Central Bureau of Statistics 1991: 268–282)). Between 1951 and 1990 Nepal received an estimated Re 85 billion (c. US\$ 2 billion) in grants and loans from foreign governments and international banks (Tiwari 1992:8), most of which went through the 'essentially extractive' structures of Nepali governmental and non-governmental organizations (Rana 1992: 7; Aryal 1992).

6 While recognizing *caste* as a key feature of social identity, one must acknowledge the growing saliency of *class* in the daily lives of Kathmandu residents. In settings such as schools, offices, suburban

residential areas, factories, and even public spaces like buses, cinemas and parks, relationships between people are now often more meaningfully construed in terms of *class* than *caste*. As Anup Pahari argued in a recent critical essay, 'The dominant social group in Nepal is increasingly . . . not a *caste*, but a *class*' (1992: 54).

7 A sizeable body of literature now exists that examines the new relations of dependence that accompany the post-Second World War transnational 'development aid' industry (e.g. Escobar 1988; 1991; Mishra and Sharma 1983; Marglin 1990).

8 I do not wish to imply that a small number of Nepalis have not for centuries constructed personal identities in contrast to (or even in imitation of) external, 'foreign', if not 'national' others. For example, Prithvi Narayan Shah, the 'Father of Nepal', clearly developed his notion of *Nepaliness* in reaction to moral and political developments on the subcontinent in the eighteenth century (Stiller 1968). On the other hand, the Ranas of the late nineteenth- and early twentieth-century constructed their identities as a national elite through a policy of foreign cultural emulation and sumptuary laws.

9 As Campbell puts it, within the realm of capitalist commodity consumerism, 'each purchase leads to literal disillusionment' (1987: 90). In more Marxist terms Haug argues that capitalist commodity production 'does not set as its aim the production of certain use-values' but rather the 'sensuous appearance', or 'semblance' of use-value (1987: 106).

10 My interest in the notion of a 'media assemblage' was sparked, in part, by Ulf Hannerz's call for the study of the 'assemblage of media' in contemporary complex cultural contexts (1986: 367). For a fuller discussion of this concept, see Liechty, forthcoming.

11 By dwelling at some length on *Teens*, I do not mean to suggest that this magazine is somehow single-handedly creating a group of youthful middle-class consumers. There are also a host of other commercial interests at work in Kathmandu hoping to produce (and reproduce) 'teens' as a specific consumer 'public' (see Liechty, 1994).

12 *Teens* readers resemble the *remaja*, or Indonesian 'teenage' readers of a popular youth-directed fan/fashion magazine called *Topchords* described by James Siegel (1986, Chapter 8). Siegel shows how print media can set into motion new 'circuits of exchange' between 'stars' and audiences and how commercial forces can capitalize on these new relations by defining the terms of exchange in an idiom of taste, fashion and consumer goods.

13 As Conrad Kottak argues, mass media 'may not tell us what to think, [but they are] very successful in telling us what to think about' (1990: 10).

14 These changes seem to parallel historical shifts in North America documented by Joseph Kett (1977). Kett notes that until the middle of the nineteenth century Americans noted no intermediate 'adolescent' phase between child- and adulthood. Children entered the work force at age 7, with 'full' incorporation for a male at around puberty (Kett 1977: 17).

15 I follow the Nepali romanization scheme used in Pradhan and Terrell (1990).

16 English words and phrases appearing between asterisks designate English words used by people while speaking in Nepali.
17 '*Smack*' in Kathmandu is brown heroin.
18 Jean Baudrillard captures some of this distancing effect in a discussion of the relationship between television and 'habitat'. In his characteristically overblown and totalizing voice, Baudrillard proclaims:

It is well known how the simple presence of the television changes the rest of the habitat into a kind of archaic envelope, a vestige of human relations whose very survival remains perplexing. . . . [A]ll that used to fill the scene of our lives [television] relegates to total uselessness, desuetude and almost obscenity.

(1983: 129)

19 One Nepali psychologist speculated that 'Westernization' in Kathmandu had done less to promote 'modern individualism' among youth than to begin a shift in their senses of primary orientation away from family groups and towards peer groups.
20 Most accounts of modern mass consumption overstate the necessity for some process of fundamental individuation that is said to accompany the rise of mass consumerism (e.g. Friedman 1989:127). In Nepal and the 'modern' West, identities based on consumer goods never *totally* replace socially derived identities. Furthermore, as Douglas and Isherwood argue, consumption is at least as much a matter of 'reciprocity' within social groups as about individuation (1979:110).
21 For example, the religious themes so common in South Asian popular films blur the boundaries between cinema and temple, and television's place in domestic space blurs the boundary between shopping arcade and home.
22 Clearly 'youth culture' in a place like Kathmandu is an area of cultural practice that is about much more than age. It is also a space where young people contest what it means to be bearers of certain class and gender identities. The historical contingencies of resource distribution, labour markets and gender politics are such that Kathmandu's 'youth culture' is largely (though not exclusively, or eternally) male and middle class.
23 See Appadurai (1990b) and Marglin (1990) on development, commercialization and the restriction of choice.
24 If for working-class young people in capitalist societies youth is a time for 'learning to labor' (Willis 1977), for those in the middle class youth is a time for 'learning to consume'.
25 'Three-wheelers' are boxy, open-air commuter vehicles – noisy and fume-ridden – that ply the roads in the Kathmandu valley transporting mostly middle-class workers and students from their homes in the suburbs to the offices and campuses of the city.

REFERENCES

Appadurai, A. (1990a) 'Disjuncture and difference in the global cultural economy', *Public Culture*, 2. 2: 1–24.
—— (1990b) 'Technology and the reproduction of values in rural western

India', in F. A. Marglin and S. A. Marglin (eds) *Dominating Knowledge: Development, Culture, and Resistance*, Oxford: Clarendon Press.

—— (1991) 'Global ethnoscapes: notes and queries for a transnational anthropology', in R. G. Fox (ed.) *Recapturing Anthropology: Working in the Present*, Santa Fe, NM: School for American Research Press.

Aryal, M. (1992) 'Women in development: what's in it for me?', *Himal*, 5. 2: 24–25.

Barthes, R. (1983 [1967]) *The Fashion System*, trans. M. Ward & R. Howard, New York: Hill & Wang.

Baudrillard. J. (1983) 'The ecstasy of communication', in H. Foster (ed.) *The Anti-Aesthetic: Essays in Postmodern Culture*, Port Townsend, WA: Bay Press.

Campbell, C. (1987) *The Romantic Ethic and the Spirit of Modern Consumerism*, Oxford: Basil Blackwell.

Caughey, J. L. (1984) *Imaginary Social Worlds*, Lincoln, NE: University of Nebraska Press.

Central Bureau of Statistics (1991) *Statistical Year Book of Nepal*, Kathmandu: CBS.

Custen, G. (1987) 'Fiction as truth: viewer use of fictive films as data about the "real" world', in M. Taureg and J. Ruby (eds) *Visual Explorations of the World*, Aachen: Edition Herodot.

Douglas, M. and Isherwood, B. (1979) *The World of Goods*, New York: Basic Books.

Escobar, A. (1988) 'Power and visibility: the invention and management of development in the Third World', *Cultural Anthropology*, 3. 4: 428–443.

—— (1991) 'Anthropology and the development encounter: the making and marketing of development anthropology', *American Ethnologist*, 18. 4: 658–682.

Fabian, J. (1983) *Time and the Other*, New York: Columbia University Press.

Fox, R. G. (1985) *The Lions of the Punjab: Culture in the Making*, Berkeley: University of California Press.

Friedman, J. (1989) 'The Consumption of Modernity', *Culture and History*, 4: 117–130.

Hannerz, U. (1986) 'Theory in anthropology: small is beautiful? The problem of complex cultures', *Comparative Studies in Society and History*, 28. 2: 362–367.

Haug, W. F. (1987) *Commodity Aesthetics, Ideology and Culture*, New York: International General.

Hepburn, S. (1993) 'Fashion and ethnic tourists in Nepal: whose authenticity is this?' Twenty second Conference on South Asia, Madison Wisconsin, November.

Kett, J. F. (1977) *Rites of Passage: Adolescence in America 1790 to the Present*, New York: Basic Books.

Kottak, C. P. (1990) *Prime-Time Society: An Anthropological Analysis of Television and Culture*, Belmont, CA: Wadsworth Publishing.

Lewis, T. (1984) 'The Tuladhars of Kathmandu: a study of Buddhist tradition in a Newar merchant community', Ph.D. dissertation, Columbia University.

Liechty, M. (1994) 'Fashioning Modernity in Kathmandu: Mass Media, Consumer Culture, and the Middle Class in Nepal', Ph.D. dissertation, University of Pennsylvania.
—— (forthcoming) '"Teens" in Kathmandu: Thoughts from Nepal on Mass Media and Consumer Subjectivity', *Public Culture*.
Marglin, S. A. (1990) 'Towards the decolonization of the mind', in F. A. Marglin and S. A. Marglin (eds) *Dominating Knowledge: Development, Culture, and Resistance*, Oxford: Clarendon Press.
Mishra, C. and Sharma, P. (eds) (1983) *Foreign Aid and Social Structure: Notes on Intra-State Relationships*, Proceedings of a Seminar, 4–5 October, Kathmandu: Integrated Development Systems.
Pahari, A. (1992) 'Fatal myth: a critique of *Fatalism and Development*', *Himal*, 5. 1: 52–4.
Pigg, S. (1990) 'Disenchanting shamans: representations of modernity and the transformation of healing in Nepal', Ph.D. dissertation, Cornell University.
—— (1992) 'Inventing social categories through place: social representations and development in Nepal', *Comparative Studies in Society and History*, 34. 3: 491–513.
Pradhan, K. B. and Terrell, G. M. (1990) *Sano Shabda Samsar*, Kathmandu: Terrell & Pradhan.
Rana, M. (1992) 'An Open Letter to the Minister', *Himal*, 5, 2: 5–7.
Rodowick, D. (1988) *The Crisis of Political Modernity: Criticism and Ideology in Contemporary Film Theory*, Urbana: University of Illinois Press.
Sharma, P. (1989) *Urbanization in Nepal*, Papers of the East–West Population Institute, no. 110, May, Honolulu: East–West Center.
Shrestha, C. B., Kharty, P.K., Sharma, B. and Ansari, H. (1986) *The Historic Cities of Asia: Kathmandu*, Kathmandu: Centre for Nepal and Asian Studies.
Siegel, J. (1986) *Solo in the New Order*, Princeton: Princeton University Press.
Simmel, G. (1950) *The Sociology of Georg Simmel*, K. H. Wolff (ed.) New York: The Free Press.
Stiller, L. (1968) *Prithwinarayan Shah in the Light of the Dibya Upadesh*, Kathmandu: Himalayan Book Centre.
Tiwari, S. R. (1992) 'Planning: never without aid', *Himal*, 5, 2: 8–10.
Williams, R. (1985) *Keywords* (revised edn), Oxford: Oxford University Press.
Willis, P. (1977) *Learning to Labor: How Working Class Kids Get Working Class Jobs*, New York: Columbia University Press.

Chapter 9

Masta Liu[1]

Christine Jourdan

Nomoa selen
Man hangaraon
Nomoa selen
Save faet
Save drink
Go begam mani
Man liu Nao

(Philip Lauts, 17 years)

In Honiara, the capital city of the Solomon Islands, there are many young boys and young men who hang around the town. Their main characteristic is being unemployed: some have lost their jobs, some have dropped out of school, others are simply waiting for the departure of the ship that will take them back to their home village. Drifting in and out of jobs, in and out of hope, they are very often on the verge of delinquency. Many of them have had some brush with the law. To the people of the Solomon Islands, they are known as the *Masta Liu*.[2]

The phenomenon of the *Masta Liu* is not new: there have been *liu* since the town first started to attract great numbers of Solomon Islanders, without being able to provide them with jobs. However it is only recently that the *Masta Liu* have become a cultural phenomenon: songs are being written about them, people talk about them: a *Masta Liu* stereotype is developing. The *liu* have become a significant segment of the urban population, not only because of their sheer numbers, but because of the influence they have on the development of the urban popular culture. Their life-style, the way they dress and talk, their taste in music and films, their outlook on life, all this gives a particular direction to social change in Honiara.

The purpose of this chapter will be to open up the myth of the *Masta Liu* that is in the process of developing in the Solomon Islands, by exploring the constitutive elements and the symbols of this subculture. The chapter will show that the *Masta Liu* subculture is not solely a direct result of the problems of development that the country is undergoing, but that it is as well rooted in the cultural tradition of some islands of the country. We may choose to look at the *Masta Liu* phenomenon as linked essentially to the unemployment of the youth, and we would not be wrong in doing so; and/or we may choose to look at it as the new form that a cultural tradition is taking, and we would not be wrong there, either. In any case, these are young people whose life-styles over the years have helped shape the urban social fabric and have given it much of its 'creolized' aspects. Young urban people participate actively in life in the town, and are constantly negotiating the cultural role they are playing. They may have been pushed to the fringes of urban economic life, but the responses they give to marginalization stress cultural agency as a means to find one's urban identity and social space. This renegotiation of identity takes place through a process of socio-cultural creolization, analogous in some ways to the processes at work in the pidginization and creolization of languages: an ongoing dialogue of cultural forms which is facilitated by the agency of individuals and which allows new meanings to be generated. In the urban scene, creativity and juxtaposition are pervasive: as with pidgins and creoles, the pace of change is dramatic.

CREOLIZATION, URBANIZATION AND AUTHENTICITY[3]

The classic ethnographies of anthropology have been predicated, and have instilled in us, an anthropological practice which accentuates, and to some extent legitimizes the exotic, the primitive, the authentic, and if possible, the unknown (Carrier 1992). Of course, all that has come from a historical context in the development of a science of the Other in which the Other could only be conceived of an accorded legitimacy if it were fundamentally different, and free from contamination by the West. Constructing an Other as dramatically different seems to have been a way by which Western Europe constructed itself; from the writings on Utopia in the Renaissance (Trouillot 1991) to the 'Noble Sauvage' of the Enlightenment (Diderot, Rousseau) and the representation of Oceania and North American Native population in the Romantic Era (Chateaubriand

1839; Pierce 1965), European literature created a spectacularized and theatrical Other. A European anthropology followed suit. Such an approach to the Other reflects an ahistorical and romantic vision of non-Western societies, and a warped conception of time that is even more puzzling in that it seems to negate the relationship that exists between time and history (Fabian 1983; Thomas 1990). Curiously, the Other that anthropology has created for itself seems to be impervious to time's arrow. Moreover, the importance that our discipline has given to time as a constituting element of culture leads us to consider as authentic what is rooted in history. As a result, the form of history that anthropology privileges for the Other is one that is immutable: a timeless history of self-reproducing structures that reinforces our very notion of authenticity. Viewed as a form immanent in things, at once derived from history but placed outside historicity, authenticity blurs our interpretations of socio-cultural phenomena: what is authentic is deemed cultural; everything else is only the result of Westernization or disintegration, and by that fact, uninteresting. For Westerners to conceive of history as static is an interesting twist of things: it partakes of the West's needs to create an Other, or a multiciplicity of Others, that would be dramatically different (Keesing 1994). Living in timelessness (dreamtime) instead of living in history (as a flow of events, actions and interpretations on the said events and actions) is radically different. And in that sense, anthropology's obsession with the dreamtime quality of a static representation of history may reveal a nostalgic effort to keep dreamtime alive, for Others and in Others, as if dreamtime captured the imaginary quality of history that may have been lost to progress.

The pristinity of cultures is an illusion directly associated with conceiving of history as stasis (dreamtime). As an illusion, it continues to be entertained in our field of studies by a reification of culture. We speak about culture the way we talk about a consumer good: whole, indivisible, homogeneous, of which each member is at once a repository and an exemplar. A culture is thus taken to have an existence in and of itself, at once essential and existential. In this conception of culture, the individual is object, and the group subject: only the group engages the world culturally, even if that means doing some adjusting whenever another manipulation of the 'authentic' becomes necessary. I will argue, however, that these adjustments are possible because of the individual's agency: in the course of social life, the individual is constantly negotiating his or her position *vis-à-vis* the group and the institutions. There exists an ongoing dialogue between individuals and groups through which each is progressively changed. It is this ongoing everyday, multi-sided process of negotiation that, on the one hand, situates the individual within the cultural milieu, and on the other, contributes to the elaboration and transformation of the cultural practices of the community. This Bakhtinian dialogue is in fact the key to social relations: it provides both the dynamics that generates broad cultural homogeneity at the level of the group, and the heterogeneity of individual practice. When it comes to cultural changes, nothing is given or fixed: individuals creatively select and appropriate different discourses and ideologies and map them (very often, partially) on to existing practices. The result is permanent hybridization (Bakhtin 1981), what I call here creolization. The positioning of individuals and the creative appropriations they make of discourses, practices and ideologies[4] do not take place within neatly bounded entities: they appear, rather, in cultural settings that Sapir (1985) would have qualified as 'spurious'.

Honiara is the epitome of the 'spurious' cultural world dreaded by Sapir and shares with many other towns and budding cities, in Melanesia and other parts of the Third World, the characteristics of undergoing rapid social changes and of being inhabited by a very young population.[5] In that kind of social world, the concept of pristinity is devoid of meaning. The *Masta Liu* of Honiara have come to turn to their advantage the cultural conflation they live in, and are expanding it. They do so by borrowing foreign cultural traits, obviously, but mainly by putting new meanings into old shells. The new reading of cultural texts allows them to find an identity niche in town, while at the same time forcing the town to recognize them. However economically and socially marginalized they may be, they have become an increasingly important element shaping the culture of the town. They manipulate and conjugate various systems of meaning (*kastom*, popular culture, the institutions they inherited from the British administration, and the forms of social relations and ideologies associated with the world system). The world of the village is no longer the only cultural anchorage they are claiming as authentically theirs.

A NEW SOCIAL CONTEXT

Honiara (population 43,000), the capital city of the Solomon Islands, was built on the remains of the military base that the American army had left on Guadalacanal after the Second World War. The Solomon

Islands were still a British Protectorate, and Honiara was organized and administered as a typical colonial port. Its main purpose was to allow for goods and merchandise to be moved in and out of the archipelago, and to orchestrate the movement of the Melanesian labour force between various islands. The social ecology of the town was very much a colonial one: British and Australian expatriates occupied the most lucrative and prestigious functions, and the Melanesian population was locked into poorly rewarded occupations. Progressively, as the protectorate moved towards self-government and later on, independence (1978), Solomon Islanders became more involved in the social organization of the town and their impact started to be felt. This was facilitated by an increase in the level of education of the population, by an amelioration of means of communications and by access to cash employment.

In the earlier years of the emergence of the town, living in Honiara was essentially a male prerogative: young men came to town looking for paid labour. As they jumped on board the recruiting ships that roamed around the various islands of the archipelago and signed up for plantation labour, young men left behind their wives and families, but most importantly, the cultural world of the village. They discovered the world of plantation work, where male-only barracks re-enacted the village men's house (Jourdan 1987). On their way back home, they stopped in Honiara in order to get some cargo, but with the hope of finding additional paid work. There, they met other men who had come to the town directly, and were struggling to survive. Once again, all-male households were organized, particularly in the Kukum labour lines, by the water front. Men pooled their meagre resources; those who earned wages subsidized those who did not, with the understanding that some ulterior repayment (*sensim* in local pidgin) would take place whenever the latter ones were able to get some money. Life was difficult, and very often characterized by despair more than by joy. The following song, written in the early 1960s, captured the disheartening loneliness of some of these men and their boredom. Frazer (1981) cites it as well.

Wakabaot Long Saenaton   Walking around in
                              Chinatown

Wakabaot Long Saenaton,   Walking around in Chinatown,
Makem kosi, angga lon kona   Finding a path, stopping in a
                              corner,

Sutiap, sekem hed	Shouting, shaking one's head,
Kikim baket enikaen	Kicking anything.
Ies, iu laf	Yes, you laugh
Haf senis, wata nating.	As if the brain is like water
Tingting baek lon iu,	I am thinking of you,
Lusim hom long taem	I have left home long ago,
Tu iia ova mi no lukim iu	I haven't seen you for over two years,
Tastawe mi no laekem iu,	This is why I do not love you,
Man garange,	I am a stupid fool,
Garange hed lusim mani.	A stupid head who lost money.
No mata mi dae lon Honiara,	It does not matter if I die in Honiara
Samting mi lusim long taem lon iu,	What we had I lost long ago
Bat sapos iu tingim lon mi,	But if you still think of me
Iu kan weit fo tu iia moa,	You have to wait for two extra years
Letem kam laet skin	Until my skin becomes
Long lilebit.	Slightly lighter.

Once they had left the village, it was very difficult for these young men to go back home without the minimum cargo or amount of money that would allow them to re-enter village life with pride. And so they stayed on, in the hope of finding even the small amount of money that would save their honour. When they did, they could go back home, and as their forebears had done in the days of the labour trade to Queensland, they could recount stories of hardship and adventures that would enhance and strengthen the young men's status in the village.

Today's *Masta Liu* are not very different, if not for the fact that they are, in general, much younger than the *liu* of the early sixties, that most have had some minimal schooling and that they now comprise girls and young women as well as men. Most come to town directly from the village: the almost obligatory transit through the plantation world that existed previously seems to have gone. The *liu* are not a homogeneous group. Age, ethnic origin (most of the sixty-four ethnic groups of the country are represented in town) and ethnic rivalries (becoming increasingly problematic for urban peace), and degree of experience in the *liu* world, are factors that create diversity. As a rule, *liu* are young people (mostly male), between the ages of 15 and 25, and are predominantly single. Interestingly, their number in town will fluctuate with the seasons. From the beginning of October, their numbers soar to peak towards the end of November and the beginning of December. In November 1993, the Honiara Town Council (the municipal authority) estimated at around 5000 the number of *liu* in town. As Christmas gets nearer, people flock into town to shop, and so do the young people. This is the time of year when delinquency and petty criminality is at its highest. Whatever household items are left unguarded outside the home at night are bound to be snatched by people who need to bring gifts back home at Christmas. Clothes left to dry on the line, plastic buckets left to drain, shoes and slippers forgotten on the front steps, all these items find their way to the village. This urban foraging is essential to the standing of the *liu* both in town and in the village.

THE *MASTA LIU*[6]

The *liu* I worked with in Honiara were for the most part employed as unskilled labourers by the Honiara Town Council (HTC) in the context of a pioneer project on employment and training of school leavers. Even though these particular *liu* were actually working at the time when the research took place, their work history reveals that they have been largely unemployed since they arrived in Honiara. Most are from Malaita (Table 1). This does not come as a surprise, for two reasons: first, Malaita is the most populous island in the country; and second, Malaita has a tradition of temporary migration that goes back to the nineenth century, when Malaitans went to Queensland and Fiji to work in the sugar cane fields (Corris 1973; Moore 1985; Saunders 1982).

This circular migration out of Malaita is compounded by the fact that the island (unlike the Central and Western islands of the archipelago), does not have large coconut plantations, cash crops or other forms of economies that could absorb the local labour force. In the old days, young men went to work on plantations within the archipelago, mainly to obtain the money that would allow them to pay the head tax that had been imposed on to them by the then British Administration (Bennett 1987). At the same time, they enjoyed the prospect of an 'exciting' life outside the social constraints and social control of the village.

Table 1 Ethnic origin of the *liu* in HTC youth project

Islands of origin	No.
Choiseul	3
Guadalcanal	4
Malaita:	
'Are'Are	2
Baegu	2
Baelelea	2
Kwai	1
Kwaio	9
Kwara'ae	15
Lau	2
Sa'a	1
To'abaita	13
Nggela	3
Total	57

Today, the reasons behind circular migration are not very different from what they were in the past. People need money, and the only way for them to get it is to search for employment, either on plantations in the island group or in urban areas. However, there are major differences. The most striking difference is that wage labour migration now involves women as well as men, where previously only men had gone away to search for wage labour. Nowadays, a woman can accompany her husband, or she can be single (Jourdan 1985). Education is the other side of the coin. Very many of the young people who reach Honiara nowadays have had some schooling, however minimal. They were sent to school by their parents with the expectation that education would make them employable at good salaries. When they come to town with a Standard 6 year of education or a Form 3,[7] they quickly realize that the level of education and

Table 2 Reasons given by informants for having left school

Reasons	No.
No schooling at all	5
Did not like going to school	18
No money for school fees	4
Either parent died	2
Failed Hicks Test (Std. 6)	22
Failed Form 3 exam	4
Still at school	2
Total	57

training they have obtained is not sufficient to give them access to the good job they expected to find. Education has let them down. Many of these young people have dropped out of school.

Part of the *liu* drama is having to negotiate constantly the expectations that one had at the onset of schooling and prior to coming to town, with the realities of the urban world. Most certainly, the transformation of the Solomon Islands' economy, schooling and the urbanization of social relations are factors that need to be taken into consideration when looking at the expansion of the *liu* phenomenon.

Young people, either school-leavers or drop-outs (Table 2) without any marketable skills, come to town, lured by the 'lights' of Honiara: cinemas, shops, crowds, sports games, big markets, takeaway food, etc. They are drawn by the desire to experience it all, or at least to see it all, and by the possibility they see in earning the necessary money that will allow them to partake of some of the goods available in the shops. In general, the items eagerly sought are food (especially rice); clothes (particularly blue jeans and fake army garb) bought either new or at the second-hand stores; cassette players; household goods, etc.

More often that not, these young and not so young people come only *wakabaot*, to take the pulse of the town, to experience the excitement and be part of the scene. An exhilarating feeling of freedom and endless possibilities invades them. It is then that one can see *oketa Masta Liu* wander about the town, in groups of up to ten, blocking the pavements, holding hands two by two, boisterous groups of young men walking down the street in search of excitement. They stop at every shop on their way, eager to look at the merchandise but afraid to be kicked out by the security guards; they check out all the cinemas only to dream in front of the preview posters (themselves an endless subject of debate as to whether or not they genuinely represent the content of the film), not even having the $2 bill that will allow them to get in; they gaze for hours on end, and without moving, at the electronic equipment displayed in the Chinese shops, without saying a word: one can read in their gaze the silent dreams they create; they make fun of the *liu* girls who giggle at them, pleased but confused by the attention they draw. The *liu* girls are more subdued in their behaviour, even though some of them have recently taken to wearing make-up and sporting a fancy hairstyle, but one can sense that the sexual playfulness of potential courtship is initiated.

Some young girls marvel at the freedom they experience at being able to wander around with their peers, and at being able to talk to the boys without facing the reprimands of their *wantok*. They relish being spared the back-breaking work in the taro (*Colocasia Esculenta*) and potato (*Ipomea Batatas*) fields that would have filled their days had they stayed in the village. All *liu*, boys and girls, will tell how easy life is in Honiara and how much they rest when they come to town. For some of them, working for small wages, or even having no money at all, seems preferable to the life of hard physical labour and general boredom that awaits them if they go back to the village.

More than boredom, what the *liu* are avoiding is the inescapability of *kastom* and the control that their kin and members of older generations have over the young ones: control over work, control over marriage through the payment of bride wealth, control over wealth through a system of reciprocal obligations, etc. Young people in the village are indulged in many ways, but are trained to take on social or marital responsibilities from a very young age. However congenial life in the village may be, young people acquire early on the sense that the community and the social ties are of overwhelming importance. In town, young people feel a sense of reprieve from the customary obligations: their autonomy, financial or cultural, depends precisely on their ability to follow customary rules only inasmuch as it allows them to remain in town in security and comfort. For many youth, *kastom* has become instrumental to their life in town. They do not bend customary rules: rather, whenever they have an opportunity to do so, they select and follow the aspects of *kastom* that can be read in urban terms. Doing so, they preserve the budding cultural autonomy that they have progressively acquired while, at the same time, they appease the anxieties that their 'unorthodox' behaviour has provoked in the mind of the older generation. Cultural autonomy exists, of course, only inasmuch as the older generation is prepared to let it happen and is not present in all realms of *kastom*; young *liu* learn quickly which aspects of tradition they can stretch with impunity, and which they will need to negotiate.

Members of the older generation humour symbolic expressions of identity that the young *liu* like to flaunt, such as clothing. Very often dressed in rags, or old clothes that need washing because they are being worn every day for lack of replacement, the *liu* are easily recognizable. Some young men wear their run-down clothes with bravado, putting on layers and layers of old rags. Some, inspired by the Rambo films they see in the local cinemas, wear bandanas around their foreheads; some, enlightened in the Reggae music of the West Indies and the Rastafarian culture, wear their hair in long dreadlocks that fall down their backs. Young *liu* enjoy all aspects of popular culture, generated locally or imported from Western or other Pacific countries. However recent it may be, this new cultural tradition is essentially urban and has caught the imagination of young urbanites very quickly. Soccer matches and rock concerts, T-shirts and videos, marches and banners, dress and hair fashion, new words and new body language, all these contribute to making the cultural world of the town increasingly complex.

In this new world, the young people have the cultural edge over the adults who, for the most part, are still enmeshed in village-related meanings and social activities, and for whom the world of the village remains the frame of reference for many symbolic and practical activities in town. Young urban people, brought up in town, are not as caught up in the world of *kastom* as their parents are; the cultural norms are more lax for them, precisely because there is no pre-established norm as to what living in town entails culturally. Young people are thus 'free' to initiate changes, or to carry further the cultural transformations that have been initiated by their parents. As I have shown elsewhere (Jourdan, forthcoming), Solomon Islanders are by no means passive consumers of imported multinational capitalist culture in prepackaged forms: they impose their own creative stamp on the Western phenomena with which they are bombarded, and they stretch or jettison the aspects of tradition that they see as inappropriate to living in town. Most elements of urban popular culture are seen as non-threatening. As they do not belong to anyone and cannot be associated with a particular ethnic group, they are perceived as culturally neutral – a form of generic culture that overcomes ethnic and generational boundaries. Young *liu* bask in the new shared meanings that give them more creative agency: in an effort to seek the control of some aspects of urban social space, they endorse new symbols and redefine *kastom*.

But for all this playfulness, many aspects of a *liu* urban reality are difficult. Poverty is the dominant key of the *liu* life. Of course, in the context of village life, the concept of poverty is irrelevant for the young people; but it becomes excruciatingly real and blatant in the urban context. As they get off the ship that brought them to Honiara, they realize quickly that they are poor. The consciousness they have of their poverty increases with the number of steps they take towards the centre of town. Poverty creeps up, as they make their way through an exhilarating but frightening world, full of strangers, noise and confusion. In town, however, poverty very often means hunger as well. Most *liu* claim that they often go hungry, and that the one thing that makes the village better than the town is the fact that they can eat plentifully and at will in the village. Many of them do not eat anything in the morning, and they often have no dinner either.

> If I get work, then I'll be happy. If I do not get work, then I'll *liu*, I'll walk around, I'll go hungry. We are constantly hungry. There is no food in the house. They [his *wantoks*] are not feeding us well. There is nothing to eat in the house.
>
> (Michael, 13 years)

Their preoccupation with food becomes an obsession at the end of the month (*long en*), when money has ran out, and when the only thing they have is a few betel-nuts that will mask the hunger pangs they feel. It is then that delinquency takes its toll: when the only hopes one has to be able to eat lie in one's ability to steal a wallet or break into a house. Most of the young *liu* have been sent to town by their parents, and have been asked to send remittances, in the form of cash, food or household goods, as soon as they get a job. But of course, because of their lack of skill and the saturation of the work market in Honiara, it takes a long time before they obtain a job. If they get one at all, it is likely to be a job that is not interesting and which pays poorly. Furthermore, tales of sheer exploitation by employers are not rare. Quickly, the young men resign their jobs and fall back into the *liu* way of life. Most were drawn to town by dreams of freedom and high financial and social expectations. But quickly, idleness, boredom, low self-esteem and despair rapidly become an everyday reality. Aware of their plight, many balance their life in the village with their life in town. It would be reasonable to go back, some say. They know that the village is their social security, but they entertain the possibility of going back as the last resource. They have to save face. In the back of their mind lies the desire to give it a last try, to stick it out, to fulfil the promises made to a wife or a father to bring some money back. And so they wait, hoping that something will come their way that will allow them, if not to realize the dreams they had upon arrival, at least to survive. Very often they find themselves at the fringes of delinquency. Many young men I interviewed said they had often been asked to join a gang of 'rascals' and break into a store or a house. Most claimed to have refused the offer. Some hinted that, out of despair and boredom, they have very often been tempted to take up the offer and go along with the group:

> Some of them asked me to join them in breaking into a store or a

house. I refused. They were angry with me. They said: Aren't you ashamed? Come, let's go and steal! But I did not want to. So I went home instead. I was lucky, because later on that evening the police got hold of them and took them to prison.

Some took up the offer and became involved in gangs of safe crackers who operated in town for quite a few years at the end of the 1980s. They seem to have enjoyed themselves very much. Silas's story is very revealing:

The first time I went to prison, it was for brawling. It was for six months. A way to try out the place. I said: Eh! it's not that bad. When I got out, I tried to find work, but I did not find any. People called me an ex con. I had no work, no money, nothing to do. I was a *liu*. So I started to hang around with tough people from my island who had been involved in all sorts of big crimes: house-breaking, burglary, safe cracking. I got interested, and it was full of adventure. So I joined them. We started to go out in gangs. They called us the safe crackers. We were four. It was fun, real good fun, because we never ran out of money. But then, they caught me again.

Not all *liu* have had that kind of experience. Their ways of making a living in Honiara are not as extreme as Silas's. In most cases, *liu* are being put up by members of their immediate family upon their arrival in Honiara. This is done according to a customary principle of balanced reciprocity. Whether they like it or not, urban relatives have to oblige. Against room and board, while looking for work, *liu* will perform small tasks in the household: they work in the garden if the *anti* has one; they look after the children when the mother is at work; they run errands for the family, etc. In many cases they are confined to the house due to lack of money, and become bored. Thus, a typical Honiara household[8] usually comprises a nuclear family plus a few kinsmen/kinswomen on either side of the family (Figure 1 (a) and (b)).[9]

Figure 1(a)   Figure 1(b)

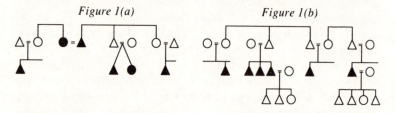

Key: Blocked out symbols represent people actually living in the household
Source: Fieldnotes, June 1989

The host family is often already an extended family by the time the young *liu* arrives. Other young members of the family have found their way to Honiara and rely on their wantoks for food and lodging. This proves to be a severe strain on the financial resources of many urban families who have to carry the burden of so many mouths to feed on a meagre salary.

Many *liu* wantoks will choose to live together in the same house. Single men, or young married men who have left their wives and children back home in the village, organize a household exclusively constituted of young men, thus reproducing the lodging patterns found in a plantation barrack. Some of the young men may be working, most are not. They share the expenses of rent, electricity and water, and pool their financial resources for food. It may happen that some *liu* who have not contributed any money for too long a time, and do not show any inclination or ability to do so, will be asked to leave the household. For example, the To'abaita household across the Vura road from where I live comprises ten men, all related to one another through kinship, and not a single woman or child (Figure 2).

Figure 2

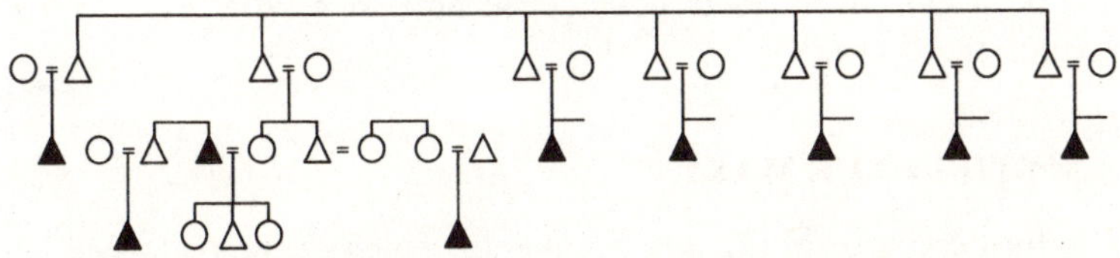

Key: Blocked out symbols represent people actually living in the household
Source: Fieldnotes, June 1989

Sometimes, *wantoks* take over the parental role and keep too close an eye on the young *liu*. Resentment builds up as the youth realizes that, even in Honiara, he or she is still under the control of the village and the family. The social autonomy they had hoped to obtain in town is not easy to obtain.

I am not too happy because they act as if they were my parents. They sermon me. Strongly. They sermon me when I go wandering around, when I *liu*, when I do not have a job, when I drink a bit.
(Andrew, 18 years)

However crowded and constraining these households may be, they nevertheless provide emotional and moral support to the young *liu*. Not all *liu* are that lucky. Some have no family in town: they have to share quarters with wantoks they may not know or with whom they do not get along. With no close kin to turn to for emotional support, these young men feel alienated in a place like Honiara. David is one of them and he tells a rather sad tale.

David is from South Malaita. He is 19 years old and the first-born of a family of five children. His parents sent him to Honiara to look for work, with, as sole luggage, a STD 6 diploma from primary school; they asked him to send some money back as soon as he got a job. The only accommodation David could find was shared crowded quarters with a group of young *liu* wantok not related to him, in the labour lines of Kukum, a sordid row of houses divided into rooms. The rooms are dark, dirty and have no cooking facilities. Adding to the sordid environment and endemic poverty, David has to put up with the heavy drinking habits and the unpredictable temper of his *wantoks*: 'I live in the labour lines. I find it very hard. The wantoks yell at me, beat me up. I have enough. There is no one from my family to whom I could go'. David, however, was lucky enough to find work at the HTC youth employment project almost as soon as he arrived in Honiara in March 1989. With a salary of $95.00 a month, he feels good to be able to send $25.00 to his parents each month.

A MYTH IN THE MAKING

The *liu* stereotype of the lazy drunkard is being counterbalanced by the testimonies I received from the young *Masta Liu* with whom I worked. Surprisingly, their first preoccupation is not with buying beer on pay-day, but rather with buying food and clothing. *Kaleko* (clothing) is the foremost item in a *liu*'s budget. In that regard, the youth of Honiara is not very different from the youth in other parts of the world. It is true that some claim to drink beer once in a while, and that two or three of them have admitted to drinking a carton of beer on pay-day, alone or with friends. But most object to being associated with excessive consumption of beer. They rightly point out that in order to drink beer, one has to have money ($2.40 for a can of Fosters; $57.60 for a pack of twenty-four cans). Excessive drinking is looked down upon by most of them. According to the observations I made of the drinking habits of some urbanites, those who are likely to drink heavily are those who have a regular salary and/or make enough money, and in general are between the ages of 25 and 40.

The young men are aware of the *liu* stereotype that prevails in town. Part of that stereotype is colourfully captured by a song that was very popular in 1989 and 1990 and aptly entitled *Masta Liu*. It was played constantly on the only radio station of the country, and served to emphasize the increasing importance of the *Masta Liu* in Honiara, while at the same time diffusing the tension that was developing between the *liu* and their *wantoks*.

Masta Liu

No garem waka	I have no work
Wokabaot long rod	I loaf along the road
Evri pipol no laekem mi,	Everybody despises me
Kolem mi pulsit man,	They call me names
Kolem mi pua man;	They call me poor
Evriwea insaet Honiara	Everywhere in Honiara
Trae askem wok plant kampani	I try to find work
Evri wan tale sore roon man.	Everybody tells me 'Sorry, wrong man'
Hed go daon, nomoa smael,	The head goes down, the smile is gone
Ating mi bon fo olsem nao.	It must be my fate.
Masta liu, masta liu	Masta liu, masta liu
Nomoa mani, no garem eniting	No money left, nothing on my name
Masta liu, masta liu	Masta liu, masta liu
Kanse nao, mi man fo olsem nao	It must be it, its my fate.
Frenim gel fo wan wiki nomoa	I had a girlfriend for a full week
Askem hem 'mi laek maritim iu'	I told her I'd like to marry her
Askem mi 'wea nao iu wok'	She asked me 'Where do you work?'
Hem no wandem mi taem mi se	She stopped wanting me when I said
Mi nomoa wok bikos mi masta liu.	That I was not working, because I was a liu.
Nomoa wok, nomoa lavu,	No work, no love

Bat mi no wari nomoa.	But I do not worry
Bat bae mi singim spesol singsing	I will sing a special song
Blo mifala pipol no garem wok	Of people like me who have no work.
Gagim nao! Masta liu, masta liu	Let's go! Masta liu, Masta liu
Hem no man nating man save had waka	A man who works hard is quite something.
Masta liu, masta liu,	Masta liu, masta liu,
Samtaem hem laki man.	Sometimes he is a lucky man.

The central theme of this song is rather similar to that of *Wokabaot long Saenataon*: unemployment, lack of money, sense of personal failure, lack of love and lack of hope. However, there is a new twist to that song, and that is the implication that unemployment has become a way of life that is widespread. In the thirty years that separate the two songs, being a *liu* has become a cultural phenomenon. The *masta liu* world and way of life is multifaceted, in a way that is not thoroughly captured by this last song. While it focuses on work, love and money and the lack thereof in a gentle and humorous way, the song fails to address a less gentle side of the stereotype, which makes room for toughness, coolness, street wiseness, laziness, as well as for panache, bravado, independence and guts. Local musketeers, the *Liu* will fight for their rights: but they will also threaten, mug or beat up anyone who happens to displease them. It is a dangerous but appealing stereotype, which many youth admire and some try to live up to. A successful robbery or break-in, a murder accomplished according to the rules of *kastom* (even if one is caught), a street fight between mobs belonging to different ethnic groups, all these fall within the category of feats that the *liu* are supposed to be good at. Gallantry, courage, honour, are part of the game which will make a 'good' *liu* stand out in the crowd and acquire a reputation. But the border with delinquency is dangerously close and many Honiarians will be prompt to blame many social evils on what they qualify as the unruliness, laziness and drunkenness of the *liu*. However, there is a certain amount of 'bonhomie' about it all in town. If people cannot help but criticize the *liu* for being potential trouble-makers, they nevertheless humour them. The indulgence is reflected through new developments in the language. People will joke and call someone a *liu* to tease them about their inactivity, their sleepiness, their brashness: *Barava man liu nao* (this is a real *liu*), they will say with a laugh. Accordingly, the word *liu* is in the process of becoming an adjective in Pidgin, encompassing various meanings according to contexts. However, whatever the context, there is always a degree of indulgence attached to the word. This forbearance and humour reveals an underlying anarchy *vis-à-vis* the established order, an order in which one seems to be only superficially involved. And it stems as well from the recognition that material and economic conditions of life in Honiara are not easy. Behind this forbearance lies a cultural obsession with social harmony. All social relations, whether between individuals or between groups, seem to be governed by a conception of social life, public and private, that privileges harmony over antagonism, and places higher value on humour over confrontation. This is illustrated by the importance still being given in town to compensatory payments as an effective mode of conflict resolution; not only does the compensation stop all litigation, but it allows the parties involved to resume their social relations as if nothing had disturbed them. Moreover, it would be against *kastom* for anyone to bring up a conflict that has been settled through compensation. The street-wise *liu*, those from Malaita in particular, always on the lookout for money, are quick to perceive the advantage they can take of this system. Claiming kinship ties and family duties and responsibilities, they will claim compensation from any man who befriends and seduces a female relative, however distantly related she may be and how little they may care for her. Unlike bride wealth payments, compensatory payments do not need to be shared amongst kin; they remain the property of the claimants and the immediate or distant family members who have become aware of the situation. It is an easy way to 'make a fast buck' and some of the more desperate youngsters will not hesitate to menace and beat up whoever refuses to pay. The situation became so extreme in town at the end of the 1980s, that the then parliament promulgated a law making it illegal to obtain compensatory payments by threatening potential payers.

Liu are exploiting the adults' indulgence towards them, as much as they are taking advantage of the rules of 'cultural harmony'. Thus doing, they constantly push back, or stretch, the limits of the acceptable and redefine the rules of interaction between adults and youths. They tilt the balance of cultural power and force the adults into a set of new cultural expectations that will provoke the demise of their own cultural legitimacy. Young people are able to do so precisely because the cultural flux so characteristic of this period in the history of Honiara leaves *tradition* and *kastom* very much up in the air. Adults can no longer use the tool of cultural ideology that has lost parts of its reasonance to coerce youth.

CONCLUSION

In their search for urban space, the *liu* are striving to find an identity of their own. In a town that was non-existent fifty years ago, urbanites, and young people particularly, have no model of urban living that could be drawn upon. Their social role as young people has been necessarily redefined by migration to town, or by the urban way of life. Tensions between generations are heightened by alterity, material difficulties and the expectations that urbanites have with regard to living in town. And they are heightened as well by the sense that the communality of experience in the past may not be sufficient, or relevant, to the shaping of a communality in the urban present. As with creolized languages, young people increase the pace and direction of change in creolized cultures. The rapidity of the change is brought about by the cultural interferences that come into play to create a new social world, which, in turn, contributes to augment its complexity. However, rapid change is facilitated by the agency of individuals and the relative freedom of individual cultural practices in a social world where dominant and rigid cultural norms give way to a constant negotiation of cultural practices. In societies such as Honiara, young *liu* put their individual and collective creating stamps on the cultural flux of the town by forcing new meanings into old shells.

NOTES

1 This research was made possible by a research grant from the Social Sciences and Humanities Research Council of Canada. I am grateful to the Government of the Solomon Islands and to the Honiara Town Council for granting me permission to undertake this research. I specially wish to thank Keith Hannigan, a Peace Corps volunteer in charge of the Liu Project in the HTC, who allowed the young Liu to spend time with me during their work time, without any financial penalty to them.
2 *Liu* is a north Malaita word from To'abaita origin. In that language it means *to wander around aimlessly*. Incorporated in Pijin, the word is either a verb or a noun with a similar semantic field. When used as a noun, it refers to those people who have no jobs and who spend their time

hanging around the town doing nothing. In Pijin, plural is not morphologically marked on the noun and accordingly my usage of the noun *liu* will be found in the unmarked form. The word has recently been associated with the adjective *Master*, and thus conveys a stronger stereotype of laziness.

3 This section is an abridged version of a longer argument that I developed in a paper entitled 'Where have all the cultures gone?: Sociocultural creolization in the Solomon Islands' to appear in J. Carrier and J. Friedman (eds) *Social Change in the Contemporary Pacific*, Harwood Press (forthcoming).

4 This creative appropriation is, to some extent, contained in Bourdieu's (1972) concept of 'habitus'.

5 The 1986 census of population states that 45 per cent of the population of Honiara is under 15 years of age.

6 Most of the information for this article was obtained while working with the young *liu* of the Honiara Town Council Youth Employment Project. This programme is a pioneer project addressing employment and training of school leavers and was devised to cater to the needs of the young male population only. No women or young girls were considered when hiring took place. As a result the sample is certainly not representative of the totality of the *liu* population in Honiara.

7 Standard 6 is the last year of primary schooling, and Form 3 is the third year of secondary school. Major examinations are set at these two levels of schooling which aim to select the few who will be accepted into the higher grades. The selection is very harsh. For example, in 1992, 8000 pupils took the standard 6 examination and only 2000 were admitted into secondary schools. Again, only 25 per cent of those who took the Form 3 examination were admitted into Form 4.

8 Honiara households have a mean of seven people per household. However, given the great extent to which circular migration is practised between the islands and Honiara, Honiara households are very fluid. Their size is constantly changing.

9 The symbols used in Figures 1(a) and (b) and Figure 2 are as follows:

△   man
○   woman
=   marriage link
| filiation link
—   siblingship link

REFERENCES

Bakhtin, M. (1981) *The Dialog Imagination*, Translated by C. Emerson and M. Holquist, Austin: University of Texas Press.

Bennett, J. (1987) *Wealth of the Solomons. A History of a Pacific Archipelago, 1800–1978*, Honolulu: University of Hawaii Press.

Bourdieu, P. (1972) *Esquisse d'une théorie de la pratique*, Genève: Droz.

Carrier, J. (1992) 'Approaches to articulation', in J. Carrier (ed.) *History and Tradition in Melanesian Anthropology*, Berkeley: University of California Press.

Chateaubriand, F.R. de (1839) *Voyages en Amérique (Moeurs des Sauvages)* Paris: Béthune and Plon.

Corris, P. (1973) *Passage, Port and Plantation. A History of Solomon Islands Labour Migration.,1870–1914*, Melbourne: Melbourne University Press.

Fabian, J. (1983) *Time and the Other: How Anthropology Makes its Object*, New York: Columbia University Press.

Frazer, I. (1981) 'Man long taon. Migration and differentiation amongst the To'abaita, Solomon Islands', unpublished Ph.D. thesis, Canberra: Australian National University.

Jourdan, C. (1985) 'Sapos iumi mitim iumi: urbanization and creolization in the Solomon Islands', unpublished Ph.D. thesis, Canberra: Australian National University Press.

Jourdan, C. (1987) 'Des plantations à la ville', *Journal de la Société des Océanistes*, 5, 2: 242–253.

—— (forthcoming) Stepping stones to national consciousness: the Solomons case', in R. Foster (ed.) *Nationalism in Melanesia*, Chicago: University of Chicago Press.

Keesing, R.M. (1994) 'Theories of culture revisited', in R. Borofsky (ed.) *Assessing Cultural Anthropology*, New York: McGraw Hill.

Moore, C. (1985) *Kanaka. A History of Melanesian Mackay*, Port-Moresby: University of Papua New Guinea Press.

Pierce, R. H. (1965) *Savagism and Civilization: A Study of the Indian and the American Mind*, Baltimore: Johns Hopkins Press.

Sapir, E. (1985) *Selected Writing in Language, Culture and Personality*, Berkeley: University of California Press.

Saunders, K. (1982) *Workers in Bondage: The Origins and Bases of Unfree Labour in Queensland, 1844–1916*, Brisbane: University of Queensland Press Scholar's Library.

Thomas, N. (1990). *Out of Time*, Cambridge: Cambridge University Press.

Trouillot, M.R. (1991) 'Anthropology and the savage slot: the poetics and politics of otherness', in R. Fox (ed.) *Recapturing Anthropology: Working in the Present*, Santa Fe: School of American Research Press.

Chapter 10

Conclusion

The 'multi' cultural of youth

Vered Amit-Talai

In a book concerned with youth and cultural production, it behoves us to pause before concluding to consider the epistemological status of a concept such as 'youth cultures'. Such an analysis must cope with broader theories of the cultural both as these have often worked to marginalize studies of youth and in the possibilities opened up by contemporary efforts at reconceptualization. The efforts at rethinking culture have involved a movement, in varying degrees, away from a conceptual triad of unity, community and difference. The shift instead to pastiche (Keesing 1994:310) and situation or activity (Goodenough 1971; 1994) suggests a view of individual cultural engagement as ordinarily involved with multiple frameworks. Or put another way, cultural production is multi-cultural regardless of whether or not the 'exotic' or the exoticized is around the corner (Clifford 1988:1).

UNITY/SOCIETY/DIFFERENCE

The notion of cultures as isolable, unitary, internally coherent wholes has come in for such trenchant criticism over the last thirty years that its repeated disavowal has taken on the overtones of a redemptive anthropological mantra, a *mea culpa* for the sins of our functionalist forefathers. Notably, at least three chapters in this volume incorporate some version of this conversion. What arouses such condemnation is the sense that such accounts of culture gloss over crucial divisions, inequalities and contradictions (Keesing 1994:306). None the less, as Virginia Caputo (Chapter 2 this volume) cogently notes, the excavation for previously silenced voices which Marxist and feminist critiques initiated has not yet succeeded in rendering children and youth audible. The problem, Caputo points out, is not that juveniles are absent from ethnographies. After all, Alice Schlegal and Herbert Barry's recent review (1991) of adolescence relied on a large corpus of extant ethnographies, providing in total 186 different cases for comparison. The problem is rather the status of these youthful appearances.

Youths appear, but as potential adults rather than in their own right. In major part this focus reflects the continuing dominance of development and socialization emphases in social science constructions of childhood and adolescence (Prout and James 1990:22). A more particular anthropological problem, however, arises out of the tendency to identify cultures with community and society (Goodenough 1971; 1994). Within such a perspective, the very concept of youth culture becomes for all intents and purposes untenable unless we can assert that youths form their own separate societies. Youth however clearly operate within a wider social network which includes relationships with people of widely varying ages and statuses. Given this embeddedness, the culture/society equation can offer only two principal options for reading youth *and* culture. One is to focus on how children and youths learn or acquire the culture of the society. Another would be to argue that the cultural constructions of youths, at most, constitute a variant of the societal or adult cultures, a kind of cultural dialect (Goodenough 1971). This latter version retains the society/culture link but allows for a greater measure of internal variability. Both these versions however privilege – although to differing extents – transmission between youth and adult, either for observing how youths learn their culture from adults or for noting the way in which they adapt adult cultures.

It is difficult to see youths in this paradigm not least because of its tendency to minimize the cultural entailment of certain kinds of variations while pushing difference to the utmost. If distinctions of domain, roles, status, organization, history, experience, power and resources are but variations on a central organizing cultural thematic, then cultural difference has to be extreme to be counted as such. In this search for what Roger Keesing terms 'radical alterity' (1994), youth cultural production is necessarily marginalized. Either its particularity is subsumed within and hence attributed to a more general cultural Other or it has to be exoticized before it can be counted as sufficiently different to be considered cultural in its own right. By this logic, youths, it seems, would have two choices: either they can be different because they are Quebeçois, Algerian, Nepali, English, etc. or they can shout their difference.

A notion of youth culture is clearly alien to a concept of shared, unitary and enclosed cultural universes. If I raise the latter concept however, it is not to pile on my own redundant denunciation of a paradigm which has been under attack for decades but to note how difficult it is to shake off its central elements. Its functionalist progenitor may have been sweepingly rejected but notions of exotic difference, unity and incorporation still turn up in some ironic theoretical locations. The subcultural exposition of the Birmingham School (see Chapter 1 and 4 by Wulff as well as Chapter 2 by Caputo, this volume for more discussion) with its emphasis on class- situated cultural production and a Gramscian conception of ideological hegemony is diametrical to the paradigm I have outlined above (Clarke *et al.* 1976). None the less, it still resorts to the old standby of the 'exotic other', criticizing undifferentiated, market imposed versions of youth culture but reserving youth subcultures only for 'coherent', highly visible and dramatic youth movements. The majority of youths who do not participate in these kinds of movements must fall back on the parent class for their culture.

'BORDERLANDS', FLUIDITY AND HYBRIDITY

There is a reactive dualism to many of the currently fashionable conceptualizations of culture which often retains the elements they critique as running subtexts . Fluidity is postulated against staticness, 'borderlands' offered in lieu of self-contained cultures, the situated subject in place of the 'exotic other'; hybridity rather than authenticity and essentialism. It is difficult to glean much about the analytical properties of these alternative metaphors beyond an insistence on their contrast to the old metaphors. *Fluid* rarely seems to mean much more than *not static*. None the less, the old culture does not seem to have disappeared despite the emphasis on reconceptualization.

When Renato Rosaldo argues against the conflation of culture with difference, it turns out that he has no intention of jettisoning the latter. Rather, what he has in mind is a cultural consciousness that recognizes middle-class, white, North American researchers as much 'visibly different' as the people with whom they do fieldwork (1989). Or in James Clifford's version: 'Now ethnography encounters others in relation to itself while seeing itself as other' (1986:23). When Rosaldo argues for a focus on border zones as 'sites of creative cultural production', he defines them as 'within and between' communities rather than in place of them (1989:208, 217). Along the same lines, Talal Asad points out that conceptions of hybridity while arguing against bounded, discrete cultural traditions none the less appear to presume their existence as the forms from which new mixtures are derived (1990). Some of the efforts at paradigmatic shift do not seem to have replaced the old version of culture so much as *added* a new set of cultural circumstances.

The difficulty, apart from the inevitable shortcomings of any model in tackling the true scope of cultural complexity, is that we do not appear to have decided exactly why we need to rethink our conceptions of culture. Does the need arise from the inadequacy of unitary, exotic versions to explain cultural process altogether? Or does the need arise from the development of new circumstances for which these versions are inadequate? The implications for the status of youth cultures are quite different. Is it only now useful to talk about youth cultures in places like the Solomon Islands, Algeria and Nepal because recent increases of wage labour, urbanization, tourism, global trade and electronic media have prompted the development of the *Masta Liu* in Honiara, 'teenagers' in Kathmandu and raï music in Oran (see chapters 9, 5 and 8 by Jourdan, Schade-Poulsen and Liechty, this volume)? Or would it have been as relevant to talk about youth cultures before the advent of these dramatic political and economic changes?

In the 1970s, the Birmingham School viewed youth culture as a 'new' phenomenon arising through the increased spending power of British youths, the greater availability of cheap, mass-produced commodities and the development of a new leisure industry. Youth culture, Clarke *et al.*(1976) argued, did not exist as such before the Second World War. The premise of this book is that careful attention must indeed be devoted to the analysis of new forms of youth cultural production. But it is also our view that a conception of culture which withholds recognition of the capacity for cultural agency from *any* category of human beings is deficient. In the midst of late twentieth-century politico-economic transformations, new youth cultural forms are certainly emerging but youths have always been cultural.

ACTIVITIES

Such a perspective requires that we do more than layer borderlands on top of communities, a complex present resting on a neat and simple past. Instead, it is important to sever the identification of culture with community conceptually as well as historically. I therefore want to pick up on Ward Goodenough's argument that culture is more usefully located in activities rather than communities, in the expectations people have of interaction and the standards of evaluation operating within a particular situation. Even in the smallest, most isolated of communities, people are engaged in a variety of activities with differing organizational requirements, roles, actors, institutions, settings and duration. Whatever the locale, people must therefore engage different sets of situated understandings and expectations (1994). Or put another way, in any society, to operate effectively, people have to be multi-cultural. This view of culture is closely associated with Wulff's conception of microcultures (Chapter 4 this volume). However, while microcultures are limited to the kinds of situations which involve small groups in regular face-to-face interaction, activities do not necessarily have to be either localized or ongoing. A national election, Olympic sports broadcast, international association, a war, a visit to ClubMed, or multinational business deals are examples of activities that are either very limited in duration, geographically dispersed or both, but none the less they predicate particular cultural rubrics.

I am not, however, trying to map out a schema of neatly compartmentalized bundles of activities, actors and cultures. There are overlaps in the composition of participants in different activities. In small, face-to-face communities, such overlaps can be more the rule than the exception. As my own study of friendship in a Montreal high school indicated, activities (See Chapter 7 this volume), can occupy overlapping physical, institutional and temporal spaces producing uneasy accommodations and thinly veiled conflicts. Such overlaps render cultural process complex in any circumstance and hence practices rarely as 'automatic and impersonal' as Bourdieu would have us believe (1977:80). The question of 'what's going on here?' and 'what should or can I do?' is seldom a plain calculation. All of this makes the descriptive labels of simple and complex cultures obfuscating rather than clarifying (Cohen 1985). Social differentiation, economic development and political incorporation have critical cultural consequences but these do not necessarily make cultural agency any more or less problematic or complicated. Indeed, for argument's sake, it is possible to contend that a highly differentiated system in which activities were sharply compartmentalized and dispersed could be culturally less ambiguous than a system in which activities more regularly overlapped in setting and personnel (ibid.).

Nevertheless, this kind of 'messiness' should not lead us to assume that there are no distinctions between the cultural agency of different activities. Indeed, what makes cultural agency problematic is the dual realization that different situations, people and actions demand divergent cultural strategies but also that the divergence must be constantly worked through. While an activity involves its own cultural *modus operandi*, no one activity exhausts the range of cultural frames or possibilities which a person handles. Each protocol is thus employed in the awareness that there are other possibilities for operation. Cultural consciousness, I am arguing, involves a pragmatic manipulation of multiplicity which imparts a constant edge of private scepticism to social action.

DIFFUSION AND CHANGE

There are thus two important levels of cultural engagement: the cultural competencies involved in the production and reproduction of forms of collective action, and the development of individual consciousness through handling multiple cultural frameworks. The two levels are certainly linked but we need to be careful to investigate rather than to presuppose the nature of that link. Expectations and protocols which emerge in one context could certainly diffuse to another activity (Goodenough 1994:267) but not necessarily or automatically. Especially in a volume concerned with a category of people customarily denied full enfranchisement, issues of power and structural constraints on autonomy and choice constantly wind around considerations of cultural process . Among these are what Ulf Hannerz called 'role-discriminatory attributes' (1980). These are attributes such as race, ethnicity, gender and of course age which, while not constituting an activity in themselves often provide its rationale or motif, determine eligibility to participate or the nature of participation. Since the constraints which can be incumbent in such ascribed characteristics are often a product of systematic inequalities, it is not surprising to find that they can also limit or shape the diffusion of cultural elements between social situations. The South London teenage girls in Helena Wulff's study (Chapter 4 this volume) could not easily export their notion of ethnic equality in the youth club where black and white girls readily mixed to encounters in other more polarized situations. Young Creoles in the Netherlands dream of being able to use the fashion and style skills they have developed on the street corner and the dance floor to fashion careers for themselves in entertainment and sports, but as Livio Sansone points out, few have succeeded (Chapter 6 this volume). As Ulf Hannerz later argued, however, these structural influences on cultural agency and process are themselves shaped and constructed by the flow of ideas, symbols and meanings (1992:14). Sansone describes a dialectical exchange between the marginalization of young Creoles in Dutch society and their efforts to create new styles and ethnicities which can provide them with an edge in symbolic negotiations with their white peers. Their resulting and recognized success in the leisure sphere has in turn strengthened the belief of many young blacks that they can only succeed in high risk 'ghetto outlets' such as sports and fashion. Since few do succeed in these ventures, this focus further accentuates their exclusion even from the limited job market available to young blacks.

Limiting the diffusion of cultural elements from one activity to another can also be a factor, however, not of relative impotence but of the attempt to assert control. In Montreal, Sally, a Royal Haven student, deliberately tried to contain concepts of gender promoted by her parents in the domestic household which were a challenge to the educational objectives she was trying to pursue at school (see Amit-Talai, Chapter 7 this volume). Cultural multiplicity should therefore not be confused with any simple notions of fluidity, at least in the sense of a free movement of ideas and information.

As Ulf Hannerz argued, the unfree flow of knowledge has been a critical aspect of a 'distributive' view of culture (1992). This approach has featured a critique of assumptions of cultural sharing with a focus on the uneven distribution of ideas and information across socially differentiated populations. To this one can add the fairly obvious point that knowledge is unevenly distributed not only in relation to the respective total cultural resources of individuals but also as a factor of the concepts they use in different activities. In other words, the issue is not only whether people have different ideas, but their situational, selective and partial use of these concepts. If we are going to examine the flow of cultural concepts as these are constituted by and in turn constitute the social structure (ibid.: 14–15), then we need to examine their distribution not only between individuals but also between social situations.

This has some significant consequences for the way in which we view cultural change, not least the kind of global diffusion which is described in a number of chapters in this volume (Jourdan, Schade-Poulsen, Liechty; Sansone, Chapters 9,5,8 and 6 respectively). These are issues which have been discussed elsewhere (Hannerz 1992; Featherstone 1990; Robertson 1992) in far greater detail and depth than I can possibly achieve here, so I do not want to belabour this subject much beyond noting that the arguments I have outlined above and the ethnographic cases in this volume support the familiar but no less critical observation that cultural change is uneven in scope and pace. The distribution of Western commodities and the cultural possibilities represented through them are now common currency in those parts of the world that anthropologists used to, and tourist boards often still do represent as exotically remote. But their wider distribution over many more people still tells us very little about the uses which are made of them, both in terms of the range of activities in which they could be incorporated or the forms in which they might be realized. For the youths who are often on the front line of global economic and political restructuring, pervasive Western images of consumption can have painfully ironic resonances in the face of shortages of jobs, resources and competing cultural claims.

There is a temptation, none the less, to view the engagement of youths with new cultural forms, both as producers and consumers, as prefiguring, however fitfully and unevenly, more comprehensive cultural transformations. Versions of this assumption run through many of the chapters in this volume, although strongly qualified by the recognition of countervailing forces. Chapters 3 and 2 by Allison James and Virginia Caputo should, however, warn us of the dangers of assuming that generational discontinuity necessarily favours the role of youths as agents of cultural change. Elementary schoolteachers in Toronto and Halifax were astonished when Caputo was able, after only a few hours of observing their pupils, to record songs which in some cases they recognized from their own childhoods but had assumed to have been erased by technological and communication changes. Caputo points out how impervious the construction of gender in these girls' chants have been to attempts over the last few decades to change the status of women. Similarly, Allison James notes the continuity of the structure and form of British children's language. In two research locations separated by years and miles, James encountered similar songs, rhymes, phrases and cadences. Words no longer used by most adults still occurred in the speech of their children taught to them by slightly older children. The very tendency to view certain practices as specific to children or youths and to be discarded when individuals reach adulthood can enhance their insularity and specificity but also their cultural conservatism. That disconnection can also minimize the wider impact of even major youthful cultural innovations marginalizing new practices as a peculiarity of temporary adolescence.

THE MULTI-CULTURAL OF YOUTH

I have approached cultural production through a three-pronged focus on, respectively, the cultural rubrics which are employed in different activities; the consciousness of manifold possibilities which emerges from multiple situational involvement, and the attributes which can constrain agency. Within such a perspective a view that youth is peculiar in status, expectations and involvement but that its incumbents are simply practising an imperfect version of adult culture is an oxymoron. An activity-oriented view of culture presumes that youthful cultural strategies will emerge from and be addressed to the exigencies of the situations in which they are implicated and the constraints which age restrictions impose on the range and nature of that involvement. I am not contending that the nature of cultural process changes abruptly from youth to adulthood. Quite the opposite, I am arguing that human beings, at any age, must be multi-cultural if they are to be 'socially effective' (Barth 1969). Youths cannot simply adopt the cultural repertoires of their parents if these are addressed to different involvements and conditions of engagement. They simply would not work. It is hardly surprising, therefore, to find that adult advice on how to handle peer pressure often sounds good out of context but falls flat *in situ*.

On the other hand, a view of cultural production as necessarily multi-cultural does not require that we limit a notion of the youth cultural to one activity. We can thus liberate ourselves from the see-saw between adult/youth interaction which has been the overwhelming concern of the socialization/development school of adolescence and the informal, highly stylized peer leisure activities on which the Birmingham School focused. Youth cultural production occurs at home, at school, at work, at play, on the street, with friends, teachers, parents, siblings and bosses, draws elements from home-grown as well as transnational influences, and intertwines with class, gender, ethnicity and locality with all the cultural diversity that such a multiplicity of circumstances compels.

Such multi-culturalism imparts to youths, as to adults, a degree of consciousness that goes beyond any one situation, an awareness that each moment is embedded within a range of cultural possibilities.

For youths, that awareness is further heightened by the unfolding of life-cycle shifts, by what Allison James calls the 'cultural experience and structuring of the passage from childhood to youth' (Chapter 3, this volume) and the imminence of further transitions. So, far from being only 'partially cultural' (Caputo, Chapter 2, this volume), youths may have an especially acute awareness of the contingent character of any cultural experience.

REFERENCES

Asad, T. (1990) 'Multiculturalism and British identity in the wake of the Rushdie affair', *Politics and Society*, 18: 455–480.

Barth, F. (ed.) (1969) Introduction to *Ethnic Groups and Boundaries*, London: George Allen & Unwin.

Bourdieu, P. (1977) *Outline of a Theory of Practice*, Cambridge: Cambridge University Press.

Clarke, J., Hall, S. Jefferson, T. and Roberts B. (1976) 'Subcultures, cultures and class', in S. Hall and T. Jefferson (eds) *Resistance through Rituals: Youth Subcultures in Post-War Britain*, London: Hutchinson.

Clifford, J. (1986) 'Introduction: partial truths', in J. Clifford and G. E. Marcus (eds), *Writing Culture: The Poetics and Politics of Ethnography*, Berkeley L.A. and London: University of California Press.

—— (1988) *The Predicament of Culture: Twentieth Century Ethnography, Literature and Art*, Cambridge: Harvard University Press.

Cohen, A. (1985) *The Symbolic Construction of Community*, London and New York: Tavistock.

Featherstone, M. (ed.) (1990) *Global Culture: Nationalism, Globalization and Modernity*, A Theory, Culture and Society Special Issue, London, Newbury Park and Delhi: Sage.

Goodenough, W. H. (1971) *Culture, Language, and Society*, A McCaleb Module in Anthropology, Reading, Mass: Addison-Wesley Publications.

—— (1994) 'Toward a working theory of culture', in Robert Brofsky (ed.) *Assessing Cultural Anthropology*, New York: McGraw-Hill.

Hannerz, U. (1980) *Exploring the City: Inquiries Toward an Urban Anthropology*, New York: Columbia University Press.

—— (1992) *Cultural Complexity: Studies in the Social Organization of Meaning*, New York: Columbia University Press.

Keesing, R. (1994) 'Theories of culture revisited', in R. Borofsky (ed.) *Assessing Cultural Anthropology*, New York: McGraw-Hill.

Prout, A. and James, A. (1990) 'A new paradigm for the sociology of childhood? Provenance, promise and problems', in A. James and A. Prout, (eds) *Constructing and Reconstructing Childhood: Contemporary Issues in the Sociological Study of Childhood*. London, New York and Philadelphia: Falmer Press.

Robertson, R. (1992) *Globalization: Social Theory and Global Culture*, London, Newbury Park and Delhi: Sage Publications.

Rosaldo, R. (1989) *Culture and Truth: The Remaking of Social Analysis*, Boston: Beacon Press.
Schlegal, A. and Barry, H. III (1991) *Adolescence: An Anthropological Inquiry*, New York: The Free Press.

Index